This book is an outstanding statement,  and resistance in Latin American and of innovative and original developm Latin Left to grapple with geopolitica on the "reconstitution" of hegemony in the Americas. – *Adam David Morton, University of Sydney*

Though an early-2000s wave of elected leftist leaders challenged US pre-eminence in Latin America, Rubrick Biegon explains, this preeminence—or "hegemony"—proved stable. This sweeping survey views twenty-first century US–Latin American relations through lenses of trade, security policy, bilateral and multilateral diplomacy, and analysis of US discourse, backing it up with innumerable examples from US officials' own words. Employing a thoughtfully constructed and richly layered theoretical framework, this book gives us important new tools with which to make sense of recent developments in hemispheric affairs. – *Adam Isacson, Senior Associate for Defense Oversight, Washington Office on Latin America*

US Power in Latin America

An original account of contemporary US–Latin American relations, this book utilises neo-Gramscian and historical materialist approaches to build a novel conceptual framework for analysing US hegemony, extending critical theory in new and exciting directions. It disaggregates US power into distinct forms (structural, coercive, institutional and ideological) to convincingly argue that the United States is remaking its hegemony in the Western hemisphere.

The first decade of the new century saw the ascendancy of leftist and centre-left forces in Latin America. The emergence and consolidation of the 'New Latin Left' signalled a profound challenge to the long-standing hegemony of the United States in the region. This book details the ways in which US foreign policy responded: defining hegemony as a dialectical relationship patterned by multiple and overlapping forms of power, it situates US policy in the context of the Post-Washington Consensus. Making considerable use of confidential diplomatic cables published by Wikileaks, it examines the interplay of different facets of US hegemony, which are inextricably bound up in the neoliberalisation of the region's political economy.

This book brings clarity to what remains an open and contested process of hegemonic reconstitution, and promises to be of interest to scholars working in a number of overlapping subject areas, including International Relations (IR), US foreign policy and Latin American studies.

Rubrick Biegon is an Associate Lecturer in International Political Economy in the School of Politics and International Relations at the University of Kent. Prior to coming to Kent, he worked as a policy analyst with a small international consulting firm based in Washington, where his reporting focused on political and economic developments in Latin America and US policy towards the region.

Routledge Studies in US Foreign Policy

Edited by Inderjeet Parmar, *City University*, and
John Dumbrell, *University of Durham*

This new series sets out to publish high quality works by leading and emerging scholars critically engaging with United States Foreign Policy. The series welcomes a variety of approaches to the subject and draws on scholarship from international relations, security studies, international political economy, foreign policy analysis and contemporary international history.

Subjects covered include the role of administrations and institutions, the media, think tanks, ideologues and intellectuals, elites, transnational corporations, public opinion, and pressure groups in shaping foreign policy, US relations with individual nations, with global regions and global institutions and America's evolving strategic and military policies.

The series aims to provide a range of books – from individual research monographs and edited collections to textbooks and supplemental reading for scholars, researchers, policy analysts, and students.

US Power in Latin America

Renewing Hegemony

Rubrick Biegon

Routledge
Taylor & Francis Group

LONDON AND NEW YORK

First published 2017 by Routledge

2 Park Square, Milton Park, Abingdon, Oxfordshire OX14 4RN
52 Vanderbilt Avenue, New York, NY 10017

Routledge is an imprint of the Taylor & Francis Group, an informa business

First issued in paperback 2019

British Library Cataloguing in Publication Data
A catalogue record for this book is available from the British Library

Library of Congress Cataloging in Publication Data
Names: Biegon, Rubrick, author.
Title: US power in Latin America : renewing hegemony / Rubrick Biegon.
Other titles: United States power in Latin America
Description: Abingdon, Oxon ; New York, NY : Routledge, 2017. |
Series: Routledge studies in US foreign policy | Includes bibliographical
    references and index.
Identifiers: LCCN 2016048336| ISBN 9781138185418 (hardback) | ISBN
    9781315644516 (e-book)
Subjects: LCSH: Latin America—Foreign relations—United States. |
    United States—Foreign relations—Latin America. | Hegemony. |
    Neoliberalism—Latin America. | Neoliberalism—United States.
Classification: LCC F1418 .B49 2017 | DDC 327.8073—dc23
LC record available at https://lccn.loc.gov/2016048336

ISBN: 978-1-138-18541-8 (hbk)
ISBN: 978-0-367-26488-8 (pbk)

Typeset in Times New Roman
by Swales & Willis Ltd, Exeter, Devon, UK

Contents

Tables

Acknowledgements

The longer-term project that culminated in this book was the product of a collaborative process of intellectual exchange as much as individual initiative. I benefited greatly from the support of friends, family members and co-workers on both sides of the Atlantic. Colleagues at the University of Kent, some of whom have moved onto pastures new, played an outsized role in shaping my research interests over the duration of the project, providing guidance and insight, as well as a great deal of inspiration. Ruth Blakeley has been an invaluable supporter, offering key advice along the way, and enhancing the inquiry from beginning to end. Doug Stokes and Jonathan Joseph also provided vital input as I sifted through the literature on power and hegemony in relation to US foreign policy. In addition, Donna Lee and, from outside Kent, Adam David Morton provided instrumental feedback at a pivotal point in the project's development, helping to refresh the work in a number of ways. I am very appreciative of conversations with Paul Ashby, Govinda Clayton, Philip Cunliffe, Charles Devellennes, Matthew Loveless, David Maher, Andrew Thomson, Harmonie Toros and Tom Watts. In Washington, Patrick Quirk read and commented on much of the writing and, along with others too many to name, helped arrange interviews during the preparatory stages of the research. I would be remiss not to thank the students on my international political economy modules for engaging with some of the themes of this book in creative and often perceptive ways.

I am grateful to the series editors, John Dumbrell and Inderjeet Parmar, for including the manuscript as part of their Studies in US Foreign Policy series. I thank the anonymous reviewers for their comments on the text, which strengthened the work in a number of ways. At Routledge, Nicola Parkin, Lydia de Cruz, Rob Sorsby and Claire Maloney helped to guide the work to completion.

Finally, I wish to acknowledge the encouragement of my wonderful and caring family. I owe my passion for politics to my parents, Glenn Biegon and Rebecca Cramer, and to my extended family members of their generation, who have done so much to support me personally and throughout my educational and professional life. I would not have been able to complete this book without the patience, understanding and unshakable optimism of my wife Sophia. Our son Andreas, who arrived in the middle of this project, has been a delightful distraction in the years it's taken to finish it, as well as my greatest source of joy.

Abbreviations

ALBA	Bolivarian Alliance for the Americas
APEC	Asia-Pacific Economic Cooperation
APRA	Alianza Popular Revolucionaria Americana
CAFTA(-DR)	Central American Free Trade Agreement(-Dominican Republic)
CAN	Community of Andean Nations
CANF	Cuban American National Foundation
CARICOM	Caribbean Community
CELAC	Community of Latin American and Caribbean States
CIA	United States Central Intelligence Agency
CRS	United States Congressional Research Service
CSIS	Center for Strategic and International Studies
DCA	Defense Cooperation Agreement
DDR	Doha Development Round
DoD	United States Department of Defense
ECLAC	Economic Commission for Latin America and the Caribbean (United Nations)
EU	European Union
FARC	Revolutionary Armed Forces of Colombia
FDI	foreign direct investment
FOL	Forward Operating Location
FTA	free trade agreement
FTAA	Free Trade Area of the Americas
G8	Group of 8
G20	Group of 20
GATT	General Agreement on Tariffs and Trade
GDP	gross domestic product
HM	historical materialism
IEMP	Ideological, Economic, Military and Political power model
IFI	international financial institution
IMF	International Monetary Fund
IO	international organisation
IPE	International Political Economy
IR	International Relations

LAC	Latin America and the Caribbean
MAS	Movement towards Socialism (Bolivia)
Mercosur	Southern Common Market
MST	Landless Workers Movement (Brazil)
NAFTA	North American Free Trade Agreement
NATO	North Atlantic Treaty Organization
NGO	non-governmental organisation
NLL	New Latin Left
OAS	Organization of American States
PdVSA	Petróleos de Venezuela, SA
PRI	Partido Revolucionario Institucional
PT	Workers' Party (Brazil)
SAP	Structural Adjustment Programme
SOE	state-owned enterprise
Southcom	United States Southern Command
SSI	Strategic Studies Institute, United States Army
TPA	trade promotion agreement
TPP	Trans-Pacific Partnership
UN	United Nations
UNASUR	Union of South American Nations
USAID	US Agency for International Development
USTR	Office of the United States Trade Representative
WTO	World Trade Organization

1 Introduction

Latin America's new left and the challenge to US hegemony

For the better part of the twentieth century, the international relations of the Western hemisphere were characterised by the dominance of the United States. The United States rose to great-power status on the heels of its 1898 war with Spain, quickly adopting a neo-colonial posture in the Caribbean basin. During the Cold War, as the United States intervened across the Americas, its pre-eminence was routinely challenged, but never in doubt. It seemed an almost natural state of affairs, at least to planners in Washington. The post-Cold War period witnessed the steady expansion of US influence. In 1994, heads of state from across the hemisphere (with the lone exception of Cuba) gathered at the first Summit of the Americas in Miami, Florida. They proclaimed their commitment to the Free Trade Area of the Americas (FTAA), an economic integration scheme based on the free market policies of the Washington Consensus. In an era of American-led globalisation, there seemed to be no alternative to Washington's hemispheric vision. The region was bound together by deepening processes of neoliberalisation, underpinned by the hegemonic power of the United States. In a well-worn trope, Latin America served as the United States' 'backyard'.

In the first decade of the twenty-first century, however, the narrative of US dominance became outmoded. The countries of the region gained increased autonomy from the superpower to the north. This trend was closely related to the 'left turn' in Latin America's politics. The rise of nationalistic leaders such as Venezuela's Hugo Chávez, Bolivia's Evo Morales and Brazil's Luiz Inácio Lula da Silva, among others, bolstered the image of an independent Latin America free from the political and economic dictates of Washington. Latin American governments created new multilateral forums that excluded the United States, undermining the centrality of the Organization of American States (OAS) to institutional co-operation. Meanwhile, the Washington Consensus had all but collapsed. The region's progressive governments began implementing policies in line with their socialist and 'populist' platforms, which, while largely market-driven, called for a greater role for the state in the economy. In this context, US policy towards the region seemed adrift. The administrations of George W. Bush and Barack Obama appeared uninterested or incapable of reversing these trends. Questions were raised about the status of US hegemony and the efficacy of US power in Washington's 'near abroad'.

For scholars and policymakers alike, the United States' geopolitical decline was connected to the rise of the region's 'new left' governments. Some suggested that Washington had 'lost' Latin America (Hakim 2006). Others perceived the beginnings of a 'post-hegemonic' hemisphere (Crandall 2011; Riggirozzi 2012; Sabatini 2012). Commentators pronounced the death of the Monroe Doctrine, which had loomed over the United States' relationship with Latin America since it was first decreed in 1823 (Erikson 2008). The venerable Council on Foreign Relations issued a report claiming that the era of US dominance in Latin America was over (2008). In recognition of this new reality, President Obama called for a 'new era' of 'true partnership' with the United States' southerly neighbours (2008). Gradually, discussion of Washington's position in Latin America was coloured by the prospect of American decline on a broader scale. As the Obama administration 'reset' America's foreign relations, it reiterated the United States' traditional commitment to an active, internationalist foreign policy. There was to be no retrenchment—not globally, nor in Latin America. Obama and his team maintained that the United States was, as before, the 'indispensable nation' (ABC News 2012). Following in the footsteps of the Bush administration, the United States would remain 'first among equals', far and away the hemisphere's most consequential actor. The 'hegemonic presumption' identified by Lowenthal (1976) decades ago was alive and well. But, given the emergence and durability of Latin America's new political bloc, what of US hegemony itself? How would it be remade?

This book engages the debates over US foreign policy towards Latin America in the post-Cold War, post-9/11 period. It builds on the (neo-)Gramscian tradition in International Relations (IR) and International Political Economy (IPE) by conceptualising hegemony as a unified, asymmetrical social relationship combing material and ideational elements of coercion, consensus-building and ideological legitimation. At times, however, Gramscian theory (like much of IR) has been inattentive to the complexities of different forms of power and, more to the point, the ways in which they are manifest in the agency of system-leading states. By overlaying multiple forms of *power* within a discussion on US *hegemony*, the book interweaves two touchstone concepts in the study of international politics. Although power is widely (and rightly) viewed as an 'essentially contested concept' (Gallie 1956; Lukes 2005) hegemony would likely fall short of this classification (because it has multiple accepted definitions in the literature). As with many concepts in the social sciences (Gerring 1999; Gray 1977), both are theory-driven, so conflicts over their meanings follow patterns determined by competing ontological and epistemological assumptions and commitments. I would argue that, paradoxically, both have been neglected despite their importance to the discipline. The book thus has two closely related aims: to detail the ways in which the United States has attempted to reconstitute its hegemony in Latin America following the region's 'left turn'; and to flesh out the relationship between these two master concepts, albeit in the circumscribed context of US–Latin American relations. It responds to recent calls in IR to get 'back to basics' in focusing on power (Finnemore and Goldstein 2013), while simultaneously wrestling with the concept's complex and multifaceted nature (Barnett and Duvall 2005; Berenskoetter and Williams 2007).

In light of these objectives, the book's contribution centres on its extension of the neo-Gramscian and historical materialist tradition(s) to the discipline's burgeoning discourse on power. It follows in a long line of critical work illuminating American imperialism/hegemony in world politics. The United States' dominance in Latin America has clearly been challenged at multiple levels of international interaction: militarily, institutionally, economically and ideologically. I argue that these strata correspond to different forms of power in the international arena. Empirically, I aim to show how the United States has sought to protect and strengthen—to renew—its hegemonic position in the Americas. This process is open-ended and non-linear, but it can be 'mapped' in accordance with the various forms of power expressed in the highly asymmetrical US–Latin American relationship. Of course, these expressions of power necessarily shape one another in profound and fluid ways, coalescing to form a hegemony that is a 'living thing', recalling the meta- phorical centaur Gramsci borrowed from Machiavelli's description of power.

In this introductory chapter I briefly review the history of US foreign policy towards Latin America. Drawing on the existing literature on Latin America's 'left turn' I also sketch the contours of the New Latin Left (NLL), as I have dubbed the region's left-leaning governments. This reading of relevant histori- cal and contemporary events sets up the book's critical theoretical intervention, which is brought into relief in the next chapter.

US policy towards Latin America in historical perspective

The re-emergence of Latin America's left coincided with the administrations of George W. Bush and Barack Obama. For much of the 2000s, US foreign policy towards Latin America was subsumed to the so-called 'War on Terror', which focused primarily on events and actors outside the hemisphere. Bush's War on Terror did contribute to the militarisation of US policy in Latin America. It placed considerable focus on Colombia, where the United States was already involved in counter-narcotics/counter-insurgency following the implementation of Plan Colombia under President Bill Clinton. By the time of Bush's re-election (2004), Latin America's left turn was increasingly defining US diplomacy and strategy in the region. After backing the failed 2002 coup against Venezuela's Chávez, the Bush administration geared its efforts towards isolating his leftist government. For some observers, the Bush administration viewed Latin America primarily through a War on Terror lens (Emerson 2010). Others emphasised the Cold War-style treatment of adversarial governments, calling attention to the fact that Bush had stocked his administration with Reagan-era officials (LeoGrande 2007). Either way, Latin America never rated high on Bush's foreign policy agenda. A com- mon refrain during the Bush (and Obama) years was that Washington had ignored Latin America (Valenzuela 2005; Wiarda 2011: 135). This book shows otherwise.

Obama's election appeared to herald a new direction. During the 2008 presi- dential contest, Obama stated that he would engage the United States' adversaries in Latin America (including the governments of Cuba and Venezuela) as part of a broader effort aimed at recalibrating Washington's diplomatic compass. There was a sense among many Latin America specialists in Washington that US policy towards the region was due for an overhaul (Lowenthal *et al.* 2009). Despite the sheen of the new president, Washington's approach to Latin America changed little under Obama, who, like Bush, failed to advance a singular project or initiative to draw together the various strands of US objectives and policies in the region. On issues of economics and security, Obama's multilateral posture obscured his commitment to a rather traditional understanding of American primacy. Even his second-term efforts at a rapprochement with Cuba—forced by the hemisphere's new political reality—unfolded as his White House pushed for sanctions on Venezuela. In hindsight, expectations of a major shift in Washington's approach were unfounded. A foray into the revisionist school of US foreign policy historiography helps explain why, while also justifying the critical theoretical assumptions framing my inquiry.

Critical IR theory and the revisionist school of US foreign policy

In spite of the disciplinary cleavages separating IR, IPE and foreign policy analysis, there is noticeable overlap between the literature on US hegemony (in the international system and global economy) and the literature on US diplomacy, strategy and behaviour. Academic analysis of US foreign policy tends to be more historical in scope, often drawing on particular case studies of American statecraft, including in relation to Waltz's (2001 [1954]) second image—that is, at the level of domestic society and within the national state. In what follows, the second image literature acts as the historical foundation for the theoretical investigation into hegemony and power. The trajectory of US–Latin American relations begs innumerable questions about the fundamental unevenness of international politics, questions that have often been marginalised through the traditional concentration on great-power wars, the balance of power, hegemonic transition and the like.

The field of IR has been characterised by grand debates between competing theoretical approaches to the study of world politics. These have generally pitted two sparring camps against each other—realists versus idealists, traditionalists versus scientists, positivists versus post-positivists. Tangential to these 'paradigm wars', IR has witnessed additional efforts to carve up the discipline's theoretical landscape. Robert W. Cox's (1981) distinction between 'problem solving theory' and 'critical theory' was highly influential. For some, Cox's formulation has grown banal (Cammack 2007), but his admonishment that all theories have 'perspectives and purposes' is a useful starting point for a project focused on the asymmetries of US–Latin American relations. Cox reminds us that 'theory is always *for* someone and *for* some purpose' and that 'there is no such thing as theory in itself, divorced from a standpoint in time and space' (Cox 1981: 128). This is worth remembering when attempting to address questions of US foreign policy given the dominance of Anglo-American perspectives in IR. Although my analysis is nested in the broad tradition of critical theory, it makes no attempt to extend (or refute) Cox's axiom. Instead, I begin here so as to highlight the inadequacies of mainstream theories to fully address the questions motivating this study. Although realist and liberal perspectives may speak to the ebb and flow of US policies towards Latin America, they are poorly equipped for an examination into US hegemony in the region, particularly as it relates to the uneven history of inter-American relations and the complexity of US power therein.

Much like IR, the study of US foreign policy is defined by sharp divisions. One prominent schism stems from competing views on US objectives in the international arena. Some scholars perceive real and indisputable changes to the purposes of US strategy. Others view the intentions of American statecraft as fundamentally inert. While the first group sees epochal shifts resulting from the end of the Cold War and the attacks of 9/11 (and hence *discontinuity* in US foreign policy objectives), the second group is inclined to approach these events as largely immaterial to the core goals underpinning US behaviour (a condition of *continuity*). In many ways, this dis/continuity divide gives shape to the multitude of debates over US foreign policy within the academy. By and large, it pits *orthodox* scholars against *revisionists*, though by no means does it exhaust the meanings of these labels. The latter tend to employ a critical outlook, whereas orthodox scholars are aligned with more conventional or mainstream approaches. The basic division here can be traced to the debates over the origins of the Cold War. As noted by Saull (2007: 53–6), revisionists stressed the expansionary character of US policy, which mirrored that of the Soviet Union in several important ways. The pioneering work of American historian William Appleman Williams did much to advance revisionist ideas (1972, 2011 [1961]). Gabriel Kolko (1988) also contributed major works in this area, as did Noam Chomsky (1994), William Blum (2003), Chalmers Johnson (2000) and Perry Anderson (2015).

Debates over the goals of US foreign policy echo IR's paradigmatic fissures, but in a way that cuts across IR's established (meta-)theories. Those operating from the perspective of discontinuity include both realists and liberals. While revisionists often draw on a Marxian approach, there are also self-proclaimed realists who adhere to the continuity thesis, which aligns them with the revisionists (Bacevich 2002). In general, however, orthodox scholars subscribe to the tenets of realism and/or liberalism. This means they accept and advance the view of a country pursuing an objective 'national interest' while adhering to and promoting liberal values. Revisionists critique this dominant narrative and its portrayal of US hegemony as largely benign. Many focus on the history of US policy in the context of 'the geo-economic and strategic interests of US (trans)national capital and the construction of a world order conducive for the long-term preservation of capitalism' (Stokes 2005: 22). Others prioritise the cultural factors that work alongside socio-economic concerns to facilitate domination or exploitation (Hunt 2009). Revisionists pay close attention to the history of US foreign policy in the 'Third World' (or 'Global South'), rife with various forms of intervention and, in some cases, outright domination; a history, in other words, characterised by US imperialism and deep hegemonic rule. This history encompasses US relations with Mexico, the Caribbean and Central and South America.

My focus on the drive of the United States to renew its hegemony in Latin America means the present book is concerned primarily with continuity. It works from the assumption that the rise of the New Latin Left has not altered the core objectives or basic priorities of US foreign policy in Latin America. It reinforces the view that, under Obama, the prospect of meaningful change in US policy was overrun by the forces of the status quo (Bentley and Holland 2014; Singh 2012). Revisionist historiography centres on the uninterrupted expansionary drive of the United States (for power and influence in the international system, if not territory) as a process underpinned by geo-economic imperatives and a concomitant ideological/discursive rationale. This narrative matches the historical experience of US involvement in Latin America. A cursory survey of the literature on US actions vis-à-vis its southerly neighbours reveals a history that undercuts many of the orthodox assumptions of realist and liberal approaches.

Revisionist and critical perspectives on US–Latin American relations

There is a large body of scholarship on the history of US foreign policy in Latin America written from a revisionist angle. This includes seminal works by Lars Schoultz (1998) and Peter Smith (2000), among others (Galeano 1973; LaFeber 1984; LeoGrande 2000; Loveman 2010). Greg Grandin (2006) has examined the history of Washington's imperialist policymaking in Latin America in light of Bush's aggressive unilateralism. Chomsky's copious writings have chronicled the offences of US policy in Central and South America in great detail (1993). As these scholars demonstrate, Latin America's geopolitical subjugation to the United States has been so thorough at times that the region has often served as a 'laboratory' for US foreign policy writ large (Grandin 2006; Kolko 1988: 96; Loveman 2010: 377; Williams 1972: 151).

The revisionist literature points us in the direction of a critical approach. However, it is worth noting that a careful reading of more orthodox interpretations helps to illuminate the imperial legacy of US policy in the region. Even though many mainstream accounts avoid the terminology of 'imperialism' and treat US hegemony as normatively unproblematic, many of these works do in fact capture the historical asymmetry between the United States and the countries of Latin America. For example, in *Exiting the Whirlpool*, former National Security Advisor and liberal scholar Robert Pastor distances himself from the revisionist accounts of Schoultz and Smith. Pastor focuses on US interest-formation at the domestic level and aims to accord additional agency to Latin American countries. Nevertheless, he acknowledges that the 'imbalance of power' in hemispheric relations did have 'pervasive effects', though he subsequently downplays their implications (Pastor 2001: ix–xii). Meanwhile, John Mearsheimer sees US hegemony in the Western hemisphere since the Monroe Doctrine as unique in its depth, so much so that he refers to the United States as 'the only regional hegemon in modern history' (2001: 141). But Mearsheimer's account divorces the United States' geo-strategic expansion (in the Americas as elsewhere) from the structural evolution of capitalism, highlighting the limitations of his realist approach. Further, he naturalises the deep domination that has characterised US–Latin American relations, which this books seeks to problematise.

Both revisionist and conventional histories have documented the extensive history of US interventionism in Latin America. As the United States rose to superpower status over the course of the nineteenth and twentieth centuries it persistently intervened in the political affairs of its closest neighbours. While many of these interventions were relatively small-scale 'police actions', the overall pattern served to augment US domination. Through covert encounters and overt military manoeuvring, the United States absorbed and quashed oppositional challenges of various kinds. Washington rebalanced its strategy over time in accordance with the adjustments made by the waves of agents seeking autonomy from the United States and its proxies. This was particularly pronounced during the Cold War. An exhaustive retelling of US interventions in Latin America would fill several volumes. The following paragraphs merely aim to sketch the contours of this interventionist dynamic using some of the more infamous examples.

Although often justified through anti-communist rhetoric, US interventions during the Cold War featured a multitude of rationales and impulses. Strategies and tactics were also heterogeneous, alternating between various forms of covert and overt coercion and subversion. In Guatemala, for example, the CIA orchestrated the 1954 overthrow of the democratic and reformist government of Jacobo Árbenz in a clandestine operation (Smith 2000: 137–9). Similar covert action was taken against the elected socialist government of Salvador Allende in the early 1970s, culminating in the *coup d'état* of General Augusto Pinochet in 1973 (Smith 2000: 172–8). In both cases, imperialist actions were justified on geopolitical grounds in part to conceal the raw economic interests of US capital.[1] That is, they were dressed up as purely anti-Soviet when they served more parochial interests as a first order of business. Throughout the Cold War, when covert actions failed, Washington turned to more overt tactics. For example, in 1965–6 US troops occupied the Dominican Republic following years of behind-the-scenes meddling. The occupation was designed to prevent the potential emergence of a 'Castroist' movement in the context of the political instability that had gripped the country following a coup against centre-left president Juan Bosch in 1963 (Smith 2000: 169–72). In 1989, with the Cold War winding down, US Special Forces invaded Panama outright to depose General Manuel Noriega, a former drug trafficking CIA asset turned 'rogue dictator'. Although Noriega had few sympathisers in the region, the governments of Latin America were uniform in their opposition to Washington's unilateral and heavy-handed operation (Blum 2003: 305–13).

The line between covert and overt actions was often blurry, as was the extent of US participation in the state-directed terrorism of the region's authoritarian governments (Blakeley 2009). This blurriness was a deliberate component of US strategy, which shifted in accordance with political changes in Latin America (and in Washington). For instance, the United States' opposition to the Nicaraguan Sandinistas went from counter-insurgency under Nixon to diplomatic criticism under Carter to barely-concealed 'covert' warfare under Reagan, all in the span of a decade or so (LaFeber 1984; LeoGrande 2000). The changes reflected both the success of the guerrilla-movement-cum-government and the sometimes-divergent proclivities of US administrations.[2] Washington often hoped to avoid open violence if possible. This thinking produced the Alliance for Progress, the Kennedy administration's answer to the Cuban revolution, which used foreign aid to stimulate social development (LaFeber 1984: 145–64; Smith 2000: 143–63). It also fuelled widespread support for the region's dictatorial regimes. In Jean Kirkpatrick's classic articulation (1982), authoritarian states were preferable to rickety liberal alternatives that were weak on communism. Washington propped-up dictatorships from the Caribbean to the Southern Cone.

The Cold War witnessed an unrelenting effort by the United States to combat revolutionary movements, popular left-wing forces and nationalist governments of the political centre (Kolko 1988: 35–40). Although the Cold War's termination did not upend the United States' fundamental *goals* in Latin America, it did lead to further shifts in strategy. Among other things, the United States' interventionist impulse was channelled through a greater emphasis on multilateralism. This was demonstrated by the US intervention in Haiti in 1994, which was carried out under the auspices of a UN Security Council resolution. On the surface, Washington's reinstatement of president Jean-Bertrand Aristide, a former priest ousted by the military in 1991, reversed the long-standing pattern in US–Latin American rela-tions. Aristide was a left-leaning adherent to liberation theology who was widely popular with Haiti's poor. His eventual restoration, backed by the OAS, seemed to portend a new era of co-operation. However, the drawn out episode laid bare a kind of 'negotiation in the service of US hegemony' that would typify this period of deepened neoliberalisation. Political and economic conditions were attached to Aristide's reinstatement in an effort to counter the class-based appeal of his 'pro-poor' programme. US opposition to Aristide and his Lavalas movement was persistent if somewhat furtive. Following his re-election in 2000, Aristide was forcefully removed from power again in 2004 in a move backed by Washington (Hallward 2007). The saga showed how consensus-building was compatible with the kind of deep hegemony exemplified by the United States in the region.

That the historical record evidences high levels of continuity in Washington's endgame does not invalidate claims of shifting policy *means*. Hegemonic states alter their 'grand strategies' to accommodate the inescapable contingencies of world politics. However, the idea that US objectives are constantly in flux appears weak when set against its overarching efforts to globalise the political economy of the Americas as a matter of priority—from the Cold War through the War on Terror, to the aftermath of the global financial crisis and Great Recession. Neoliberalism reached a crescendo during the Washington Consensus but remains intact, its 'non-death' conspicuous in the United States' economic and trade pol-icy, as seen in Chapter 3. This (neo)liberalisation drive has also underpinned the United States' security policy (Chapter 4), its multilateral agenda (Chapter 5) and its promotion of democratic values (Chapters 5 and 6). The historical lineage is substantial, and the packaging of coercive, diplomatic and ideological power in the service of a geo-economic logic bears resemblance to the Open Door strategy of early American imperialism (Williams 1972). The similarities are sufficient to carry forward the revisionist argument, allowing the present study to update the continuity thesis for the early twenty-first century.

Of course, this is not to imply that the international relations of the Americas are somehow static. On the contrary. The new century has witnessed unforeseen uncertainties in inter-American relations, driven mainly by the shifting political winds in Latin America itself. In summarising these transformations, the following section outlines the significance of the NLL as a counter-hegemonic force in the Western hemisphere.

The emergence and consolidation of the New Latin Left

In its political culture, Latin America is situated within the Western tradition. The left–right model of understanding and classifying politics has an enduring applicability to the Latin American context. Stemming from, among other things, its idiosyncratic social cleavages, the region's political peculiarities are apparent enough. Questions of race, ethnicity, gender, ecology and nationality simmer alongside the dynamics of class conflict. New areas of concern reinvigorate older debates about the appropriate role for the state in the economy. Meanwhile, the international politics of the Americas features new powers (namely Brazil and, from outside the hemisphere, China), casting doubt on the status of the United States' long-standing regional hegemony. Through all of this, the left–right spectrum remains a salient (if limited) heuristic in the study of Latin America.

A left turn in Latin American politics

Latin America's politics were moulded in the fires of the Cold War. Histories of that period paint a picture of a continent beset by ideological struggle, in which nearly all political concerns were subsumed to the left–right conflict that tracked the superpower rivalry (Brands 2012; Grandin 2004). The polarisation of the Cold War was real, but the conflict's culmination did not consign the left–right model to the dustbin of history. Rather, the post-Cold War period witnessed the stunning ascendency of the 'free market' right across Latin America, while the left was put on the defensive by the sudden collapse of 'actually existing socialism'. As discussed by Jorge Castañeda in *Utopia Unarmed* (1994), the consolidation of conservative rule led to an identity crisis on the left. Although left-leaning forces were instrumental in ending the military dictatorships of the Cold War and putting the region back on the path towards liberal democracy (Grandin 2004), they seemed incapable of formulating persuasive alternatives to the primacy of the unbridled market. 'To a considerable degree', wrote Castañeda, 'the most damaging effect of the Cold War's conclusion on the Latin American left' was in its 'generalized perception of defeat'. At the same time, 'the conditions in Latin America that gave birth and recognition to the left in the past (were) as pervasive as ever' (Castañeda 1994: 240).

By the mid-2000s, the political pendulum was in full swing. Confronting the reality of a globalised capitalism with no immediate alternative, Latin America's politics came to be defined by the rise of the progressive left, a remarkable reversal of post-Cold War trends. From 2000 to 2012, fourteen Latin American countries elected left-leaning presidents. The majority replaced centre-right leaders, and many subsequently won re-election. Journalists referred to this as the 'Pink Tide', with pink representing a lighter version of the red typically associated with the left. Although the gendered connotations of the colour pink in this context render the moniker problematic (with pink signifying a feminised and therefore 'softer' type of politics), it did capture one key aspect of Latin America's shift: namely, that the new left-wing governments were far removed from the revolutionary movements of the Cold War. By and large, they operated within the frameworks of liberal democracy and market economics. Although these governments evoked socialism, developmentalism and social democracy, the new left was 'new' partly because it emerged at a time when democratic institutions were well-established. In the context of open elections, the NLL materialised largely in response to the deepening process of neoliberalisation that took hold from the 1970s onward. It was this anti-neoliberal tinge which best expressed the novelty of Latin America's left turn, and which best offered contrast with the political currents of the centre and right (Panizza 2009).

Because there is disagreement over how to categorise specific politicians and parties along the left–right spectrum, any allocation of membership in the NLL is bound to be somewhat partial. For the purposes of this study, the national governments included in this grouping are those with executive leaders who (1) self-identified as being on the (centre-)left and (2) defeated candidates with more conservative (pro-market) ideological positions in socio-economic policy. Despite the fact that it developed close ties to some NLL governments (namely Venezuela), Cuba isn't included, as it has maintained essentially the same government for decades. Additionally, it should be noted that most analyses of the Pink Tide are limited to *Latin* America, which excludes the English-speaking Caribbean (but includes Mexico and Lusophone Brazil).

By no means did Latin America's left turn conquer the continent. Several countries maintained governments of the centre and right, including Mexico and Colombia, the second and fourth largest economies in the region, both of which remained important allies of the United States. Furthermore, political trends can change in turnabout fashion. For some observers the Pink Tide crested in the mid-2000s, giving way to the rise of the centre (Shifter 2011). By 2010, left-leaning presidents governed approximately two-thirds of the population of Latin America (Weyland 2010: 1). As the centre shifted leftward, conservative politicians were forced to adapt. For example, following Álvaro Uribe's right-wing government in Colombia, his successor, the more moderate Juan Manuel Santos, deepened relations with Venezuela and entered into peace talks with the FARC (the Revolutionary Armed Forces of Colombia, a Marxist guerrilla group). Towards the end of Obama's tenure, electoral victories for the centre-right in Argentina and for the opposition in Venezuela, coupled with the 2016 ouster of Dilma Rousseff in Brazil, suggested the Pink Tide was receding. With a newly ascendant right, leftist forces appeared fatigued (Zibechi 2016). Nonetheless, the left's generational resurgence had greatly altered the landscape of Latin America as a whole, shaping expectations and rewriting assumptions in the new century.

Table 1.1 The New Latin Left: leftist and centre-left presidents elected in Latin America, 2000–15

Country	President	Party	Tenure*
Argentina	Néstor Kirchner	*Partido Justicialista* (PJ) Justicialist Party (Peronist)	2003–7
	Cristina Fernández de Kirchner	*Partido Justicialista* (PJ) Justicialist Party (Peronist)	2007–15
Bolivia	Evo Morales	*Movimiento al Socialismo* (MAS) Movement toward Socialism	2006–
Brazil	Luíz Inácio Lula da Silva	*Partido dos Trabalhadores* (PT) Workers Party	2003–11
	Dilma Rousseff	*Partido dos Trabalhadores* (PT) Workers Party	2011–16*
Chile	Ricardo Lagos	*Partido Socialista* (PS) Socialist Party	2000–6
	Michelle Bachelet	*Partido Socialista* (PS) Socialist Party	2006–10, 2014–
Ecuador	Rafael Correa	*Alianza Patria Altiva y Soberana* (*Alianza PAIS*) Alliance of the Proud and Sovereign Fatherland	2007–
El Salvador	Mauricio Funes	*Frente Farabundo Martí para la Liberación Nacional* (FMLN) Farabundo Martí National Liberation Front	2009–14
	Salvador Sánchez Cerén	*Frente Farabundo Martí para la Liberación Nacional* (FMLN) Farabundo Martí National Liberation Front	2014–
Guatemala	Álvaro Colom	*Unidad Nacional de la Esperanza* (UNE) National Unity of Hope	2008–12
Haiti	Jean-Bertrand Aristide	*Fanmi Lavalas* Lavalas Family	1991, 1994–6, 2000–4*
Honduras	Manuel Zelaya	*Partido Liberal* Liberal Party	2006–9*
Nicaragua	Daniel Ortega	*Frente Sandinista de Liberación Nacional* (FSLN) Sandinista National Liberation Front	2007–
Paraguay	Fernando Lugo	*Alianza Patriótica por el Cambio* (APC) Patriotic Alliance for Change	2008–12*
Peru	Ollanta Humala	*Partido Nacionalista Peruano* Peruvian Nationalist Party	2011–16
Uruguay	Tabaré Vásquez	*Frente Amplio* (FA) Broad Front	2005–10, 2015–
	José Mujica	*Frente Amplio* (FA) Broad Front	2010–15
Venezuela	Hugo Chávez	*Partido Socialista Unido de Venezuela* (PSUV) United Socialist Party of Venezuela	1999–2013
	Nicolás Maduro	*Partido Socialista Unido de Venezuela* (PSUV) United Socialist Party of Venezuela	2013–

Note

* Tenure represents time in office as of September 2016. Rousseff, Aristide, Zelaya and Lugo were forced from office before the end of their terms (Aristide twice).

Commentary on the NLL ranged from polemical jeremiads to staid policy briefs. There was a widespread tendency to classify Latin America's various new left governments—to group them together in accordance with their differing governing styles and/or policy preferences. Because these forces were far from monolithic, observers sought to distinguish amongst the members of the NLL by placing them at differing points along the ideological spectrum, or by contrasting the temperaments of the various national leaders. In general, this categorisation took the form of a 'typology of two', an approach employed by Castañeda in an oft-cited *Foreign Affairs* article. Using normative language, he outlined the contours of a 'right left' and a 'wrong left'. The former was 'open-minded, reformist, and internationalist', whereas the latter was 'nationalist, strident, and close-minded' (2006: 29–42). For Castañeda, the 'right left' (Brazilian President Lula and Chilean President Bachelet) was moderate, cosmopolitan and politically and economically orthodox, while the 'wrong left' (i.e. Venezuelan President Chávez and Bolivian President Morales) was radical, populist and semi-authoritarian. I explore the merits of a dichotomous approach below.

A great deal has been written on the agents of the NLL, including national leaders. Unsurprisingly, Hugo Chávez garnered the most attention (Gott 2005; Kozloff 2006). However, Brazil's Lula also generated substantive interest, as did Evo Morales of Bolivia. In many respects, the NLL began with the region's vibrant social movements, and analysis of these groups has been interwoven into the broader discussion on the new left. Detailed studies carried out by Petras and Veltmeyer (2011), Raúl Zibechi (2012) and Eduardo Silva (2009) demonstrated the ways in which social movements in Latin America resisted neoliberalism, thus creating the conditions for the re-emergence of progressive governments. The rise of the NLL led to a re-examination of the status of neoliberalism in the region, with some reaching the conclusion that Latin America was entering a post-neoliberal age (Grugel 2009; Sader 2011). The re-emergence of the left has also been associated with a rise in nationalism, a phenomenon that dovetailed with a surge in anti-*Yanqui* 'anti-Americanism'.

Multiple lefts: a typology of the NLL

Much of the literature on Latin America's new left aimed to distinguish between the different national currents that comprised it as a regional trend (Castañeda and Morales 2008; Weyland 2010). This was based on economic and financial policies, leadership styles, attitudes towards democracy and foreign relations, among other criteria. The usual breakdown was between the 'radicals' (Venezuela chief among them) and the 'moderates' (with Brazil the leading example). The radicals were widely labelled populists, while the moderates avoided this association. This basic binary had variations tethered to different normative conclusions. It surfaced in much of the academic literature on the political shifts in Latin America, contributing to a broad understanding of the 'Pink Tide' as a wave of two lefts. Polemical and journalistic writings celebrating, condemning or downplaying the trend proliferated as it grew more pronounced. Although the 'typology of two' has merits, it is true that the NLL is characterised by a wider diversity (Cameron and Hershberg 2010). With conditions differing on a country-by-country basis, it is unsurprising that governments sharing common ideological tendencies diverged on policy matters. However similar, they came to power for particularised reasons.

At the same time, the regional nature of the political shift is indisputable (Panizza 2009; Sader 2011). Given that the NLL emerged in the context of deep neoliberalisation, analytical distinction should align with the degree of receptiveness to, or rejection of, neoliberalism itself. I therefore define the two main blocs within the NLL as *anti-neoliberals* and *neoliberal reformers*. The anti-neoliberal bloc comprises the governments of Bolivia, Ecuador and Venezuela, while the remaining members of the NLL (including, most prominently, Brazil) are more accurately understood as neoliberal reformers. Argentina and Nicaragua occupy a kind of middle ground. Although they correspond to particular countries often viewed as being on opposite sides of the moderate/radical split, these two groups, or tendencies, are best seen as ideal-typical. A more fluid categorisation reflects the actuality of Latin American politics, in which diverse leftist forces are constrained by pre-existing structures of varying scope and depth.

In addition to pursuing divergent policies in the socio-economic realm, the NLL as a whole appeared highly accommodating of (and even supportive of) a plurality of political strategies. And, when it comes to the details of state behaviour in fiscal and monetary affairs, researchers point to the 'ample diversity of specific policies' applied by leftist politicians, a trend that 'underscores the considerable pragmatic blending that goes on' (Tussie and Heidrich 2008: 62). In monetary policy, exchange policy (currency valuation), fiscal positioning (after debt payments), debt administration, social expenditures, support for free trade agreements with the United States, and support for regional economic integration, among other things, the NLL has been 'ecumenical', making it difficult at times to conceptualise 'the phenomenon of the new left in a dichotomous fashion'. The differences that criss-cross NLL governments call into question the basic moderate/radical binary, while failing to fully undercut the unity interwoven in the NLL's diverse policy positions. Overall, there has been 'a clear turnaround from the confidence in the cure-all ability of markets' as well as 'the emergence of a pragmatic belief in a role for state management' (Tussie and Heidrich 2008: 62–4). In other words, as summarised by Jean Grugel, 'all of Latin America's left democrats are, in different ways, concerned to strengthen state authority in the social and economic domains' (2009: 45). Although the state never really 'retreated' under the Washington Consensus, the NLL redirected it towards a renewed sense of purpose in social and economic policy.

That there are important differences between the various NLL governments is fairly intuitive given the diversity of the Latin American countries governed by centre-left administrations. Important though they are, these differences do not negate the similarities or abrogate the conceptual utility of the left turn as a meaningful development in the politics of the hemisphere. 'Despite differences in manner, Latin American governments have committed themselves to a common agenda of economic diversification, regional integration, and development policies that spur not just growth but equality' (Grandin 2006: 242). It was the definitiveness of the left turn as a regional trend that made it significant from an inter-American perspective. In William Robinson's assessment of these debates:

> There *are* two Lefts: one that dominated the pink tide and sought to reintroduce a mild redistributive component into the global capitalist program in the region, and a more radical one that sought a more substantial transformation of social structures, class relations, and international power dynamics.
>
> (2008: 293–4)

But the left turn was not wholly defined by this schism. In fact, Robinson saw it as both symbolic of 'the end of the reigning neoliberal order' and demonstrative of the 'limits of parliamentary changes in the era of global capitalism' (2008: 290).

The differences between the anti-neoliberal governments of the new left and those classified as neoliberal reformers must not be overplayed. That several members of the NLL straddled the two groups reinforces this notion; for instance, many analysts sought to place Argentina's Kirchner and Fernández de Kirchner governments somewhere between the Chávez and Lula 'poles', and others did the same with the Sandinista government of Nicaraguan President Ortega. Moreover, the distinction loses some of its cogency when applied to the foreign policies of the NLL states, particularly in the regional arena. The governments of Venezuela, Bolivia and Ecuador maintained strong ties with those of a more 'moderate' bent. Chávez and Lula had an amiable and productive relationship, particularly in light of their supposed rivalry for symbolic leadership of the region. On issues of trade, for example, there was widespread co-operation. As examined in Chapter 3, opposition to the FTAA was relatively consistent among anti-neoliberal and reformist governments, effectively felling the US-backed proposal.

The anti-neoliberals: Chávez and the Bolivarian bloc

Elected in 1998, Hugo Chávez became the most potent symbol of the region-wide turn to the left. Chávez epitomised the 'radical' or 'populist' elements of the NLL, garnering much media attention for his flamboyant style and larger-than-life character. Chávez's personalised movement presented itself as explicitly anti-neoliberal from the very beginning, even if, in practice, the Venezuelan state under Chávez was slow to break with the tenets of neoliberal orthodoxy. Chávez routinely condemned 'savage neoliberalism', a conjunction that was prominent in his rhetorical repertoire (Kozloff 2006: 56). The discourse of anti-neoliberalism that enveloped Chávez, his supporters (referred to as *Chavistas*) and the Venezuelan government overlaid the implementation of economic policies that countered the Washington Consensus. Over his 14 years in office, Venezuela was the exemplar post-neoliberal country, and Chávez the anti-neoliberal agent *par excellence*. Using Venezuela's oil wealth, he exercised influence on the international stage, including as the leader of the region's 'anti-American' states. Venezuela's influence was channelled through the Bolivarian Alliance for the Americas (ALBA).

The discourse of Bolivarianism (which invokes Simón Bolívar, South America's independence hero) was constitutive of Chávez's nationalist, anti-imperialist and pan-Latin American appeal (Gott 2005; Kozloff 2006). His death from cancer in 2013 raised questions about the future of the Bolivarian project, both in Venezuela and regionally. Although Nicolás Maduro, Chávez's chosen successor, was subsequently elected to a full term, his narrow victory raised the prospect of divisions within Venezuela's Chavista coalition. Within a few years, mismanagement and macroeconomic turmoil had reversed the momentum of the 'Bolivarian Revolution'.

To a degree, Chávez's marriage of socialist rhetoric with redistributive and developmentalist policies served as a model for other leaders in South America, particularly in the Andean region. President Evo Morales of Bolivia and President Rafael Correa of Ecuador were widely seen as those leaders closest to Chávez, so much so that they were often portrayed as his 'protégés'. Although this involved the vague characterisation of Morales and Correa as underlings of the Chávez juggernaut, the linking of the three leaders was not without merit, as they shared an explicitly anti-neoliberal praxis (Sader 2011). It is clear that, within the diversified NLL, the Venezuelan, Bolivian and Ecuadorian governments formed something akin to an anti-neoliberal bloc. This is not to say that the other left-leaning governments of the region did not, at times, challenge neoliberalism, or that the Andean members of the NLL represented a revolutionary break with capitalism. Rather, it is simply to state that that which gave Latin America's new left its 'newness' and its 'leftness' was demonstrably stronger in certain circumstances.

Among other similarities, Venezuela, Bolivia and Ecuador are major producers and exporters of hydrocarbons. Their development strategies have been characterised by an extractivism that rests heavily on the oil, gas and mining industries (Kennemore and Weeks 2011; Webber 2015a). In Bolivia and Ecuador, leftist administrations drew support from vibrant peasant and indigenous-based social movements, a role played by the more clientelistic Chavistas in Venezuela. All three countries ratified new constitutions in an effort to incorporate groups long excluded from political decision-making. These changes allowed politicians to remain in office for extended periods of time by abolishing term limits. Following Chávez, Morales and Correa routinely affirmed their commitment to 'Twenty-first Century Socialism'. Notwithstanding the terminology, the extractivist nature of this model provided scope for the further penetration of transnational capital. It fostered new political tensions as popular forces came in conflict with NLL governments in Bolivia and Ecuador (Webber 2015a, 2015b), while in Venezuela the state's dependence on petroleum revenues led to prolonged crisis amidst the declining oil prices of the post-Chávez era.

Even within the anti-neoliberal faction of the NLL important differences exist. In Venezuela, politics were quickly polarised around the figure of Chávez himself. Anti-neoliberal and class-based social movements, as well as the political opposition, operated largely in reference to Chávez's Bolivarian 'project' and, more to the point, Chávez's central position within the new order. Meanwhile, Morales and Correa governed with the tenuous support of highly autonomous social movements; anti-systemic groups that brought down several pro-Washington Consensus presidents (Petras and Veltmeyer 2011; Silva 2009). (As a leader of the national coca growers' union, Morales himself was instrumental in Bolivia's protest movement.) Additionally, Venezuela's massive oil reserves 'make it the only country in the region with a truly independent source of wealth, and this (gave) Chávez increased manoeuvrability'. In contrast, 'even with the limited bargaining power produced by Bolivia's natural-gas reserves, Evo Morales (was) forced to moderate his anti-neoliberal aspirations' (Clearly 2006: 46). And although Ecuador is one of South America's largest oil producers, the country's proven reserves are but a fraction of those found in Venezuela.

The neoliberal reformers: Brazil and the moderates of the NLL

If Chávez exemplified the NLL's anti-neoliberal faction, Brazilian President Luiz Inácio Lula da Silva embodied the more reformist aspects of Latin America's left turn. Lula, who governed from 2003 to 2011, was a metallurgist and union organiser before helping to found Brazil's Workers' Party (PT). Known as the country's first 'worker president', and a committed socialist for most of his career, Lula came under criticism from PT activists and Brazil's social movements for his perceived willingness to capitulate to the country's macroeconomic status quo. 'The strategic case against Lula is that he compromised too much on economic policy, so that a conservative, market-friendly approach made it hard to achieve real social reform' (Bourne 2008: 229). In moving to the centre, Lula won two elections after failing to gain the presidency in three previous attempts. During the 2002 campaign, Lula issued a highly publicised 'Letter to the Brazilian People' to calm international financial markets' apprehension about the prospects for a PT government. The letter clarified that the incoming administration was prepared to forfeit its anti-neoliberal platform to avoid the risks associated with macroeconomic instability, a pattern that held throughout Lula's tenure (and that of his PT successor, Dilma Rousseff). Specifically, the letter stated that Lula would respect business contracts and continue to abide by the conditions of the country's existing financial arrangement with the International Monetary Fund (IMF). Lula's 'commitment to economic orthodoxy could be seen as a case of a left-wing leader abandoning radical policies under overwhelming economic constraints' (Panizza 2009: 216–17).

In contrast to Chávez, Lula metamorphosed into a reformer operating largely within the parameters of neoliberalism. Although his government maintained tight control over public expenditures and prioritised Brazil's external debt payments, Lula insisted that fiscal austerity did not imply full compliance with the neoliberal model. Yet even his signature social programme, the *Bolsa Familia* (Family Grant) initiative, which centred on monthly stipends to poor families, was an extension of programmes implemented by the previous (neoliberal) government. Similar dynamics can be seen in other parts of the Southern Cone, especially in Chile and Uruguay, where 'parties of the left . . . have become increasingly integrated into the existing political system and have moved from the radical left towards the centre-left' (Panizza 2009: 223). Though they implemented economic and social policies that challenged the Washington Consensus in important ways, the majority of NLL governments adhered to this cautionary, ostensibly piecemeal approach. In general, however, 'there would appear to be insufficient reason for affirming that these countries . . . are in a process of "transition from neo-liberalism"'. In the case of Brazil's PT government, this was demonstrated by the 'undeniably neo-liberal nature of the macroeconomic policies it has implemented', including continued liberalisation of the financial sector (Sánchez *et al.* 2008: 66–7).

If Venezuela's exceptionalism is defined by its oil wealth, Brazil occupied a unique position within the NLL based on its status as South America's largest economy. Under the governments of Lula and Rousseff, Brazil consolidated its standing as a leader of the Global South in a variety of forums, including the WTO. The country has used the Mercosur customs union to curry influence in South America. It is one of the BRICs, alongside the major economies of Russia, India and China. To the consternation of much of the PT rank-and-file, the management of Brazil's rise to regional power status was prioritised at the expense of socio-economic development and wealth redistribution (Bandeira 2006). As the PT downplayed its traditional emphasis on social and economic justice, Lula justified such a turn on pragmatic grounds—a pragmatism that was extended to cover the country's foreign policy. There was relative stability in Brazil's foreign relations from the 1990s through the 2000s. Lula's foreign economic policy did not represent a radical break from that of previous administrations. Rather, his administration was focused primarily on adjusting Brazil to 'the new realities imposed by global capitalism and the need to form coalitions with other countries in similar conditions to advance the international interests of the Brazilian capitalist class' (Flynn 2007: 11). At the same time, the PT retained a residual emphasis on its social agenda. The lack of a major shift notwithstanding, Brazil's more assertive foreign policy placed it on a path of antagonism with US hegemony. This pattern holds for the NLL as a whole. These governments cannot be understood as 'revolutionary' in the classical sense. But their search for autonomy in important aspects of the policy arena suggests that, collectively, their emergence marked a clear-cut counter-hegemonic moment in inter-American relations.

Plan of study

At its core, this study is a historical analysis of US foreign policy at a crucial juncture in US–Latin American relations. In this vein, it is informed by historical materialism (HM), which involves an understanding of 'history in the sense of being concerned with not just the past but with a continuing process of historical change' (Cox 1996: 88). This process unfolds dialectically. History, in this view, is constantly in motion, full of tensions and contradictions, and of the actions and reactions of co-dependent agents and concepts (Harvey 2010: 11–47). As a philosophical disposition, the dialectic precludes the total separation of the hegemon from its subordinates. Hegemony involves some amount of pushback, or resistance, which is internal to the arrangement. It requires a counter-hegemony that is both constitutive of the hegemonic order and a potential threat to its durability, depending on the contingencies of human agency. The following chapters offer an in-depth explication of this interlocking relationship. The discussion is sensitive to the intrinsic complexity of processes of change/stasis in the politics of the Western hemisphere.

Inspired by critical theory, the research draws on interpretivist methodologies. But while it cannot be classified as positivist or rationalist, it is also distinct from constructivism and post-positivism. This is because the 'analytical paradigm' overlaying the study encompasses a 'realism of assumptions' in its basic precepts (Hay 2002: 29). In other words, the ontology here is realist. A number of scholars have commented on the compatibly of critical realism with historical materialist theory (Brown 2007; Joseph 2007). Without wading into the deeper debates over positivism, post-positivism and critical realism, I assume that social phenomena exist 'out there' in the real world, irrespective of our attempts to study or label it as such. Importantly, critical realism allows for the analysis of both discursive and extra-discursive phenomena. In the present study several methodological tools are used, including various forms of textual analysis (both discourse and content analysis). These track different forms of power using the framework delineated in Chapter 2.

The methodology flows from the book's philosophical realism of assumptions. It requires an acknowledgement of the ontology on which the inquiry is built, including in relation to the agent–structure problem. Although the hegemony/counter-hegemony dialectic sets up the framework, its implications for the structures and agents at play are less than obvious; the parsimony of hegemony as a concept derives from the fact that it bridges (or sidesteps) the agent–structure divide. Let me clarify my position here. If US hegemony in Latin America is understood as a *set of asymmetrical power relations* between agents (the US state; Latin American governments; classes and other subnational [and transnational] groups), this arrangement is conditioned by various structures (the inter-state system, the transnational/global economy). These structures are (re)created through purposeful human action, the parameters of which are set by the (pre-existing) structures themselves. I take structures and agents to be co-determined, or 'mutually implicated' (Wight 2006: 121). Because this project investigates US policy, its desiderata lies primarily on the agentic side of the agent–structure divide. The agent at the centre of the story is the US state. The counter-hegemonic agents are the 'member-states' of the NLL. Their shared structural space is the inter-American system, which includes formalised institutions of co-operation (such as the OAS) as well as deeper, unobservable structures (the global[ising] political economy). The 'statist' inflection of the analysis is not meant to obscure the importance of sub- and transnational actors. For historical materialists, the state is always a site of contestation and a reflector of class dynamics, even if, as noted by Ellen Wood, 'the global economy as we know it today is still constituted by national entities' (2002: 17).

Moreover, my empirical focus on the United States is not meant to downplay the agency of Latin Americans. Indeed, the role of Latin American leadership and diplomacy in the historical shaping of inter-American relations is often overlooked, and should not be discounted (Long 2015; Tulchin 2016). In fact, this book argues that this tendency has become more pronounced in the twenty-first century. Structural shifts have reconfigured the regional context, creating opportunities for Latin American governments both economically and politically. Examples abound, and are examined in detail in the following chapters, especially in relation to the hemisphere's new international organisations. Brazil's work to institutionalise the BRICs grouping represents one notable case. Even after Brazil's economic boom subsided in the mid-2010s, the BRICs framework continued to pay dividends as the country forged deeper ties with Asia (Stuenkel 2016). A more institutionalised forum had ramifications for the wider region, as well. The BRICs-led New Development Bank, established in 2014 and capitalised at $100 billion, provides an alternative to the IMF and World Bank, one that may prove more consequential than other relatively recent institutional interventions due to the active involvement of China.

The agency of the United States, like that of Latin American states, is expressed via different forms of power. These necessarily overlap, shaping one another in important ways. For instance, it is difficult to consider US structural power without referencing the formal institutions (e.g. free trade regimes, the IMF) used to codify and lock-in neoliberal patterns of economic production. Similarly, it is problematic to discuss US coercive power in Latin America without also addressing the ideological construction of 'radical populism' (or drug trafficking) as a threat to the United States and its interests. Agency requires intentionality. To understand the drive by the United States to rebuild its hegemony in Latin America, we must assess the goals and intentions of the US state. In this vein, my analysis begins with the official texts of US foreign policymaking. This includes statements and speeches by government officials in the executive branch, including in the Departments of State and Defense (DoD), as well as the Office of the US Trade Representative (USTR) and the United States' Permanent Mission to the Organization of American States. The posture statements of Southcom (US Southern Command, the Pentagon's unified command structure for Latin America [bar Mexico]) and monographs published by the Army's Strategic Studies Institute (SSI) shed light on US security strategy in Latin America. Congressional Research Service (CRS) reports and statements from relevant congressional committees and sub-committees show the perspective(s) of the legislative branch.

In 2010, the whistle-blower website Wikileaks published over 250,000 secret, classified and confidential diplomatic cables from US embassies, consulates and interest sections around the world. In effect, the cable dump created a massive archive of contemporary primary documents virtually unparalleled in the study of international politics. In contrast to on-the-record statements, public documents and the like, the cables provided an 'unfiltered' view of official opinion. They opened a panorama onto the 'actual' perspective(s) and position(s) on many of the foreign policy issues of the 2000s, within the State Department and in the embassies' consultations with other actors and agencies. Cables classified as 'top secret' or higher were not released. As noted by one journalist, 'diplomatic cables are versions of events. They can be speculative. They can be ambiguous. They can be wrong' (Keller 2011). And yet, there is no doubt as to the utility of the material for researchers. I make significant use of these cables in this book, thousands of which pertained to US policy in Latin America. While relevant cables were always analysed and triangulated in conjunction with other sources of information, they give the research a depth that would not have existed without their timely release.

Conclusion

The Western hemisphere is fraught with the historical baggage of the subordination of those countries 'beneath the United States', to borrow from Schoultz (1998). The critical and revisionist approaches discussed in this chapter are far from uniform, but they speak to gaps in an orthodox view that is ill-equipped to grapple with the legacy of a dynamic that goes by several names: dominance, aggression, expansion, empire, etc. A critical approach tackles head-on the implications of the asymmetry captured in these terms. For reasons further spelled out in the following chapter, and by building on the heterogeneous (neo-)Gramscian theoretical tradition, I conceptualise this as hegemony. The ascendency of the NLL was a watershed moment for Latin America, for inter-American relations and for the political economy of the Americas precisely because it called this legacy into question. By considering Latin America's contemporary challenge to US hegemony alongside the theoretical problematic of hegemonic reconstitution, we gain a richer understanding of the variegated power of American foreign policy at a time when many assume that power is dissipating. What follows is an attempt to capture the fullness of the concept of hegemony and the tensions inherent in its actualisation.

Notes

1 In Guatemala, Árbenz had carried out land reform policies that threatened the vested interests of the United Fruit Company, a powerful US-based firm with close ties to the Eisenhower administration. In Chile, Allende had moved to nationalise the country's lucrative industrial and mineral companies, prompting opposition from several prominent US companies, including ITT, Anaconda and Kennecott Copper. The overthrows of Árbenz and Allende were also intended to prevent the Guatemalan and Chilean governments from drifting into the Soviet camp. This rationale was commonplace during the US's various interventions in Latin America during the Cold War, and formed a core part of Washington's foreign policy in the region.

2 The Carter administration's nominal focus on human rights represented the greatest departure in this regard. Although these changes impacted policy, and reflected considerable shifts in the attitude of the US public following the period of the Vietnam War, Carter's human rights policy was subsumed to the logic of the Cold War and the imperatives of US hegemony. Moreover, in the last two years of his term in office, Carter relinquished his human rights agenda for a more traditional security approach.

References

ABC News (2012). 'Obama Says He Restored America's Image as "Sole, Indispensable Power"', 19 January. Available online at http://abcnews.go.com/blogs/politics/2012/01/obama-says-he-restored-americas-image-as-sole-indispensable-power/ (accessed 30 August 2015).

Anderson, P. (2015). *American Foreign Policy and its Thinkers*, London: Verso.

Bacevich, A. (2002). *American Empire: The Realities and Consequences of US Diplomacy*, Cambridge, MA: Harvard University Press.

Bandeira, L. A. M. (2006). 'Brazil as a Regional Power and Its Relations with the United States', *Latin American Perspectives*, 33(3): 12–27.

Barnett, M. and R. Duvall, eds (2005). *Power in Global Governance*, Cambridge: Cambridge University Press.

Bentley, M. and J. Holland, eds (2014). *Obama's Foreign Policy: Ending the War on Terror*, London: Routledge.

Berenskoetter, R. and M. J. Williams, eds. (2007). *Power in World Politics*, New York: Routledge.

Blakeley, R. (2009). *State Terrorism and Neoliberalism: The North in the South*, London: Routledge.

Blum, W. (2003). *Killing Hope: US Military and CIA Interventions since World War II*, revised edition, London: Zed Books.

Bourne, R. (2008). *Lula of Brazil: The Story So Far*, London: Zed Books.

Brands, H. (2012). *Latin America's Cold War*, Cambridge, MA: Harvard University Press.

Brown, C. (2007). 'Situating Critical Realism', *Millennium*, 35(2): 409–16.

Cameron, M. and E. Hershberg, eds (2010). *Latin America's Left Turns: Politics, Policies, and Trajectories of Change*, Boulder: Lynne Rienner.

Cammack, P. (2007). 'RIP IPE', Papers in the Politics of Global Competitiveness, No. 7, Institute for Global Studies, Manchester Metropolitan University e-space Open Access Repository.

Castañeda, J. (1994). *Utopia Unarmed: The Latin American Left After the Cold War*, New York: Vintage Books.

Castañeda, J. (2006). 'Latin America's Left Turn', *Foreign Affairs*, 85(3): 28–43.

Castañeda, J. and M. Morales, eds (2008). *Leftovers: Tales of the Latin American Left*, London: Routledge.

Chomsky, N. (1993). *Year 501: The Conquest Continues*, Boston: South End Press.

Chomsky, N. (1994). *World Orders, Old and New*, New York: Columbia University Press.

Clearly, M. (2006). 'A Left Turn in Latin America? Explaining the Left's Resurgence', *Journal of Democracy*, 17(4): 35–49.

Council on Foreign Relations (2008). *US–Latin America Relations: A New Direction for a New Reality*, New York: Council on Foreign Relations.

Cox, R. W. (1981). 'Social Forces, States and World Orders: Beyond International Relations Theory', *Millennium*, 10(2): 126–55.

Cox, R. W. (1996). *Approaches to World Order*, Cambridge: Cambridge University Press.

Crandall, R. (2011). 'The Post-American Hemisphere: Power and Politics in an Autonomous Latin America', *Foreign Affairs*, 90(3): 83–95.

Emerson, R. G. (2010). 'Radical Neglect? The "War on Terror" and Latin America', *Latin American Politics and Society*, 52(1): 33–62.

Erikson, D. (2008). 'Requiem for the Monroe Doctrine', *Current History*, 107(706): 58–64.

Finnemore, M. and J. Goldstein, eds (2013). *Back to Basics: State Power in a Contemporary World*, Oxford: Oxford University Press.

Flynn, M. (2007). 'Between Subimperialism and Globalization: A Case Study in the Internationalization of Brazilian Capital', *Latin American Perspectives*, 34(6): 9–27.

Galeano, E. (1973). *Open Veins of Latin America: Five Centuries of the Pillage of a Continent*, New York: Monthly Review.

Gallie, W. B. (1956). 'Essentially Contested Concepts', *Proceedings of the Aristotelian Society*, 56: 167–98.

Gerring, J. (1999). 'What Makes a Concept Good? A Criterial Framework for Understanding Concept Formation in the Social Sciences', *Polity*, 31(3): 357–93.

Gott, R. (2005). *Hugo Chávez and the Bolivarian Revolution*, London: Verso.

Grandin, G. (2004). *The Last Colonial Massacre: Latin America in the Cold War*, Chicago: Chicago University Press.

Grandin, G. (2006). *Empire's Workshop: Latin America, the United States, and the Rise of the New Imperialism*, New York: Owl Books.

Gray, J. (1977). 'On the Contestability of Social and Political Concepts', *Political Theory*, 5(3): 331–48.

Grugel, J. (2009). 'Democracy after the Washington Consensus', in *Governance after Neoliberalism in Latin America*, edited by J. Grugel and P. Riggirozzi, New York: Palgrave: 217–30.

Hakim, P. (2006). 'Is Washington Losing Latin America?' *Foreign Affairs*, 85(1): 39–53.

Hallward, P. (2007). *Damning the Flood: Haiti, Aristide, and the Politics of Containment*, London: Verso.

Harvey, D. (2010). *A Companion to Marx's Capital*, London: Verso.

Hay, C. (2002). *Political Analysis: A Critical Introduction*, Basingstoke: Palgrave.

Hunt, M. (2009). *Ideology and US Foreign Policy*, revised edition, New Haven: Yale University Press.

Johnson, C. (2000). *Blowback: The Costs and Consequence of American Empire*, New York: Owl Books.

Joseph, J. (2007). 'Philosophy in International Relations: A Scientific Realist Approach', *Millennium*, 35(2): 345–59.

Keller, B. (2011). 'Dealing with Assange and the Wikileaks Secrets', *The New York Times Magazine*, 26 January. Available online at www.nytimes.com/2011/01/30/magazine/30Wikileaks-t.html?pagewanted=all (accessed 30 August 2015).

Kennemore, A. and G. Weeks (2011). 'Twenty-First Century Socialism? The Elusive Search for a Post-Neoliberal Development Model in Bolivia and Ecuador', *Bulletin of Latin American Research*, 30(3): 276–81.

Kirkpatrick, J. (1982). *Dictatorships and Double Standards: Rationalism and Reason in Politics*, New York: Simon & Schuster.

Kolko, G. (1988). *Confronting the Third World*, New York: Pantheon.

Kozloff, N. (2006). *Hugo Chávez: Oil, Politics, and the Challenge to the US*, New York: Palgrave.

LaFeber, W. (1984). *Inevitable Revolutions: The United States in Central America*, New York: W. W. Norton & Company.

LeoGrande, W. (2000). *Our Own Backyard: The United States in Central America 1977–1992*, Chapel Hill: University of North Carolina Press.

LeoGrande, W. (2007). 'A Poverty of Imagination: George W. Bush's Policy in Latin America', *Journal of Latin American Studies*, 39(2): 355–85.

Long, T. (2015). *Latin America Confronts the United States: Asymmetry and Influence*, Cambridge: Cambridge University Press.

Loveman, B. (2010). *No Higher Law: American Foreign Policy and the Western Hemisphere since 1776*, Chapel Hill: University of North Carolina Press.

Lowenthal, A. (1976). 'The United States and Latin America: Ending the Hegemonic Presumption', *Foreign Affairs*, 55(1): 199–213.

Lowenthal, A., T. Piccone and L. Whitehead, eds (2009). *The Obama Administration and the Americas: Agenda for Change*, Washington, DC: Brookings Institution Press.

Lukes, S. (2005). *Power: A Radical View*, second edition, New York: Palgrave.

Mearsheimer, J. (2001). *The Tragedy of Great Power Politics*, New York: W. W. Norton & Company.

Obama, B. (2008). 'A New Partnership for the Americas'. Available online at http://obama.3cdn.net/ef480f743f9286aea9_k0tmvyt7h.pdf (accessed 30 August 2015).

Panizza, F. (2009). *Contemporary Latin America: Development and Democracy Beyond the Washington Consensus*, London: Zed Books.

Pastor, R. (2001). *Exiting the Whirlpool: US Foreign Policy toward Latin America and the Caribbean*, second edition, Boulder: Westview Press.

Petras, J. and H. Veltmeyer (2011). *Social Movements in Latin America: Neoliberalism and Popular Resistance*, New York: Palgrave.

Riggirozzi, P. (2012). 'Region, Regionness and Regionalism in Latin America: Towards a New Synthesis', *New Political Economy*, 17(4): 421–43.

Robinson, W. I. (2008). *Latin America and Global Capitalism: A Critical Globalization Perspective*, Baltimore: Johns Hopkins University Press.

Sabatini, C. (2012). 'Rethinking Latin America', *Foreign Affairs*, 91(2): 8–13.

Sader, E. (2011). *The New Mole: Paths of the Latin American Left*, London: Verso.

Sánchez, F., J. M. B. Neto and R. M. Marques (2008). 'Brazil: Lula's Government: A Critical Appraisal', in *The New Latin American Left: Utopia Reborn*, edited by P. Barrett, D. Chavez and C. Rodríguez-Garavito, London: Pluto Press: 42–69.

Saull, R. (2007). *The Cold War and After: Capitalism, Revolution and Superpower Politics*, London: Pluto Press.

Schoultz, L. (1998). *Beneath the United States: A History of US Policy toward Latin America*, Cambridge, MA: Harvard University Press.

Shifter, M. (2011). 'A Surge to the Center', *Journal of Democracy*, 22(1): 107–21.

Silva, E. (2009). *Challenging Neoliberalism in Latin America*, Cambridge: Cambridge University Press.

Singh, R. (2012). *Barack Obama's Post-American Foreign Policy*, London: Bloomsbury.

Smith, P. (2000). *Talons of the Eagle: Dynamics of US-Latin American Relations*, second edition, Oxford: Oxford University Press.

Stokes, D. (2005). *America's Other War: Terrorizing Colombia*, London: Zed Books.

Stuenkel, O. (2016). 'Why Brazil Shouldn't Turn Its Back on the BRICS', *Americas Quarterly*, 28 June. Available online at www.americasquarterly.org/content/why-brazil-shouldnt-turn-its-back-brics (accessed 22 August 2016).

Tulchin, J. S. (2016). *Latin America in International Politics: Challenging US Hegemony*, Boulder: Lynne Rienner.

Tussie, D. and P. Heidrich (2008), 'A Tale of Ecumenism and Diversity: Economic and Trade Policies of the New Left', in *Leftovers: Tales from the Latin American Left*, edited by J. Castañeda and M. Morales, London: Routledge: 45–65.

Valenzuela, A. (2005). 'Beyond Benign Neglect: Washington and Latin America', *Current History*, 104(679): 58–63.

Waltz, K. (2001 [1954]). *Man, the State, and War: A Theoretical Analysis*, New York: Columbia University Press.

Webber, J. (2015a). 'Revolution against "Progress": Neo-Extractivism, the Compensatory State, and the TIPNIS Conflict in Bolivia', in *Crisis and Contradiction: Marxist Perspectives on Latin America in the Global Political Economy*, edited by S. J. Spronk and J. R. Webber, Leiden: Brill: 302–33.

Webber, J. (2015b). 'Ecuador's Impasse', *Jacobin*, 30 August. Available online at www.jacobinmag.com/2015/08correa-pink-tide-gramsci-peoples-march/ (accessed 22 August 2016).

Weyland, K. (2010). 'The Performance of Leftist Governments in Latin America: Conceptual and Theoretical Issues', in *Leftist Governments in Latin America: Successes and Shortcomings*, edited by K. Weyland, R. Madrid and W. Hunter, Cambridge: Cambridge University Press: 1–27.

Wiarda, H. (2011). *American Foreign Policy in Regions of Conflict: A Global Perspective*, New York: Palgrave.

Wight, C. (2006). *Agents, Structures and International Relations: Politics as Ontology*, Cambridge: Cambridge University Press.

Williams, W. A. (1972). *The Tragedy of American Diplomacy*, New York: W. W. Norton & Company.

Williams, W. A. (2011 [1961]). *The Contours of American History*, London: Verso.

Wood, E. M. (2002). 'Global Capital, National States', in *Historical Materialism and Globalization*, edited by M. Rupert and H. Smith, London: Routledge: 17–39.

Zibechi, R. (2012). *Territories in Resistance: A Cartography of Latin American Social Movements*, Oakland: AK Press.

Zibechi, R. (2016). 'Progressive Fatigue?' *NACLA Report on the Americas*, 48(1): 22–7.

2 The powers of US hegemony

A framework for analysis

Introduction: hegemony, imperialism and decline

'Increasingly', wrote historian Charles Maier in the aftermath of the 9/11 attacks, 'Americans talk about themselves, and others talk about America, as an empire' (2002: 28). The wars in Afghanistan and Iraq coincided with an explosion of interest in the United States as an imperium (Cox 2003; Mabee 2004; Nexon and Wright 2007). Critical scholars had long grappled with the (neo-)imperialist characteristics of US foreign policy. Many sought to place the unilateralist militarism of Bush in a broader historical setting, while also connecting the evolution of US policy to the global capitalist economy (Colás and Saull 2006). On the right, some commentators began calling for a more robust American imperialism (Ferguson 2004). Occasionally, they were supported by liberals who saw empire as a path to humanitarian intervention (Ignatieff 2003). More often, liberals were sceptical of this imperial turn, viewed as a departure from the prudential tradition of American statecraft (Ikenberry 2002). Meanwhile, many neoconservatives advocated the unbridled application of American power while rejecting the proposition that the United States was, in fact, an empire (Krauthammer 2002/3). This denial was shared by policymakers, who argued that the United States had 'no empire to extend or utopia to establish', in the words of President Bush (2002). The debate shifted as neoconservative hubris gave way to declinist anxieties and concerns over imperial overstretch. In a flash, the United States saw its unipolarity dissolve from definitive fact to speculative proposition.

The American public is famously averse to seeing the country as an empire, and the post-9/11 period did not kill this exceptionalist mythology. However, the style and actions of the Bush administration did precipitate a re-think of American pre-eminence. Perplexingly, Latin America was an afterthought to this new imperial discourse. As outlined in Chapter 1, the history of US interventionism in Latin America is extensive, and it persisted after the Cold War. Although Washington's attention was squarely on the Middle East, events around the time of the Iraq War laid bare the challenges confronting the United States in its 'near abroad'. In 2001, Argentina, darling of the IMF and its Washington Consensus prescriptions, experienced a stunning economic and political collapse. The Bush administration's support for the 2002 coup in Venezuela backfired as Chávez regained power just days after his ouster. That year, Lula was elected president of Brazil, prompting Congressman Henry Hyde, chairman of the House International Relations Committee, to declare an 'axis of evil' in Latin America comprising Cuba, Venezuela and Brazil (Forero 2003). In Colombia, the United States' counter-narcotics/counter-insurgency strategy against leftist guerrillas was reframed as counter-terrorism. In Haiti, Washington backed the forceful overthrow of left-leaning president Aristide amidst widening instability. Drug violence in Mexico snowballed. The United States unveiled the Mérida Initiative, modelled on Plan Colombia, further militarising its southern border.

The United States remained, and remains, the most powerful actor in the international relations of the Western hemisphere, so much so that its dominance is often taken for granted. I contend that the fullness of this asymmetrical relationship is best conceptualised as hegemony rather than imperialism. The two terms are related, and, at times, their transposable use has been cause for confusion. Empire and hegemony are ambiguous in the social/cultural vernacular, meaning it is worthwhile to distinguish between them. Modern imperialism has often been tied to a particular stage in the development of capitalist economies. Following past systems of colonialism, it is seen as a more direct form of rule. It is more territorial, as captured in the idea of an 'imperial centre' (Williams 1988 [1976]: 159–60). Hegemony, by contrast, 'is not limited to matters of direct political control but seeks to describe a more general predominance which includes, as one of its key features, a particular way of seeing the world and human nature and relationships'. Hence 'an emphasis on hegemony and the hegemonic has come to include cultural as well as political and economic factors', as expressed in 'active forms of experience and consciousness' (Williams 1988 [1976]: 144–6). Across the social sciences, hegemony is intimately associated with the writings of Antonio Gramsci.

The concept of hegemony allows for an analytical focus on the construction of consent and consensual relations, including through international institutions, and for an accounting of the non-territorial aspects of US rule. It also incorporates ideational/ideological phenomena. In short, the concept fosters a more complete analysis of the United States' place in the world. I define hegemony as an *asymmetrical social relationship patterned over time by the multiple and overlapping forms of power in international relations*. Hegemony involves both consent and coercion. It implies a tenuous and ever-changing balance between the two. It invites forms of resistance that track those forms of power which shape and reshape the social relationship between the hegemon and its subordinates. In fact, hegemony *requires* a counter-hegemony that is both constitutive of the hegemonic relationship and a potential threat to its durability (the nature of which is contingent on the agency of counter-hegemonic forces). Here, then, is another difference with imperialism. The *hegemony/counter-hegemony dialectic* effectively puts hegemony *in motion*. Its dynamism does not preclude the continuity of US objectives within this dialectic, as explained previously. It should be noted that, following the reflectivist, Gramscian variant of historical materialism, this is a non-teleological dialectic. If the winning of an empire represents the endpoint of imperial expansion, hegemony is a more fluid, almost iterative process. The synthesis of hegemonic reconstitution is not a permanent resting place but a new beginning.

If imperialism implies a certain degree of determinism, hegemony is more accommodating of contingency. This is an especially important distinction when it comes to US foreign policy, for it acknowledges that the messiness of domestic politics can impact the trajectory of American power. As intricately pointed out by diplomatic historians of various stripes, the nature and scope of the United States' global role in the twentieth century was not inevitable; it was shaped by those individuals in positions of official authority—shaped, in other words, through 'statecraft'. That continuity represents the dominant pattern (as explained in Chapter 1) does not negate the need to analyse the actions and ideas of the executive in the (re)constitution of hegemonic relationships (as adopted in the present book's focus on the Bush and Obama administrations). Leadership matters. Debates amongst politicians, policy elites and intellectuals matter (Anderson 2015; Milne 2015). Additionally, as a liberal democracy, the values and beliefs expressed in the wider public discourse matter. Understanding US hegemony means coming to grips with the 'sense of power' that permeates American society, to borrow from John Thompson's (2015) historical account. The normative feeling that the United States *should* play an outsized role in world affairs grew alongside its material power capabilities, but not always in linear or straightforward ways. I deal with this primarily through the notion of ideological power, as outlined below, which aims to capture the diffuseness of this cultural understanding of American hegemony.

My conceptualisation of hegemony should not be read as an attempt to dismiss the discussion of US imperialism that exploded onto the scene after 9/11. The notion of empire remains relevant in part because it captures the structural logic underpinning Washington's actions in the global political economy. Moreover, it can be said that waves of US imperialism (including military interventions) fed into and consolidated broader relations of hegemony (Anderson 2015; Go 2007). There is, after all, an unavoidably territorial aspect to *geo*politics, even as the spaciality of international relations is contested through multiple forms of 'geo-power', in Ó Tuathail's rendering (1996). Just as empire entails militarised forms of coercion that function geographically, hegemony's 'armoured' enforcers need space from which to operate, even if, as stated by Agnew (2005: 52), 'US hegemony has been based on a rejection of territorial limits to its influence, as would necessarily come with empire'. Although American hegemony isn't constrained by geography, its various strategic commitments require a physical presence. This has led to an expansive and expensive network of bases that stretch across the globe, conjuring empires of bygone eras and—coupled with setbacks in the Middle East—exacerbating 'the problems of number one in relative decline', to paraphrase Paul Kennedy (1987: 514). While the Bush years saw a vibrant debate over empire, the Obama presidency coincided with ruminations on a 'post-American world' (Zakaria 2008).

Insofar as US hegemony *is* related to territory, the Western hemisphere has been sacrosanct. US militarism reached its zenith in the early twentieth century, when the Caribbean was turned into a veritable 'American lake'. However, the decades that followed showed little let up in US-directed violence, notwithstanding the 'Good Neighbor' policy of the Franklin Roosevelt era. During the Cold War, the periodic overthrow of leftist and nationalist governments, along with persistent military support for rightist authoritarian regimes, lubricated a deeper, longer-lasting asymmetry, which coloured the region's return to electoral democracy. Washington utilised coercive pressure while also constructing a consensual system of multilateral co-operation, as expressed in the OAS, the Alliance for Progress and the Inter-American Development Bank. The United States strengthened its focus on multilateral consensus-building after the Cold War (as seen in NAFTA and the attempted FTAA), a pattern which largely held in the post-9/11 environment. (On the day of 11 September 2001 the OAS had gathered in Lima, Peru to adopt the Inter-American Democratic Charter.) This is not to say that coercion disappeared from US policy. On the contrary, the role of the US military remains an important part of the hemispheric landscape, as explored in Chapter 4. But hegemony means more than military might, a point on which IR scholars generally agree, even as they carve out widely divergent definitions of the ubiquitous term.

Theorising US hegemony

There are two predominant views of hegemony in conventional IR scholarship. In realist language, hegemony refers to a situation in which one state is *dominant* over others. This dominance is determined largely by a country's resource base. In liberal theory, however, hegemony is akin to *leadership*. Liberals emphasise the formal institutional arrangements that protect the hegemon's position while benefiting from international co-operation. For both realists and liberals, hegemony is the outcome of rational behaviour among egoistic states. In this view, hegemony represents a relatively steady and predictable order, one that is benign, even desirable. Although it has fallen out of favour, hegemonic stability theory, 'which argues that international economic openness and stability is most likely when there is a single dominant state', was 'the most prominent approach among American political scientists for explaining patterns of economic relations among the advanced capitalist countries' in the decades following the Second World War (Webb and Krasner 1989: 183).

Hegemony can never be entirely, exclusively *political*. As written by Susan Strange, to understand contemporary international relations one must pay attention to 'both the dominant international political system of states' and 'the global production structure' (1996: 24). Realist and liberalist approaches tend to take material resources as the basis of states' power capabilities, but, all too often, adherents have demurred from examining the processes of economic production that determine the capacity of hegemonic states to act qua hegemons. Of course, there are exceptions to this, as was the case with Strange herself. IPE is littered with attempts by scholars to grapple with the (geo-)economic foundations of hegemonic states and the numerous issues that overlap the world economy and international relations more broadly. Robert Gilpin was influential in this regard. In his earlier work, Gilpin articulated a rationalist, materialist view of hegemony as a particular type of imperial structure in the international system, which could be contrasted with bipolar and balance of power structures. Under hegemony, 'a single powerful state controls or dominates the lesser states in the system' (Gilpin 1981: 29). Turning his attention to the world economy, Gilpin reconciled his statist view of hegemony with the importance of market interactions. In the 1980s, Gilpin was weighing the decline of American hegemony (1987: 343–408). By 2000, however, he was emphasising the centrality of the United States to the construction and maintenance of an explicitly *global* capitalism (Gilpin 2000). In a similar realist vein, Layne (2007) has elucidated the importance of the United States' 'Open Door' strategy to the formation of a globalised economy, which, in turn, serves US interests. Or, in Mastanduno's phrasing (2009), the United States has been both 'system maker and privilege taker' within the world economy, devising a liberal order while simultaneously reaping the advantages that stem from its architectural role.

For obvious reasons, a great deal of scholarship on hegemony has been written with the United States as its focal point. John Ikenberry, for instance, has tailored his theorising to the United States' leadership of the liberal order after the Second World War. An open, rules-based system serves US interests and creates public goods that benefit the broader international community. This explains the United States' construction of the UN, the Bretton Woods institutions, NATO, etc. It is American authority that nurtures liberal values, which are realised through American leadership. Liberal historians emphasise the costs associated with this activist, 'world-making' foreign policy, connecting it to cultural factors embedded in the American public and cultivated by its leaders and statesmen (Milne 2015; Thompson 2015). Against more imperial notions of hegemony advanced by realists like Gilpin, Ikenberry writes that 'liberal hegemony is hierarchical order built around political bargains, diffuse reciprocity, provision of public goods, and mutually agreeable institutions and working relationships' (2011: 26). In this narrative, the benevolence of US power makes possible an open, stable and relatively lawful order. However, Ikenberry's view is necessarily limited in scope, a point he acknowledges in writing: 'In some parts of the developing world—including Latin America and the Middle East—American involvement has often been crudely imperial' (2011: 27). What's more, major concepts in the rationalist lexicon (interest, power) are often bracketed-off; they are made unproblematic. In contrast, critical scholars have staked their intervention on problematising those aspects of international relations left unopened in conventional scholarship.

This summary of IR's rationalist mainstream is meant to convey a simple point: there are trade-offs associated with different theorisations of grand ideas like hegemony. I argue that the weight of the phenomena downplayed or ignored in mainstream approaches overwhelms any benefit derived from defining hegemony in a more limited fashion. Whereas rationalist approaches may be parsimonious, I hope to draw out the concept's complexity. Hegemony involves multiple layers of social experience that bind actors to each other and to the structures that mould their existence (Joseph 2002). It involves elements of domination and leadership, but also includes the structures and discourses that make domination or leadership possible. Any conceptualisation that misses one or more of the elements needed to sustain such patterned asymmetry is inadequate. For example, although Gilpin situates hegemony alongside capitalism, he does so in an atomistic way, reifying the state in the global economy. Moreover, rationalist theories tend to focus on the material capabilities of states to the detriment of those factors that Strange called 'intangible' (1996: 23) and which others might call (inter)subjective, ideational or discursive. This is unsatisfying not because material factors are somehow unimportant, but because a framework that focuses solely on such factors is incomplete in attending to the depth of hegemony—to the layers of social experience implied by the concept itself. Finally, realist and liberalist theories of US hegemony tend to focus on relations among core 'Western' states. Their normative implications are far thornier when we consider the history of US policy in Latin America and the wider Global South.

US hegemony from a neo-Gramscian perspective

For Antonio Gramsci, hegemony was a highly nuanced concept. In his *Prison Notebooks*, the Italian political theorist and communist tactician developed a dialectical version of hegemony to explain the dynamics of Italy's class system, a theorisation that involved the 'unity of theory and practice' as realised through a 'historical process'. For Gramsci, hegemony brings together the philosophical and the politico-practical in a way that echoes Marx's arguments about 'ideas becoming a material force' (1971: 333). He writes that hegemony 'supposes an intellectual unity and an ethic in conformity with a conception of reality that has gone beyond common sense and has become, if only within narrow limits, a critical conception' (Gramsci 1971: 333–4). Common sense here is a 'traditional' or 'popular conception of the world' that envelops the subaltern classes (Gramsci 1971: 197–9). Far from a given, however, common sense is contested terrain (Gramsci 1971: 325–6; Hall 1986). Hegemony is deepened when particular common sense understandings serve the leadership position of the dominant group. Beyond ideology or 'false consciousness', hegemony 'is seen to depend for its hold not only on its expression of the interests of a ruling class but also on its acceptance as "normal reality" or "commonsense" by those in practice subordinated to it' (Williams 1988 [1976]: 145).

The utility of Gramsci's definition of hegemony stems from its dialectical linkage of the cultural sphere to an objective and pre-existing material reality. This is seen in his discourse on Leninist strategy. Gramsci writes about 'the philosophical importance of the concept' as well as 'the fact of hegemony' (that is, the Soviet Revolution) as brought to fruition by political agents. He states: 'Hegemony realised means the real critique of a philosophy, its real dialectic.' The philosophical and the politico-practical ('Marx and Ilich', or 'science and action') 'express two phases' of the same thing and 'are homogenous and heterogeneous at the same time' (Gramsci 1971: 381–2). This reading of Gramsci necessarily rejects his theorising as fundamentally idealist, as is often construed in post-Marxist or post-structural deployments of Gramscian concepts (Laclau and Mouffe 2001). In the terminology of IR/IPE, the Gramscian meta-theoretical approach creates the scope to jointly examine the material and ideational aspects of social reality, in much the same way that it calls for the mutual consideration of coercion, consent and ideological legitimation.

The concept of hegemony is 'both complicated and variable' within Gramsci's work (Williams 1988 [1976]: 145). Its application to the study of inter-state relations can cause confusion. Does hegemony rest on the economic resources needed for military supremacy? Or is it about the acceptance of a given state as the commonsense 'leader' among a group of nations? The answer is that it is both at once—and more, because different forms of power are needed to stabilise the hegemonic process, and to balance the (counter-)powers of subordinate actors. The hegemony of the United States, for example, involves the discursive and insti- tutional construction of consensus, but rests on the 'hard power' of its military preponderance. In a sense, the Gramscian concept bridges realist and liberal under- standings. In Gramsci's evocation of Machiavelli's Centaur (1971: 169–70), it is a creature that is half-beast and half-man, an allegorical reference that highlights the layered nature of power as something involving both force and consent. As elaborated by Robert Cox, hegemony means above all 'a unity between objective material forces and ethico-political ideas . . . in which power based on dominance over production is rationalized through an ideology incorporating compromise or consensus between dominant and subordinate groups' (1977: 387). In the con- text of the international system, then, hegemony is an arrangement which creates consensus-based power/legitimated domination, albeit one that is never fully severed from the capability to coerce through force. Consent must be protected by the 'armour of coercion' (Gramsci 1971: 263).

There is a substantial body of literature analysing US hegemony from a (neo-) Gramscian perspective, and there are important analytical differences within the collage of theorists influenced by Gramsci's ideas (Gill 1993; Robinson 1996; Rupert 1995). It is not my intention to gloss over the dissimilarities. I agree with Morton that, while there is no 'correct' reading of Gramsci, this does not license limitless interpretations (2007: 16). I use 'Gramscian' to emphasise the histori- cal materialist origins of his thinking and 'neo-'Gramscian to acknowledge the extension of his ideas to international relations, a move which has been subject to reappraisal from a segment of critically inflected IR scholarship (Ayers 2008; Germain and Kenny 1998). Against the various charges of this literature, I main- tain that the advantages of the neo-Gramscian tradition are readily apparent in its openness to the multiple forms of power in the international politics of North/South relations. It allows for analysis of the discursive components of US hegemony in Latin America in a way that does not treat such phenomena as wholly detached from more 'concrete' politico-economic factors. Simultaneously, it avoids a reductionist analysis of ideational factors as merely 'superstructural' reflections of a material base while accounting for the importance of class and economic pro- duction in international relations. And, although applications of Gramsci vary in

IR, they are broadly compatible in opening up the concept of power to illuminate the 'moving parts' in hegemonic relationships (including counter-hegemonies, as represented by the NLL).

Gramscian theory brings together structure and agency in a way that positions them as co-determining yet distinct. It is the asymmetry between the hegemon and its subordinates that drives the dialectical process forward towards a (momentary) 'synthesis', from hegemony to counter-hegemonic resistance to hegemonic reconstitution. Although it is (re)shaped through the interplay of dominant and subordinate agents, this asymmetry is captured and distilled via extant social structures. From a critical realist perspective, Joseph argues that hegemony should be seen as the relationship between social groups and structures, not just between dominant and subordinate groups (2002: 1–4, 128–9). Any analysis of the power(s) of the United States as an actor must reference existing institutions, discourses and structures. These phenomena (co)determine the ability of the United States to actualise its power in the international arena, whether coercive or consensual, direct or indirect. As noted above, the conceptual move from imperialism to hegemony occasions the prioritisation of consensus, which is nevertheless underpinned by force. In practice, consensus in international relations exists between those in charge of policy. In other words, it does not automatically extend to subordinate groups 'below' the state (to cover the entirety of civil society). Recalling the importance of common sense, however, this is a goal of hegemony in its ideological machinations. The tensions involved in maintaining such a consensus will become clearer in the discussion on the Washington Consensus, below.

Finally, Gramscian IR/IPE allows for the theorisation of resistance to hegemony, called *counter-hegemony* by scholars working in this tradition (though Gramsci didn't use this term). For Randolph Persaud, 'resistance and counter-hegemony are too often seen as responses to the embedded interests already formed, rather than theorized as dialectically defining the conditions which make hegemonic practices historically "necessary" in the first place'. It is more accurate, he notes, to understand hegemony and counter-hegemony as 'a simultaneous *double movement*, the consequence of which is the reciprocal configuration of each other' (Persaud 2001: 49). Resistance to domination is part and parcel of hegemony itself, a dynamic that, in the international sphere, helps to intuit the special significance of hegemony as opposed to more overt types of imperialist rule. The need for some amount of consensus within a hegemonic relationship is born out of the resistance to domination that is thrown up by arrangements of governance that are completely lacking in consent from within the subordinate group. Counter-hegemony is expressed through the various forms of power that layer the asymmetrical social relations found in the international arena.

US foreign policy and the global political economy

I have defined hegemony as an asymmetrical social relationship patterned over time by multiple and overlapping forms of power. This definition is mute on the utility of hegemony (and power) in international relations. Although power is not *exclusively* instrumental, it is nonetheless expressed, or manifest, via agency. This begs several questions. What are asymmetrical power relationships in the international system *for* (to the degree that power is 'for' anything at all)? Are hegemons motivated simply to maintain their hegemony? Or is hegemony a means of obtaining security, prosperity, prestige and/or other 'benefits' or 'goods'? In other words, how is US hegemony related to its 'national interest(s)'? This section engages these issues by building on the Gramscian perspective outlined above, linking it more directly with US policy. (The power problematic is fleshed out in the following section.)

In the logic of the hegemony/counter-hegemony dialectic, the hegemon is compelled to entrench and remake its asymmetrical position. To a degree, when challenged 'from below', the reconstitution of hegemony becomes its own end. Additionally, however, from the perspective of historical materialism, hegemony in the international system must be situated alongside global capitalism. As capitalist relations of production secure the United States' coercive capabilities (through the differentiated allocation of material resources), capitalist social relations help constitute the United States as a particular kind of actor. The United States comes to view its hegemony as natural, the commonsense extension of its continental march of 'manifest destiny'. Its wealth is taken as a sign of heavenly blessings from above (Hunt 2009). This ideology is closely related to structural power, as we will see, which pulls the United States to act in ways that reinforce the very structures that fashion its advantageous position. Foreign policy, as an expression of the agency of the US state, can work (within limits) to fortify and/or reconfigure the structures of global capitalism. But to what end?

Historical materialism has stimulated a powerful—if disjointed—critique of the nexus between US foreign policy and the international political economy. Competing analyses of the nature of the global/international capitalist system posit different implications for the role of the United States therein. This debate was reinvigorated by the publication of Hardt and Negri's *Empire* (2000). The book's unique synthesis argued that the imperialism of the past had given way to a new imperial form of sovereignty based on the decentred, de-territorialised processes of capitalist globalisation. Proclaiming the end of the modern imperialism of the nation-state, Hardt and Negri heralded a new postmodern order in which the agency of the US government was becoming relatively inconsequential, if not totally insignificant. 'Against such (older) imperialisms', they wrote, 'Empire extends and consolidates the model of a network power'. It has a 'universal', 'boundless' and 'inclusive architecture' which pits 'powers and counterpowers' against one another in a way that has 'nothing to do with imperialism' in its traditional sense (Hardt and Negri 2000: 166–7). A truly global capitalism meant a new global politics.

Highly provocative, Hardt and Negri's hypothesis was premature if not fanciful, even as it sharpened the debate over globalisation. A similar line of reasoning can be seen elsewhere in the historical materialist literature, chiefly among scholars focused on the transnationalisation of capital, class and/or political rule.

The work of William Robinson is paramount in this regard. For Robinson, globalisation is an 'epochal shift' in the history of capitalism, which marks the 'transition from a *world* economy to a *global* economy' (2004: 2). By this Robinson means that globalisation is best seen as a pivotal, transitional phase of capitalism driven by the rise of transnational capital, which is increasingly decentralised and highly mobile. This new structural arrangement marks a qualitative change. In Robinson's understanding, it has led to the creation of a transnational capitalist class and an emerging transnational state, to which the US state is subsumed. Rather peculiarly given his wider argument, he writes that 'the empire of capital is headquartered in Washington', alluding not only to the US state but the international financial institutions (IFIs) based in the city (Robinson 2004: 140). He agrees with Hardt and Negri that earlier forms of imperialism have lost relevance; that the emerging global order lacks a centre; and that power is no longer mediated primarily through the nation-state.

Robinson's theorising downplays the importance of the United States to the formation of the globalised order as it actually exists. As put by Stokes, although 'Robinson contends that the US state continues to be the global hegemonic capitalist state', he also argues that the United States 'now acts as the central agent of transnational capital, rather than having a nationally grounded ruling class' (2005: 227). With Washington now serving the transnational capitalist elite, it would seem that US hegemony is no longer *US* hegemony, a perplexing proposition in a world still marked by national borderlines. This is made more problematic when considering Robinson's argument that 'globalization is not a project conceived and planned at the level of intentionality' (Robinson 2002: 26), a statement seemingly at odds with his earlier work, which proffered a trenchant critique of US foreign policy in the Global South (regarding the promotion of polyarchy as the political component of neoliberalism). Recent work on the global crisis reinforces his theoretical commitment to a global capitalism divorced from the currents of inter-state competition. He notes that the crisis's appalling symptoms (from pauperisation to an upsurge in neo-fascism) have elicited an emerging 'global police' presence, acknowledging the importance of US interventionism in this dynamic. But he rejects the centrality of US power by eliding the reality of *US* interests, which (supposedly) get washed away in the transnationalising trends of globalisation (Robinson 2014: 99–103). Robinson's account of the emerging global order loses sight of the inter*national* dynamics that continue to shape it.

In contrast, Peter Gowan emphasises the ways in which the contemporary international economic order is a product of US policy. For Gowan, globalisation is a euphemism for a neoliberal monetary and financial regime erected by the United States as a tool of statecraft. Dubbed 'the Dollar-Wall Street Regime', Gowan argues that the liberalisation of the international financial system consolidated the US dollar as the principal world currency, a move that, among other things, allowed the United States to backhandedly benefit from international financial crises, such as the East Asian crisis of the late 1990s. Indeed, dollar hegemony has produced a myriad of benefits for the United States. He writes:

the process of globalization has been driven most crucially by the enormous political power placed in the hands of the American state and of US business through the particular type of international financial and monetary system and associated international financial regime that was constructed—largely by the US government—in the ashes of the Bretton Woods system.

(Gowan 1999: xi)

In turn, what is called 'globalisation' has served the geopolitical ends of the United States as a national entity. Thus, in many respects, Gowan is making a more 'realist', state-centric argument against the globalisation thesis of historical materialists like Robinson.

I would contend that, as Hardt and Negri and Robinson fail to appreciate the role of the United States in the construction and maintenance of globalisation, Gowan omits key structural changes in a globalising capitalism. Transnationalisation is proceeding, but 'the growing disparity between the global economy and the territorial nation-state in no way signals the end of capitalism's need, however contradictory, for a spatially fragmented political and legal order' (Wood 2002: 36). Ultimately, as argued by Stokes, the aims of US foreign policy are embedded in a 'dual logic': the United States pursues the interests of its own national capital while also consolidating a particular global economic system in the interests of international capital—which, to be sure, is becoming increasingly transnational (Stokes 2005: 218). This is a 'both/and' rather than 'either/or' position regarding US strategy vis-à-vis the 'levels' of capitalism. The dual logic argument brings clarity to the discussion of the relationship between the United States and globalisation, which Rupert and Solomon define as 'the continuation and intensification' of long-standing processes of 'internationalization of commodity production and capital accumulation' (2006: 7). In this view, 'a Gramscian-inflected HM enables an understanding of globalizing capitalism, its relations of power structures of governance, as the product of struggles—at once material and ideological—among concretely situated social agents' (Rupert and Solomon 2006: 79). Prominent amongst these agents is the US government. Indeed, 'contemporary capitalist globalization and US power are intimately entwined' (Rupert and Solomon 2006: 131), as evidenced by Washington's efforts to uphold its trade and investment privileges within a global order supportive of capitalist production writ large.

Neoliberalism and global capitalism

If HM scholars are split on the nature of the global political economy and its relationship to US foreign policy, they are fairly uniform in their critique of neoliberalism as a variant of late capitalism and its periodisation alongside 'globalisation'. For Tickell and Peck, 'neoliberalization, like globalization, should be thought of as a contingently realized process, not as an end-state or "condition"'; in other words, it is a 'process of political-economic change, not just (an) institutional outcome' (2003: 165). Tickell and Peck demonstrate that neoliberalism evolved in stages, from 'proto-neoliberalism' (the intellectual crystallisation of anti-Keynesianism and the critique of embedded liberalism), to 'roll-back neoliberalism' (the Reagan and Thatcher 'revolutions' built on privatisation, liberalisation, monetarism and the assault on trade unions) and 'roll-out neoliberalism' (the global consolidation and naturalisation of the ideology of the market). In the context of the Americas, one might ask whether, given the rise of the NLL, neoliberalism has entered into a more defensive posture. As noted in Chapter 1, there is discussion of 'post-neoliberalism' in Latin America. And, whereas the global financial crisis of 2007–9 was believed by some to signal the end of neoliberal ascendency, the fallout has been considerably more complex, leading some to contemplate the 'strange non-death of neoliberalism' (Crouch 2011).

The (proto-)neoliberalism outlined by Tickell and Peck began with the writings of the economists Ludwig von Mises, Friedrich Hayek and Milton Friedman, who did much to advance the 'classical liberal' or 'laissez-faire' version of 'free market' ideology during the twentieth century. These ideas came in for very different treatment in Karl Polanyi's classic work, *The Great Transformation* (2001 [1944]). Critics of neoliberalism have drawn on Polanyi to gain insight into the intellectual pedigree of market liberalism, its deficiencies and its historical origins and implications. The conceptual centrepiece of Polanyi's account is the 'double movement', which holds that, as capitalist relations advance and the so-called 'self-regulating market' is propelled forward, the negative social effects generated by the move to a laissez-faire economic order create an attendant backlash. For Polanyi, the self-regulating market is but a utopian idea, a powerful trope which, despite innate contradictions, constitutes the essence of liberal economic thought. Through 'the extension of the market organization', a process of disembedding takes hold, in which the economic 'sphere' is removed (though never completely) from its societal nest (Polanyi 2001 [1944]: 79). This leads to a variety of social and political problems that beget a 'counter-movement' which, in turn, activates checks on the market's extremes. A balance of sorts is eventually reached, as 'society protect(s) itself against the perils inherent in a self-regulating market system' (Polanyi 2001 [1944]: 80).

There is much in Polanyi's cogent critique which can enrich a more explicitly historical materialist analysis of neoliberalism. David Harvey, for example, writes that Polanyi's 'diagnosis' of 'neoliberal utopianism'—as a process 'doomed . . . to be frustrated by authoritarianism, or even outright fascism'—is 'peculiarly appropriate for our contemporary condition' (2005: 37). Polanyi's insight into the ways in which neoliberalism reduces 'freedom' to the 'freedom of enterprise' is particularly instructive for Harvey, as is the related but often overlooked point that the state never truly disappears, or fully retreats, under a neoliberal order. Harvey (2005: 2) builds on Polanyi to dissect the ideational aspects of neoliberalism:

> Neoliberalism is in the first instance a theory of political economic practices that proposes that human well-being can best be advanced by liberating individual entrepreneurial freedoms and skills within an institutional framework characterised by strong private property rights, free markets, and free trade. The role of the state is to create and preserve an institutional framework

appropriate to such practices. The state has to guarantee, for example, the quality and integrity of money. It must also set up those military, defence, police and legal structures and functions required to secure private property rights and to guarantee, by force if need be, the proper functioning of markets. Furthermore, if markets do not exist . . . then they must be created, by state action if necessary. But beyond these tasks the state should not venture.

Harvey notes that, in addition to the *values* and *ideas* of the supposedly unfettered market, neoliberalism has a tangible history as a political-economic force that has proliferated across the world stage. He writes that 'neoliberalization was from the very beginning a project to achieve the restoration of class power' (2005: 16). It involved, and continues to involve, elites overturning 'embedded liberalism' and the welfare state through 'accumulation by dispossession', or the separation of that from which individuals/groups already have (e.g. the removal of peasants from their land). Essentially, accumulation by dispossession is class-based plunder akin to the primitive accumulation theorised by Marx. It includes privatisation, or the transferring of property from the public sphere to private ownership. It also includes processes of commodification (of 'the commons', for instance) and financialisation, both of which serve a redistributive function favouring capital at the expense of labour.[1] By inserting class into the discussion, Harvey broadens the critique of neoliberalism beyond Polanyian limitations to match the realities of a phenomenon that is, in the final analysis, an offshoot of the capitalist mode of production.

Keeping in mind the strictures of capitalism, it is important to point out that there are tensions inherent in the neoliberal project. In terms of the neoliberal state, this includes problems of economic policy related to the rise of monopolies and oligopolies; market failures and harmful externalities; the imbalance of information in market transactions; and the instability wrought by technological dynamism (Harvey 2005: 67–70). As uncertainties grow more pronounced, the retreat of the state in some areas creates effects which require increased attention in adjoining areas. Then there are the antinomies of capitalism itself, which processes of neoliberalisation may exacerbate. Asymmetries of information interfere with the ability of the archetypal 'rational actor' to reach a decision that is in its objective best interest, making market interactions more opaque than they should be according to neoliberal theory. These asymmetries are often widened by new technologies developed in the service of capital, a dynamic that further aggravates social inequalities. The invention of the Internet, to cite one obvious example, has become emblematic of neoliberal globalisation's capacity for 'creative destruction', as financial crises spread at the speed of wireless telecommunications. This is despite the fact that the Internet is simultaneously seen as egalitarian and even emancipatory in some circles.

Undoubtedly, the experience of the crisis of the late 2000s lends much to this hypothesis. From a Marxian standpoint, it was not merely a financial meltdown and concomitant credit crunch, in which 'wealth' was created out of the smoke and mirrors of the money economy before vanishing into thin air.

Financial mismanagement and manipulation were undoubtedly part of the story. More fundamentally, however, the crisis can also be seen as one of overproduction and/or underconsumption, which was created by a prolonged period of stagnating real wages, rising inequality and the drive for accumulation by dispossession (as seen in the predatory lending and foreclosures in the US housing market, for example). The spread of the tumult echoed the contagion of the East Asian financial crisis of the late 1990s. Both episodes demonstrated the interconnectedness of the world's economies in an era of heightened transnationalisation. The crises also showed how these globalising trends are interlocked with neoliberalism, while demonstrating that the state remains the ultimate protector of the economic status quo. In the United States, the United Kingdom and elsewhere, it took strict state action to save the flailing banking system from complete collapse. Thus, and as discussed below, the implications of capitalism's crises are contingent on how they are understood and acted upon by agents, including governments.

The contradictions of neoliberal capitalism do not remain confined to an economic sphere detached from socio-political relations. Its economic outcomes have a track record of producing social crises which engender a backlash against the policies of deregulation, privatisation, financialisation, liberalisation and austerity; crises which bleed over into the arena of politics proper as dissatisfied forces attempt to 're-embed' the market in society, in the spatial metaphor of Polanyi's counter-movement. One does not have to strain one's eyes to see this occurring in Latin America, so thoroughly subjected to neoliberalism from the 1970s onward.[2] 'Eventually', wrote Kenneth Roberts, 'the contradictions of the new model—particularly the tension between democratic citizenship and social exclusion—would create fault lines along which resistance could mobilize' (Roberts 2008: 336).

> Recent changes in Latin America thus continue a historical pattern of cyclical fluctuation between the political exclusion and incorporation of popular majorities, along with a tradition of contention of the terms of the incorporation itself—terms that largely define the character of democratic regimes and the breadth, depth and content of citizenship rights . . . These dynamics of contention are heavily conditioned by attempts to politicize or depoliticize social inequalities, and to regulate or unshackle market forces.
>
> (Roberts 2008: 329)

As the antimonies of neoliberal production created social uncertainty throughout Latin America, popular forces responded through a wave of social movement activism (Petras and Veltmeyer 2011; Silva 2009; Zibechi 2012). This fed three main channels of opposition: confrontational protest, based largely around a resurgent peasantry; electoral politics, which shifted governments to the left; and localised alternative development strategies, as captured in the proliferation of NGOs in the region. These movements formed largely in response to neoliberalism (though they also descended from earlier waves of protest), making the neoliberal state the main site of class struggle. Unable or unwilling to confront capitalism directly, popular movements nevertheless destabilised the Washington Consensus. The model had failed to live up to its promise to grow the economy, reduce poverty and stimulate development (Kiely 2007). Ideologically, it began taking on water as the region veered from crisis to crisis. The devaluation of the Mexican peso spurred capital flight and a major recession in 1995 as the Zapatista rebellion dramatised the struggle against neoliberalism, garnering widespread attention and solidarity. Contagion from the East Asian financial crisis hit Brazil and then Argentina as the decade came to an end, with implications for much of South America. The Andes saw a wave of social protests over natural resources and privatisation, including Bolivia's gas and water wars.

William Robinson's account of the structural contradictions of global capitalism links the ideological disconnect produced by the neoliberal model to its material realities as a politico-economic project. These global, interrelated contradictions include: overproduction (underconsumption); social polarisation; the crisis of state legitimacy; and the crisis of ecological (un)sustainability (Robinson 2004: 147, 2014). Robinson anticipates the demise of neoliberalism and its replacement with an alternate model (a kind of global neo-Keynesianism), in part to protect the viability of capitalist production from the oppositional forces gathering in its interstices (2004: 162–78). This described the situation in much of Latin America from the 1990s into the 2000s, when rapid social polarisation and growing difficulties of social reproduction generated a new cycle of popular resistance (Robinson 2008: 226–359), paving the way for the NLL. Although many of the groups had decades-long histories (such as Brazil's Landless Workers Movement [MST]), others grew up alongside the electoral emergence of the NLL (Argentina's *piqueteros*, for instance, which were associated largely with the 2001–2 crisis). The general picture is one of popular movements gathering momentum and fuelling the shift in electoral politics. This was most acutely symbolised by the Morales government in Bolivia, which came directly from that country's *cocalero* movement. The degree to which these groups were 'co-opted' by the politicians of the NLL is an unsettled question, one that lends credence to the notion of passive revolution, in Gramscian language (Morton 2007).

From the vantage of historical materialism, the various interrelated tensions of neoliberalism unfold dialectically. Necessarily open-ended, this dialectic is comprised of curvilinear turning-points on the way to an unfinished synthesis. The inherent structural tensions of neoliberalisation are not fully manifest until they are internalised at the level of agency; in other words, contradictions don't become full-blown *crises* until they are understood as such—and acted upon accordingly. As stated by Mark Blyth:

> what constitutes an economic crisis *as a crisis* is not a self-apparent phenomenon . . . Agents must argue over, diagnose, proselytize, and impose on others their notion of what a crisis actually *is* before collective action to resolve the uncertainty facing them can take any meaningful institutional form.

> (2002: 9)

Policy elites in Latin America and Washington understood the economic problems of the late 1970s and 1980s as attributable to the developmentalist state and import substitution industrialisation, leading to hyperinflation and the so-called 'Third World debt crisis'. The Washington Consensus was born out of this diagnosis. It prescribed a set of 'solutions' that masked the class dynamics of neoliberalism's roll out. Subsequent tensions were translated into crises by groups with different political agendas. The forces of the NLL targeted slow economic growth and widening inequality following Latin America's 'lost decades' of neoliberal 'development' (Panizza 2009). Even before the global crisis, the Washington Consensus was collapsing on its 'home turf'.

Then came the crash of 2008 and the Great Recession, which, for some, called into question both capitalist globalisation and the durability of US hegemony. Originating at the epicentre of global capitalism, the scope of the downturn was extraordinary, setting off a wave of economic uncertainty unseen since the Great Depression. It bedevilled simplistic explanations. As policy elites argued over the nature of the crisis and how best to respond, Washington contributed to various reform efforts to protect the global economic system. The smooth transition from the G8 to the G20 (a forum that includes Argentina, Brazil and Mexico along with other major Southern economies) hinted at a more inclusive global governance. G20 members created a Financial Stability Board to regulate global markets. They moved to triple the lending capacity of the IMF, reallocating voting shares within the institution so that the 'emerging powers' would have a greater say in its policies. There would be no clean break with the existing architecture of the global economy (Helleiner 2010; Kahler 2013). And yet, coming on the heels of the Iraq quagmire, the meltdown on Wall Street spawned considerable reflection on the imminent end of American pre-eminence. In a widely circulated piece, John Gray (2008) compared the financial crisis to the fall of the Berlin Wall, arguing that it was part of a 'historic geopolitical shift' which would see 'America's fall from power'. Critical scholars were generally sceptical of this hypothesis. 'As pundits of every persuasion once again blur the lines between a capitalist crisis and the decline of the US empire', wrote Panitch and Gindin, 'it is especially important to recognize the central role which the American state continues to play in reproducing global capitalism' (2012: 331). This holds particular resonance for the Americas, the original 'site' of the Washington Consensus. Buried in the discussion of issues of global concern, the tumult queried the United States' enduring promotion of neoliberal capitalism in Latin America. Was the hemisphere on the cusp of a truly *Post*-Washington Consensus era?

Neoliberalism and US policy in Latin America: the (Post-)Washington Consensus

In recent decades, efforts to entrench US hegemony were closely tied to the neoliberalisation of Latin America's political economy. The stability of the neoliberal model remains a cornerstone of US policy. Washington's stated policy goals (democracy promotion, economic integration) are wrapped up in the dual logic of neoliberalisation, which serves US interests while also producing an increasingly transnational capitalism. The NLL emerged mainly as a response to the socio-economic shifts of the 1970s–1990s, meaning there is some historical unpacking needed at this juncture of the analysis. It was the 'Nixon shock' and the collapse of the Bretton Woods system of fixed exchange rates that paved the way for globalisation through the unleashing of financial capital (Gowan 1999). US foreign policy guided this unfolding process through the end of the Cold War, when Washington's diplomacy and foreign aid policies embraced the democratisation of the Global South and the former Soviet Union. The institutional 'face' of neoliberalism came to the fore. Under the Clinton administration, democracy promotion became the overarching principle of the United States' globalisation strategy, supplanting 'containment' as Washington's foreign policy motto.

For all the talk of democratisation, US policy towards the South in the post-Cold War era was driven by the consolidation of its transnational economic project. It consisted of the promotion of polyarchy, or 'low-intensity democracy', as a top-down system conducive to the realisation of the broader aims of economic liberalisation (Robinson 1996: 36–7). Of importance here is the notion of consent and its relative absence under the authoritarian governments supported by the United States during the Cold War. Robinson demonstrates how the consistencies in US economic objectives were translated into the promotion of polyarchic neoliberalism in the changed geopolitical milieu of the post-Cold War world. Support for elections, yes, but also staunch opposition to the demands of the popular classes. This type of elite-led consensual rule was promoted both covertly and overtly by the US government and the IMF and World Bank, including through the implementation of Structural Adjustment Programmes (SAPs). Here, Robinson's handling of US foreign policy coincides with the dual logic outlined by Stokes. He 'simultaneously analyse(s) "democracy promotion" as a *United States* policy intended to secure *US* interests *and* argue(s) that this policy responds to an agenda of a *transnational* elite' (1996: 11–12; italics in original). Updating this hypothesis, Robinson noted that, as the transition to polyarchy in Latin America frayed, casting uncertainty on the idea of 'market democracy', the United States continued to support the region's transnational elite through 'an ever deeper alignment with local authoritarian political forces and paramilitary groups' (Robinson 2006). In addition to funding the repressive capacity of the Colombian and Mexican governments, Washington backed coups in Venezuela (2002), Haiti (2004) and Honduras (2009). One could argue that this reliance on coercive power further aggravated the ideological tensions of neoliberalism, which, in the dominant narrative of the United States and its elite allies, was inseparable from a consent-based (liberal) democratic system. A major component of this larger discourse was, of course, the Washington Consensus, which began to crack amidst the antinomies of an expanding neoliberal capitalism. As some observers contemplated its passing from the scene (Gore 2000; Held 2005; Rodrik 2006), others spoke increasingly of a *Post*-Washington Consensus, which, as addressed below, was only marginally different from the original.

The Washington Consensus was coined by economist John Williamson in 1989. It originally pertained to Latin America, though it was later extended to encompass the broader 'developing world' as well as the former Soviet bloc. It consisted of ten policy reforms: fiscal discipline; re-ordering of public expenditure priorities; tax reform; liberalisation of interest rates; competitive exchange rates; free trade; liberalisation of inward foreign direct investment; privatisation; deregulation; and enhanced property rights (Williamson 2008). The Consensus was synonymous with 'neoliberalism' and 'market fundamentalism', though Williamson himself understood these terms differently (2008: 22). Its name is telling. It was the *Washington* Consensus not because its tenets were somehow proprietary to Washington, or because it lacked support outside of the United States. Rather, the name reflected the 'commonsense' status of the reforms within Washington's institutional landscape, from the US Treasury to the IMF, World Bank and Inter-American Development Bank. Moreover, the US state and its institutional partners *used* the incontrovertibility of the Consensus as a rhetorical and ideological *tool* to entrench the on-going neoliberalisation of Latin American economies.

The history of the Washington Consensus is fraught with contested meanings and interpretations (Williamson 2008). In the Americas, differences stemmed from divergent structural interests among the various agents at play (from US government agencies and transnational elites to the NLL). The Washington Consensus came to mean different things to different people. A paradigm of 'responsible policymaking' in Washington and in many Latin American capitals, popular sectors viewed the Consensus as an odious, imperialist imposition. To the degree that an actual small 'c' consensus existed amongst the hemisphere's technocratic elite, it co-existed with the various meanings of the capital 'C' Consensus, which constituted the broader discourse of economic restructuring in US–Latin American relations. As written by Panizza:

> the issue is not to determine the neoliberal nature of the (Consensus), but to show how, under the appearance of a highly codified and prescriptive policy agenda, there was a surplus of meaning that left it open to interpretation, contestation and redefinition by friends and foes alike (and even by its own author).

(Panizza 2009: 13)

The language of the Washington Consensus infused, legitimated and naturalised the neoliberalisation of the countries of Latin America, while also connecting this process to the foreign economic policy of the United States. Politically, then, it 'cut both ways'. Williamson was later to lament that his label constituted a 'propaganda gift' to the left (2008: 20).

If Williamson was the conveyor of the Washington Consensus, the Post-Washington Consensus is attributed largely to Joseph Stiglitz. In 1998, Stiglitz, then Chief Economist at the World Bank, delivered a major speech in which he stated that the policies of the Washington Consensus were incomplete and 'sometimes misguided'. However, he added, they 'provided some of the foundations for well-functioning markets' (Stiglitz 1998). The Post-Washington Consensus was to be different because 'it emphasize(d) broader goals for macroeconomic policy (including long-term sustainable growth and equity), a wider range of economic policy instruments (including prudential regulations and other microeconomic tools . . .), and a balanced role for markets and government (as opposed to minimizing the role of the state)' (Serra *et al.* 2008: 12). Governments should help markets work better, but 'there are government failures, just as there are market failures' (Stiglitz 2008: 47). Under the Post-Washington Consensus, economic governance was to be market-oriented. A fundamental break with the reigning orthodoxy wasn't necessary or desirable.

If anything, the Post-Washington Consensus was hazier than its forerunner. For Stiglitz, the revamped Consensus needed to feature 'more than an economic agenda' (2008: 45). It had to pay greater attention to issues of socio-economic distribution and institutional reform. It also needed to deliver on (market-based) economic growth as a prerequisite for social development. The global financial crisis solidified some of the more Keynesian elements of the 'new' consensus already coming to the fore (the IMF tacitly embracing capital controls, for instance). According to Birdsall and Fukuyama, by 2008 most developing countries 'had reduced their exposure to the foreign financial markets by accumulating large foreign currency reserves and maintaining regulatory control of their banking systems. These policies provided insulation from global economic volatility and were vindicated by the impressive rebounds in the wake of the recent crisis' (2011: 46). In their view, the financial collapse and resulting global recession further damaged the Washington Consensus 'brand', a process underway in Latin America well before then. Williamson acknowledged that the global crisis had created a 'Keynesian situation'. At the same time, Williamson noted that people had been proclaiming the death of the Consensus since it was first proclaimed (*Washington Post* 2009). Its basic prescriptions, he claimed, were untainted, even if the economic performance of its Latin American adherents had been mostly disappointing (Williamson 2005).

The Post-Washington Consensus coincided with new economic options for NLL states. The 2000s saw a commodities boom driven by rising demand from the BRICs and other fast-growing countries in Asia and elsewhere. Latin American and Caribbean (LAC) countries looked to forge new commercial ties with partners outside of the Western hemisphere, loosening their traditional reliance on North American markets and capital. In particular, the dynamic emergence of Chinese markets for Latin American primary goods meant that trade flows increased by substantial margins; between 2000 and 2014, bilateral trade between China and the LAC region increased twenty-two-fold (ECLAC 2015: 77). As prices rose, South American producers were supplying a larger portion of the energy resources and raw materials needed for China's industrial output. These materials included, most notably, crude oil, iron ore, copper, aluminium and zinc. Chinese foreign investment in Latin America also spiked, concentrated in the oil and gas and mining sectors, although this remained a relatively small segment of China's overall FDI (ECLAC 2015; Jenkins 2012: 1341–3; Ray *et al.* 2016). The growth in Latin American exports to China also encompassed foodstuffs to meet growing food consumption among the Chinese workforce; it wasn't just the extractive industries that benefited from the commodities boom, but also the region's sizable agro-industrial sector—namely producers of soybeans and soybean oil, coffee, sugar, bananas, beef and poultry. Global commodity prices recovered after a dip during the Great Recession, but by the early- to mid-2010s it was clear that 'the period of ever-increasing commodity prices (had) come to an end', as stated by one IMF researcher (Gruss 2014: 3).[3] In conjunction with less robust growth in China, growth in much of the LAC region slowed considerably, with some countries (including Brazil and Venezuela) entering into recession.

New interdependencies led analysts to consider an emerging 'triangular' pattern across Sino–US–Latin American relations (Ellis 2012; Gallagher 2016; Tokatlian 2008), one that, despite the obvious asymmetries, was largely beneficial to Latin American countries. While some saw the potential for a 'new dependency' to crystallise (Jenkins 2012), many in the region believed they stood to 'benefit from trade diversification, foreign direct investment, low-cost imports, and growth in sectors that (were) complementary to China's trade with the region' (Roett and Paz 2008: 16). This carried over into the diplomatic arena, as well, where Beijing was emphasising South–South co-operation at a time when Washington's agenda was increasingly unpopular. Conversely, however, with respect to the export of

Table 2.1 Average annual GDP growth at constant values, 2003–20: world and select countries and regions

	2003–7	*2008–9*	*2010–14*	*2015–20**
World	5.1%	1.5%	3.6%	3.8%
Developed countries	2.8%	−1.6%	1.5%	2.2%
Developing countries	7.7%	4.5%	5.2%	4.9%
United States	2.9%	−1.5%	2.1%	2.5%
Developing and emerging Asia (including China)	9.5%	7.4%	7.1%	6.5%
LAC	4.9%	1.3%	3.1%	2.4%

Source: Adapted from ECLAC (2015: 10); based on IMF data.

Note
* Projections.

Table 2.2 China's share of LAC exports by sector, 1994–2014

	1994	*1999*	*2004*	*2009*	*2014*
All exports	1%	1%	3%	7%	10%
Agriculture	3%	3%	8%	10%	14%
Extraction	<1%	1%	5%	12%	19%
Manufacturing	<1%	<1%	1%	2%	3%

Source: Adapted from Ray *et al.* (2016: 3); based on UN Comtrade data.

manufactured goods, China was widely viewed as a competitor. Cheaper Chinese imports could adversely impact domestic producers in national and regional markets. Moreover, the newer commercial linkages meant that a severe slow-down in China would likely lead to the further contraction of economic options for Latin American policymakers. For better or worse, China mattered more to Latin America than it ever had. This is not to say that China's economic impor-tance to the region eclipsed that of the United States. As of 2015, the United States was far and away the largest market for LAC exports (followed by the European Union and then China) as well as the largest single source of imports (ECLAC 2015).

Notwithstanding the ideological echoes between Beijing's ruling Communist Party and certain factions of the NLL, Sino-Latin American relations remained, on the whole, pragmatic. The Chinese were careful to stress that they weren't attempting to challenge US hegemony in the Americas, and the prevailing per-spective in Washington was that China's influence in the Western hemisphere was largely benign—though this was not the uniform position (Ellis 2012; Jenkins 2010; Roett and Paz 2008). Important to this discussion was the Chinese devel-opment model, sometimes called the 'Beijing Consensus', which emphasised state-led innovation strategies and policy independence from Western IFIs (Ramo 2004; Williamson 2012). Although the applicability of the Beijing Consensus to the Latin American context was dubious in some ways (it seemed to advocate an authoritarianism that was inconsistent with Latin America's vibrant democratic currents, for example), its focus on South–South co-operation and the creation of a multipolar international political economy resonated with leaders. Interest in the Beijing Consensus reinforced the notion that the heady days of the Washington Consensus were long gone. The global financial crisis of 2008–9 only heightened the perception that the neoliberal model was severely lacking as a pathway to sustained and equitable economic development; this thinking wasn't limited to the Global South.

Even as elite opinion in the North moved begrudgingly away from 'market fundamentalism', however, this did not entail the wholesale abandonment of neoliberalism, broadly defined. The Post-Washington Consensus was perhaps milder in its advocacy of neoliberal policies—a kind of 'neoliberalism lite'. As noted, it allowed for state intervention to address market failures. 'Inevitably, the policy prescriptions of the new consensus (were) more vague and less explicit than those of the old', making it 'imperative to stress that the gradually forming post-Washington consensus remain(ed) deeply conservative in fiscal and monetary matters', from liberalisation and deregulation to free trade (Fine *et al.* 2003: xvii). International agenda-setting was to stay with the Washington-based IFIs (Onis and Senses 2005). Moreover, the framework was incredibly loose, prompting Stiglitz (2008) himself to ask whether a Post-Washington Consensus consensus actually existed. Undoubtedly, the field of development economics had changed since the early 1990s, and these changes impacted US foreign economic policy at some level. However, the Bush and Obama administrations remained committed to the core tenets of neoliberal orthodoxy in their dealings with Latin America.

This was seen virtually across the board, from trade promotion to the disapproval of 'statist' or 'populist' programmes, as documented in the following chapters.

As outlined in Chapter 1, the NLL emerged in opposition to the Washington Consensus. The degree to which the NLL successfully challenged the neoliberal model is a matter of some debate. What is certain is that the election of left-leaning governments scaled-back the already-dwindling ideological purchase of the Washington Consensus, and in a way that underwrote the success of left-ist and centre-left parties. This unravelling was dependent on the NLL chipping away at the consensual properties of the paradigm, problematising its policies on a regional level. In this way, the NLL gained coherence in the politics of the Americas. As a result, US foreign policy in the age of the New Latin Left coa-lesced around a Post-Washington Consensus that, in terms of actual content, was reminiscent of the original, albeit woollier and marginally more 'Keynesian'. US behaviour 'evolved' in reaction to the anti-neoliberalism of the NLL while main-taining the goal of a globalised regional political economy. This 'evolution' was witnessed not only in its trade policy (as documented in Chapter 3), but also in its military strategy (Chapter 4) and within key multilateral institutions, including the OAS (Chapter 5). It was also seen in Washington's diplomatic efforts to undercut the ideological appeal of the NLL's reformist and radical agendas (Chapter 6). The gathering counter-hegemony elicited a response which stretched across the powers of the US state as the leading actor in intra-hemispheric relations.

The powers of hegemony

Critical theory engenders a sophisticated approach to the reconstitution of US hegemony in Latin America. This encompasses its ability to internalise the counter-hegemony of the NLL. Additionally, as the Washington Consensus was a major part of the ideological apparatus of neoliberal capitalism in the Western hemisphere, neo-Gramscian IR/IPE is well-suited to probe its 'disintegration' amidst the structural 'contradictions of global capitalism' (Robinson 2004: 167). The Washington Consensus was a 'veritable Gramscian consensus around the neo-liberal project', created and held together by the 'organic intellectuals' of the 'transnational capitalist class' (Robinson 2003: 322–5). Although US hegemony is entwined with the (Post-)Washington Consensus, the United States' asym-metrical relationship with Latin America involves much more. Gramsci himself accounted for the violence of power in his theorising. It is not for nothing that he chose to frame political contestation in terms of warfare (as in wars of position and wars of manoeuvre). As noted by his editors, that Gramsci 'concerned himself with the sphere of "civil society" and of "hegemony" . . . cannot be taken to indi-cate a neglect of the moment of political society, of force, of domination' (1971: 207). His understanding of power, developed while in prison, was attuned to its instrumentalist dimensions.

Few would argue that power begins and ends with the ability of an actor to unyieldingly bend another to their will. The application of Gramscian thought to IR moved the discipline towards an understanding of power based on cultural and productive factors in addition to politico-military force, a welcome development indeed. One might expect power to have been dissected to the point of exhaustion in IR, but this has not been the case. Scholars have shied away from the density of power, often preferring parsimony over the concept's inconvenient intricacies. In mainstream approaches, power is often truncated so that it is presented almost exclusively in Weberian or Dahlian terms, as the ability of an actor to achieve a goal or realise a desired outcome. As noted by Strange (in an adaptation of Cox's dictum), 'the treatment of power' in IR/IPE is 'usually *for* something, in that it sustains one perspective, and the prescriptions that go with it, more than rival ones' (1996: 24). The complexity of power as a concept should be embraced, not obscured.

This section foregrounds power as a way of animating hegemony's moving parts, allowing for a closer relation of hegemony to US foreign policy. I take power to be fundamentally *social* rather than merely instrumental. Power cannot be reduced entirely to something 'possessed' by actors and subsequently wielded over others. It takes different *shapes*; it has different *forms*. In international relations, different kinds of power are used/manifest in different ways. Scholars see power differently because there are different kinds of power 'out there' in the 'real world'. Context matters. If hegemonic relationships are built on certain types of power, it is conceivable that separate forms of power are needed to renew them. A viable analytical framework must have the ability to disentangle the various forms of social power that pattern hegemonic relationships over time, from the deployment of coercion to the construction of consent, to the (re)shaping of the structures and discourses that are (co-)constitutive of national actors and their foreign policies. When dealing with system-leading states, such an approach must illuminate the ways in which different types of power coalesce to protect, augment and/or recreate hegemonic relationships.

Barnett and Duvall define power as 'the production, in and through social relations, of effects that shape the capacities of actors to determine their own circumstances and fate' (2005a: 8). They write that 'power does not have a single expression or form' (2005a: 3). Their taxonomy delineates four discrete types of power: *compulsory*, *institutional*, *structural* and *productive*. Barnett and Duvall maintain that their taxonomy improves on previous attempts to classify power—that it is analytically more systematic and conceptually more general—because it is organised around what they see as power's 'critical dimensions' (2005a: 8). There are two cleavages producing the taxonomy's four categories. The first dimension asks whether power works through social *interactions* or processes of social *constitution*. The idea of interaction presupposes fully constituted actors who have control over how they behave in relation to others. In contrast, the constitutive position within this dimension focuses on that which precedes subjectivity. In relation to more traditional understandings of power, the social interaction position corresponds to 'power over', whereas power in processes of constitution is analogous to 'power to' (Barnett and Duvall 2005b: 45–7). The second dimension pertains to the degree of specificity of the social relations at play. It asks: how immediate and straightforward are the social relations that give expression to power? Is this relationship direct and tangible, or is it distant and relatively difficult to ascertain? This must be asked not only of the space between actors, but also of the space between actors and the mechanisms that constitute them as such (e.g. structures, discourses). In short, this dimension of power has much to do with the (social/temporal/physical) 'distance' between the structural and agentic phenomena that shape the totality of social experience, be it of an interactive or constitutive nature (Barnett and Duvall 2005b: 47–9).

Barnett and Duvall's taxonomy was constructed to compartmentalise forms of power in IR. It is a logical starting point for the present study, since my desiderata involves the hegemony of the United States in the contested space of Latin America. However, since the United States (as a pre-constituted actor) is my departure-point for analysis, the focus on US *policy* also shows the limits of the taxonomy, because Barnett and Duvall's notions of structural and productive power would seem to downplay the role of agents in reinforcing the constitutive properties of both structures and discourses. Additionally, and despite its constitutive dimension, Barnett and Duvall's typology runs dangerously close to reproducing the problems of reification (of the state) that have plagued IR since the rise of Waltzian neorealism, if not before. My framework thus explicitly engages interdisciplinary debates on power. Michael Mann's (1986) sweeping historical sociology is crucial here because it is invested in the *sources* of the social power of the state. Like Barnett and Duvall, Mann puts forward four separate types of power: *ideological, economic, military* and *political* (his IEMP model). Whereas Mann strives to avoid placing these types of power inside a totality (of 'society'), preferring instead to see them through the lens of overlapping networks, my aim is to show how various forms of power coalesce as hegemony. Mann uses his IEMP model to critique the contradictions of Bush-era policy in *Incoherent Empire* (2003), arguing that the inconsistencies in American power would doom its post-9/11 militarism. I invert this argument to demonstrate the ways in which US power is synthesized in a revamped regional hegemony, one that extends beyond its outsized coercive leverage.

My concern with the (potential) durability of American power is shared by Bryan Mabee. He explicitly blends Mann's work with that of Barnett and Duvall to comprehensively reassess the conditions confronting US policy in the early twenty-first century. Mabee writes that 'to properly understand American power, we need to further consider the interrelation of these (and other) different perspectives', adding that, by integrating various aspects of the 'power debates' we gain a 'better understanding of the ways in which the US expresses power internationally' (2013: 64–5). These debates encompass the political science and interdisciplinary literature on the four 'faces' of power initiated by Robert Dahl (1957), expanded upon by Bachrach and Baratz (1962), refined and extended by Steven Lukes (2005) and comprehensively reformulated in the influential writings of Michel Foucault (1977). This lineage—stretching from the four faces of power through Mann's IEMP model and Barnett and Duvall's taxonomy—feeds into my own framework, which relocates this 'typology of four' inside Gramsci's concept of hegemony. Though the types of power that make up US hegemony are conceptually distinct, they do not function independently of one another. The remainder of this chapter spells out the different forms of American hegemonic power. The chapters that follow detail how these overlap and shape one other in the practices of hegemonic renewal.

My power framework, constructed to explicate US agency, is actor-oriented. Though it does not deny the power of structures, discourses and ideologies to enable, constrain and constitute actors, the principal focus is on the use of these mechanisms and spaces by the United States. The framework specifies four forms of power: *structural*, *coercive*, *institutional* and *ideological*. It uses three typological dimensions to disaggregate these four types of power. These dimensions employ distinct if complementary physical/spatial metaphors to highlight the various ways in which distinct forms of power operate alongside one another in (potentially) synergistic ways.

- The first dimension is based on the *proximity* of the social relationship between the mechanism and its effects on interaction. It posits four 'levels' from immediate to direct to indirect to diffuse. This is similar to Barnett and Duvall's degrees of specificity (i.e. direct versus indirect; see above, pp. 47–48). These levels give order to the scheme presented in Table 2.3.
- The second dimension concerns the social *mechanism* through which power is manifest: structure, coercion, consensus, discourse. These media of power correspond to the levels of social proximity of the first dimension. The various mechanisms here engender different logics through which social realities and relations are produced and effected.
- The third dimension is based on the social *sphere* of agential interaction. These are different spaces or arenas of international relations: economy, geopolitics, institutions, ideology. The inspiration here is Mann's analytical model of diverse yet overlapping socio-spatial networks. These spheres intersect and interlink but stop short of constituting an unproblematic 'totality' of international relations.

The labels 'structural', 'coercive', 'institutional' and 'ideological', as chosen from among the terms on Table 2.3, provide descriptive clarity while relating my typological categories to the extant literature. The categories can thus be positioned alongside those of Mann's IEMP model and Barnett and Duvall's taxonomy, with the caveat that this analogous arrangement does not imply full equivalence between these conceptualisations (Table 2.4).

Table 2.3 The dimensions of US hegemonic power

Social proximity	Social mechanism	Social sphere
Immediate	Structure	Economy
Direct	Coercion	Geopolitics
Indirect	Consensus	Institutions
Diffuse	Discourse	Ideology

Table 2.4 Locating the US hegemonic power framework in existing debates

US hegemony framework	Mann's IEMP model	Barnett and Duvall
Structural	Economic	Structural
Coercive	Military	Compulsory
Institutional	Political	Institutional
Ideological	Ideological	Productive

My framework starts with structural power because it is the immediacy of structural-economic relations that constitutes the hegemon as such; just as the category 'master' cannot exist without that of 'slave', and just as the capitalist and worker constitute one another dialectically, the hegemon must, by definition, have subordinates. In other words, a structural-economic advantage is *necessary* to hegemony (though far from sufficient), and in a way that the other forms of power are not. The expression of hegemonic power in its other guises is inseparable from this immediate structural requirement. But we see straightaway how the forms of power in the framework are interlocking and overlapping because the other forms of power are indispensable to the maintenance of this structural advantage, which nevertheless exists a priori. This is consistent with the realist ontological commitments of historical materialism, the meta-theoretical scaffold on which the framework's categories 'hang together'.

Structural power

To reiterate: my framework begins with structural power because it is necessary to hegemony in the ontology of historical materialism. Structural power provides the conditions for an actor to exercise its coercive power, to build consensus through institutions and to legitimate its position via ideology. In my understanding of structural power, the (economic) structures themselves express power in the *immediate* sense, while agents work within structural limits to shift or shore-up said structures. Barnett and Duvall define structural power as the 'direct and mutual constitution of the capacities of actors', the most overtly Marxian face of power in their taxonomy (Barnett and Duvall 2005a: 18–20). This is in contradistinction to other usages of the term, including that of Susan Strange, who focused on security, production, credit and knowledge as distinct structures of world politics (1988: 43–134). However, Strange's work reminds us that the power to shape structures often rests with states, even in a global economy that features intergovernmental institutions and multinational firms.

Through their own internal mechanisms, structures proximately create agents and imbue them with material interests and capabilities. But this is not an exclusively one-way relationship. Of importance here is the *co-constitutive* dynamic between structures and agents (although the directness of this relationship applies chiefly to the impact of structures on agents). Because structures tend to allocate differential capacities to different actors based on their positioning within the structural milieu, inequality is an essential part of structural power. Structures are also constitutive in that they shape the subjectivities of actors, which, in this view, spring from their structurally-given position in the social environment. Actors thus have a tendency to see their social position as natural, even though this may entail an acceptance of inequality and their subordinate status. The classic examples used to illustrate this form of power are the master–slave and capital–labour relationships.

The structure of global capitalism is paramount to the structural power perspective, as opposed to, for example, the anarchical structure of the international system. This is because it is the 'structure of global capitalism (that) determines the capacities and resources of actors' and 'shapes their ideology, that is, the interpretive system through which they understand their interests and desires' (Barnett and Duvall 2005a: 19). Barnett and Duvall note that, although Gramscians prioritise the structural power of capitalism, this does not mean they necessarily dismiss other types of power. Utilising their taxonomy, Mark Rupert writes of 'the dialectical interdependence of structural and ideological-discursive or productive forms of power, as well as their enactment in institutional contexts and exercises of compulsory power' (2005: 212). He points out that, in the context of the asymmetric distribution of capabilities, agency is *necessary* to the re-production of extant structures.

My understanding of structural power refers to the constitutive properties of structures while foregrounding the ability of states to shape those structures through economic policy. In this guise, Chapter 3 examines US trade policy in Latin America in the age of the NLL. Although free trade agreements (FTAs) can be viewed as institutional arrangements, the agency of the United States expressed in FTAs works to advance economic neoliberalisation, with implications for the structures of transnational capitalism in the Western hemisphere. I trace Washington's support for 'free trade' from the collapse of the FTAA through the procurement of the Central American Free Trade Agreement (CAFTA) and bilateral FTAs with Chile, Peru, Panama and Colombia. Institutions like ALBA and Mercosur are important parts of this story because they undercut the viability of the FTAA. Co-ordinated opposition notwithstanding, the United States has attempted to reconstitute its hemispheric free trade drive through the Trans-Pacific Partnership (TPP), which would connect participating American markets to those in East Asia.

Coercive power

Similar to the 'first face' of power in the political science literature, coercion is the most intuitive form of power in the field of IR. It is based on Robert Dahl's definition of power as 'the ability of A to get B to do what B otherwise would not' (1957: 202). Barnett and Duvall call this compulsory power, 'direct control over another'. This image of power has several key features. It implies an element of conflict between the powerful and the disempowered, meaning the interests of A and B diverge in some important way. It also implies that actor A has the resources necessary to compel B to do something that B wouldn't do otherwise. This, in turn, suggests that B has fewer resources at its disposal than does A. Dahl's definition also suggests intentionality on the part of A, whose actions (in most scenarios) are designed and carried out to compel B to do something against B's wishes (Barnett and Duvall 2005a: 13–15). However, for Barnett and Duvall, 'compulsory power need not hinge on intentionality'. They use the example of 'collateral damage' to illustrate this point, writing that 'power still exists when those who dominate are not conscious of how their actions are producing unintended effects' (2005a: 14). Those killed through collateral damage directly experience the force of the action regardless of the actor's intentions.

The potency of this particular example serves as a reminder that, in international relations, power frequently *is* about violence and physical coercion. Indeed, the logic here calls to mind 'hard power' in Joseph's Nye's famous hard/soft dichotomy. Hard power, for Nye (1990: 31), is the 'command power' that rests on inducements ('carrots') and/or threats ('sticks'); in contrast, soft power is 'the ability to get what you want through attraction rather than coercion or payments' (Nye 2004: x). Although hard power need not imply the exercise of physical violence, this type of force certainly qualifies. Because force can operate in various ways, Mann's notion of military power is important in refining my understanding of coercive power. For Mann, military power is the concentrated ability to inflict lethal violence (2012: 11–12). Of the various forms of power in international politics, military coercion is most closely associated with states, and the United States remains far and away the most formidable military actor on the world stage. Its military resources are central to its formulations of 'grand strategy' and its broader efforts at statecraft, two concepts that would seem to depend on hard power resources. Coercive power can remain latent in the social relations between actors. As a resource, it provides states with 'leverage', giving them the ability to directly shape particular outcomes.

In Chapter 4, I examine the United States' military strategy in Latin America as the foundation of its coercive power. The election of NLL governments engendered changes in a number of areas. This was reflected in the strategic posture of the US Southern Command (Southcom), the Pentagon's unified command structure for Latin America. Specifically, I examine changes to US basing strategy and the reconstitution of a naval fleet for Latin America. I also investigate Washington's diplomatic and institutional response to the military coup in Honduras in 2009. The coercive power expressed in geopolitics is made possible by other forms of power in the framework. Importantly, the anti-neoliberal members of the NLL (Venezuela, Bolivia and Ecuador, the last of which 'ejected' the United States from its military base in the country) were viewed as radical and anti-American, and thus potential threats to US interests in the region; indeed, they were constructed as such in the discourse on populism, as explored in Chapter 6. In Honduras, President Zelaya made overtures towards populism by joining ALBA (the Venezuelan-led Bolivarian Alliance) and pursuing 'statist' economic policies. Although the OAS attempted to rectify the Honduran coup and resolve the crisis there, this effort, carried out amidst US ambivalence, proved unsuccessful.

The fissures between Washington and the OAS over the issue of the Honduran coup help to pivot the book towards institutional power, the subject of Chapter 5.

Institutional power

Institutional power is less intuitive than coercive power, partly because institutions can be formal or informal. The key feature is that institutions 'mediate' between actors. This makes institutional power indirect. In effect, actor A works through the rules and procedures of a given institution to guide, steer or constrain actor B. Barnett and Duvall define institutional power as 'actors' control over socially distant others' (2015a: 15–17). Although there is a long lineage of studies in IR pertaining to the impact of international organisations on world politics, Barnett and Duvall are careful to distance their version of institutional power from conceptualisations that focus on (1) the power of institutions as actors in their own right, and (2) the role of institutions in constituting actors. The key is that, while institutional power, like coercive power, works via interactions between fully constituted agents, institutional power is less direct because of the 'space' between states and institutions and—more to the point—between the states working *through* institutions to interact with other states.

Even when resource-rich and militarily-dominant states work through institutions, they do not *possess* those institutions. Institutions enjoy some level of autonomy. In the case of formal international organisations (IOs), they have their own mechanisms of behavioural constraint that work independently of the states that fund them. IOs have their own internal biases, and can create 'winners and losers' based upon their own internal logic. Institutions can also 'lock-in' a particular international order, 'freezing' it in time. This has been the case with many post-war IOs, such as the UN and the IMF. States, of course, are generally the architects of IOs, though other agents may contribute to the processes in which these institutions are conceived and made operational. States generally must consent to their participation in these formal rules-based organisations. There is a consensus mechanism at work here as states converge on acceptable rules that may not be 'optimal' for any single actor (trade agreements are a good example). Co-operation through institutions reinforces consensus as dialogue and negotiation produce mutually-agreed-upon rules that constrain participating actors. While states powerful in structural and/or coercive terms can certainly refuse to adhere to these rules, this does not mean that IOs are merely tools of such states. Indeed, 'weaker' states can use institutions to push back against prevailing practices or outcomes to try and shift the consensus itself. This includes constructing new organisations of diplomatic co-operation. Consensus is not static, nor is it synonymous with 'harmony'.

Chapter 5 focuses on institutional power through an examination of the OAS, the Western hemisphere's oldest and most prominent inter-governmental body. Located in Washington, the OAS has traditionally been viewed as little more than an instrument of the United States. However, under the executive leadership of José Miguel Insulza, a former member of Chile's socialist government, the OAS was brought in alignment with the NLL. Nascent US efforts to reform the OAS have focused on strengthening its more traditional liberal or polyarchic functioning (with democracy promotion and human rights understood and presented in opposition to populism). Furthermore, regional co-operation has increasingly moved *away* from the OAS, in the direction of newly-created institutions that *exclude* US participation. The countries of Latin America have emphasised intra-Latin American co-operation at the expense of inter-American co-operation with the Northern hegemon. The new regional organisations (CELAC, UNASUR, ALBA) focus on both security and economic issues. ALBA, for example, in concert with a reinvigorated Mercosur, undercut the FTAA, a US-backed economic integration scheme. We see, then, how the loss of institutional power can impact the structural power of a hegemonic state. Moreover, the consensus-making of institutional power is more than procedural. It is deeply ideological, and thus crucial to hegemony itself.

Ideological power

Ideological power is the most diffuse form of power in the US hegemony framework. It operates beyond the control of specific actors through the mechanism of discourse. Barnett and Duvall term this 'productive power', which, like structural power, is constitutive. It pertains to the ways in which discourses shape actors' self-understandings and interests, 'real' or perceived. In contrast to structural dynamics, however, this variant of power functions in a less direct, less tangible manner. It is found in difficult-to-grasp aspects of social experience like norms, customs and networks. Its diffuseness is expressed in 'the constitution of all social subjects . . . through systems of knowledge and discursive practices of broad and general social scope' (Barnett and Duvall 2005a: 20). The emphasis here is on signification, meaning and identity (as seen in categories surrounding the 'self' and 'other'), making it, in general, post-structuralist. Power, in this conceptualisation, runs *through* those discursive phenomena that produce identities, ideas and knowledge. This is often expressed via the organisation of discursive categories into binaries, such as 'democratic' versus 'autocratic', 'civilised' versus 'backward', 'north' versus 'south', and so on. In the ideological sphere, discourses work to create (and undermine) notions of common sense as key features of political contestation (Rupert 2003). The reproduction of prevailing common sense ideas (against other, rival understandings) helps facilitate more direct or 'concrete' uses of power. It feeds into the consensual side of social relations, as prevailing ideas become the basis of formalised institutions of governance.

Discourse encompasses speech and written texts, but it is more than language itself. It covers all cultural practices (symbols, images, meanings, representations and articulations) that undergird—and in fact produce—social subjectivity and social knowledge. Barnett and Duvall's definition of productive power allows for contingency and agency—for the ability of subjects to (re)ascribe meaning to themselves and the world around them. I draw primarily on this aspect of discursive/ideological power while avoiding the claim that language practices in the social world are purely instrumental. Closely associated with constructivist, post-structuralist, postcolonial and feminist research programmes, discursive power (as is the case with other forms of power) can be incorporated into theoretical traditions with distinct philosophical commitments. While I readily concede that discourse and ideology are not one and the same (Purvis and Hunt 1993), I see them as intertwining concepts insofar as they relate to each other and to other forms of social power. But I label this *ideological* power for several reasons. I am concerned primarily with the ways in which discourses *legitimate* the expressions of power in other guises. Additionally, as discussed in Chapter 1, I don't accept discourse as exhaustive of the social sphere. Discursive phenomena must be analysed in relation to the extra-discursive realm (Fairclough 1992; Jackson 2005). Finally, I aim to foreground the use(s) of discourse by the United States in analysing the official texts of its foreign policy, with an eye towards the various constructions that reinforce US ideological power.

For the purposes of this book, the discursive construction of Latin American populism is central to US ideological power, cutting across the wider empirical discussion that follows. In the context of the international relations of the Americas, populism is often defined in relation to nationalism, statist economic policies, anti-Americanism and/or anti-imperialism. But populism is not a self-evident or objective condition. It is a contested construct that is contingent on the meanings associated with related, contrasting concepts like liberal democracy and responsible, 'commonsense' policymaking. I examine the construction of populism in Chapter 6, focusing on the collocations of 'false populism' and 'radical populism' in US diplomatic and policy discourse. The discussion allows for an extra-discursive element to the populist phenomenon, helping to connect ideological power to the other forms of power in the framework. Advancing the discussion from earlier chapters, for instance, populists are defined in part through their opposition to the 'hard power' of the US military and to US-backed free trade policies. Populist governments are construed as hostile to democracy and US interests, and in a way that is part and parcel of the good left/bad left schism mentioned in Chapter 1. Because populism is normatively objectionable, it serves as a means of condemning those governments who pursue an anti-neoliberal, 'anti-American' path (the 'bad left'). Additionally, the populist construct contributes to the renewal of US hegemony by legitimating US actions against the NLL's 'radical' members in economic, geopolitical and institutional settings.

Conclusion

The powers of the United States combine to (re)produce relations of hegemony vis-à-vis the subordinate countries of Latin America. These relations involve not only the agential capacities of the United States but also the path-dependent aspects of the pre-existing structures of its hegemonic rule. Hegemony, then, encompasses both specific foreign policy projects and the deeper social processes that enable these projects to take hold. It is put in motion and shaped through different forms of power—immediate and diffuse, direct and indirect—which operate in different spheres of international politics, and through differing mechanisms of interaction. These overlap and play off of one another, but must be kept distinct for purposes of analytical clarity. To analyse US hegemony in Latin America is to recognise this layered complexity. It requires an acknowledgement that hegemony is a series of co-determining and overlapping socio-power relations rather than a fixed object of examination. In other words, hegemony is an ongoing process rather than a stationary order. Its renewal does not signal a final resting point. Rather, this re-constitutive moment is analogous to the crest of a wave that ebbs and flows in the tumult of political struggle and counter-struggle. With this in mind, I reiterate the importance of Gramscian hegemony as a conceptual starting point. Indeed, to bring the discussion in this chapter full circle, its utility lies in the fact that, unlike imperialism, the hierarchical relations implied in the concept assume a built-in element of ongoing opposition.

This book does not offer a new theory of power. It does not posit universal truths on power in international relations, nor does it advance claims about specific ways in which various forms of social power are co-constitutive or mutually imbricated across time and space. Solid theoretical grounding is a prerequisite to utilising the schematic categories outlined above. I have identified mine as Gramscian historical materialism, with the relevant realist ontological commitments and reflexive epistemological orientation. I am not subsuming the multifaceted and contested nature of power to this theoretical approach, which generally prioritises the structural power of capitalism. Rather, I apply my framework alongside the philosophical commitments of this broader scaffold. This is in the spirit of a more flexible critical approach, one based on the view that the neo-Gramscian tradition in IR, like its more conventional competitors, has been less-than-fully-attentive to the complexity of power in its myriad forms. The following chapters trace the detailed texture of power at an important juncture in the international relations of the Western hemisphere. The aim is to illuminate the ways in which various forms of US power coalesce to reproduce a hegemony that is paradoxically both precarious and durable. This cannot be done without acknowledging that US hegemony has indeed been cast in doubt. Power and resistance are 'mutually implicated because the social relations that shape the ability of actors to control their own fates are frequently challenged and resisted by those on the "receiving end"' (Barnett and Duvall 2005a: 22–3). Although my analytical focus is on the United States, its power in the Americas can only be understood in relation to those actors pushing back against the scope and expression of that very power.

Notes

1 A major concept in Harvey's thought, accumulation by dispossession can be described as a fragmented version of capital accumulation similar to Marx's primitive (or original) accumulation. The state often plays an active role in accumulation by dispossession, which, in addition to privatisation, commodification and financialisation, can be pursued through the manipulation of crises and changes to tax codes (Harvey 2005: 178–9).

2 The world's first experiment with neoliberalism unfolded in Chile under the dictatorship of Augusto Pinochet. Pinochet, who was installed in a US-backed coup in 1973, used neoliberal policies to dismantle the democratic socialism of his predecessor, Salvador Allende.

3 Most economists date the cycle of high commodity prices as beginning in 2003 and ending in 2011. Even after the end of this cycle, prices for many key commodities remained above where they had been for much of the 1990s and early 2000s.

References

Agnew, J. (2005). *Hegemony: The New Shape of Global Power*, Philadelphia: Temple University Press.

Anderson, P. (2015). *American Foreign Policy and its Thinkers*, London: Verso.

Ayers, A. J., ed. (2008). *Gramsci, Political Economy, and International Relations Theory: Modern Princes and Naked Emperors*, New York: Palgrave.

Bachrach, P. and M. Baratz (1962). 'Two Faces of Power', *American Political Science Review*, 56(4): 947–52.

Barnett, M. and R. Duvall (2005a). 'Power in Global Governance', in *Power in Global Governance*, edited by M. Barnett and R. Duvall, Cambridge: Cambridge University Press: 1–32.

Barnett, M. and R. Duvall (2005b). 'Power in International Politics', *International Organization*, 59(1): 39–75.

Blyth, M. (2002). *Great Transformations: Economic Ideas and Institutional Change in the Twentieth Century*, Cambridge: Cambridge University Press.

Birdsall, N. and F. Fukuyama (2011). 'The Post-Washington Consensus', *Foreign Affairs*, 90(2): 45–53.

Bush, G. W. (2002). Graduation Speech at West Point, 1 June. Available online at http://georgewbush-whitehouse.archives.gov/news/releases/2002/06/20020601-3.html (accessed 18 July 2013).

Colás, A. and R. Saull, eds (2006). *The War on Terrorism and the American 'Empire' after the Cold War*, London: Routledge.

Cox, M. (2003). 'The Empire's Back in Town: Or America's Imperial Temptation— Again', *Millennium*, 32(1): 1–27.

Cox, R. W. (1977). 'Labor and Hegemony', *International Organization*, 31(3): 385–424.

Crouch, C. (2011). *The Strange Non-Death of Neoliberalism*, Cambridge: Polity.

Dahl, R. (1957). 'The Concept of Power', *Behavioral Science*, 2(3): 201–15.

ECLAC (Economic Commission for Latin America and the Caribbean) (2015). 'Latin America and the Caribbean and China: Towards a New Era in Economic Cooperation', May.

Ellis, R. E. (2012). 'The United States, Latin America and China: A "Triangular Relationship"?', Inter-American Dialogue Working Paper, May.

Fairclough, N. (1992). *Discourse and Social Change*, Cambridge: Polity Press.

Ferguson, N. (2004). *Colossus: The Rise and Fall of the American Empire*, London: Penguin.

Fine, B., C. Lapavitsas and J. Pincus, eds (2003). *Development Policy in the Twenty-First Century: Beyond the Post-Washington Consensus*, London: Routledge.

Forero, J. (2003). 'Latin America's Political Compass Veers toward the Left', *The New York Times*, 19 January: A4.

Foucault, M. (1977). *Discipline and Punish: The Birth of the Prison*, New York: Vintage Books.

Gallagher, K. (2016). *The China Triangle: Latin America's China Boom and the Fate of the Washington Consensus*, Oxford: Oxford University Press.

Germain, R. and M. Kenny (1998). 'Engaging Gramsci: International Relations Theory and the New Gramscians', *Review of International Studies*, 24(1): 3–21.

Gill, S., ed. (1993). *Gramsci, Historical Materialism and International Relations*, Cambridge: Cambridge University Press.

Gilpin, R. (1981). *War and Change in World Politics*, Cambridge: Cambridge University Press.

Gilpin, R. (1987). *The Political Economy of International Relations*, Princeton: Princeton University Press.

Gilpin, R. (2000). *The Challenge of Global Capitalism: The World Economy in the 21st Century*, Princeton: Princeton University Press.

Go, J. (2007). 'Waves of Empire: US Hegemony and Imperialistic Activity from the Shores of Tripoli to Iraq, 1787–2003', *International Sociology*, 22(1): 5–40.

Gore, C. (2000). 'The Rise and Fall of the Washington Consensus as a Paradigm for Developing Countries', *World Development*, 28(5): 789–804.

Gowan, P. (1999). *The Global Gamble: Washington's Faustian Bid for World Dominance*, London: Verso.

Gramsci, A. (1971). *Selections from the Prison Notebooks*, New York: International Publishers.

Gray, J. (2008). 'A Shattering Moment in America's Fall from Power', *Guardian*, 28 September. Available online at www.theguardian.com/commentisfree/2008/sep/28/usforeignpolicy.useconomicgrowth (accessed 2 September 2015).

Gruss, B. (2014). 'After the Boom—Commodity Prices and Economic Growth in Latin America and the Caribbean', IMF Working Paper, August.

Hall, S. (1986). 'The Problem of Ideology: Marxism without Guarantees', *Journal of Communication Inquiry*, 10(2): 28–44.

Hardt, M. and A. Negri (2000). *Empire*, Cambridge, MA: Harvard University Press.

Harvey, D. (2005). *A Brief History of Neoliberalism*, Oxford: Oxford University Press.

Held, D. (2005). 'At the Global Crossroads: The End of the Washington Consensus and the Rise of Global Social Democracy?' *Globalizations*, 2(1): 95–113.

Helleiner, E. (2010). 'A Bretton Woods Moment? The 2007–2008 Crisis and the Future of Global Finance', *International Affairs*, 86(3): 619–36.

Hunt, M. (2009). *Ideology and US Foreign Policy*, revised edition, New Haven: Yale University Press.

Ignatieff, M. (2003). 'The Burden', *The New York Times Magazine*, 5 January.

Ikenberry, G. J. (2002). 'America's Imperial Ambition', *Foreign Affairs*, 81(5): 44–60.

Ikenberry, G. J. (2011). *Liberal Leviathan: The Origins, Crisis, and Transformation of the American World Order*, Princeton: Princeton University Press.

Jackson, R. (2005). *Writing the War on Terrorism: Language, Politics and Counter-Terrorism*, Manchester: Manchester University Press.

Jenkins, R. (2010). 'China's Global Expansion and Latin America', *Journal of Latin American Studies*, 42(4): 809–37.

Jenkins, R. (2012). 'Latin America and China—A New Dependency?' *Third World Quarterly*, 33(7): 1337–58.

Joseph, J. (2002). *Hegemony: A Realist Analysis*, London: Routledge.

Kahler, M. (2013). 'Rising Powers and Global Governance: Negotiating Change in a Resilient Status Quo', *International Affairs*, 89(3): 711–29.

Kennedy, P. (1987). *The Rise and Fall of the Great Powers*, New York: Vintage Books.

Kiely, R. (2007). 'Poverty Reduction through Liberalisation? Neoliberalism and the Myth of Global Convergence', *Review of International Studies*, 33(3): 415–34.

Krauthammer, C. (2002/3). 'The Unipolar Moment Revisited', *The National Interest*, 70: 13–18.

Laclau, E. and C. Mouffe (2001). *Hegemony and Socialist Strategy: Towards a Radical Democratic Politics*, second edition, London: Verso.

Layne, C. (2007). *The Peace of Illusions: American Grand Strategy from 1940 to the Present*, Ithaca, NY: Cornell University Press.

Lukes, S. (2005). *Power: A Radical View*, second edition, New York: Palgrave.

Mabee, B. (2004). 'Discourses of Empire: The US "Empire", Globalisation and International Relations', *Third World Quarterly*, 25(8): 1359–78.

Mabee, B. (2013). *Understanding American Power: The Changing World of US Foreign Policy*, New York: Palgrave.

Maier, C. S. (2002). 'An American Empire? The Problems of Frontiers and Peace in Twenty-First-Century World Politics', *Harvard Magazine*, November/December: 28–32.

Mann, M. (1986). *The Sources of Social Power Volume 1: A History of Power from the Beginning to A.D. 1760*, Cambridge: Cambridge University Press.

Mann, M. (2003). *Incoherent Empire*, London: Verso.

Mann, M. (2012). *The Sources of Social Power Volume 3: Global Empires and Revolution*, Cambridge: Cambridge University Press.

Mastanduno, M. (2009). 'System Maker and Privilege Taker: US Power and the International Political Economy', *World Politics*, 61(1): 121–54.

Milne, D. (2015). *Worldmaking: The Art and Science of American Diplomacy*, New York: Farrar, Straus and Giroux.

Morton, A. D. (2007). *Unravelling Gramsci: Hegemony and the Passive Revolution in the Global Political Economy*, London: Pluto Press.

Nexon, D. and T. Wright (2007). 'What's at Stake in the American Empire Debate', *American Political Science Review*, 101(2): 253–71.

Nye, J. S. (1990). *Bound to Lead: The Changing Nature of American Power*, New York: Basic Books.

Nye, J. S. (2004). *Soft Power: The Means to Success in World Politics*, New York: Public Affairs.

Ó Tuathail, G. (1996). *Critical Geopolitics: The Politics of Writing Global Space*, London: Routledge.

Onis, Z. and F. Senses (2005). 'Rethinking the Emerging Post-Washington Consensus', *Development and Change*, 36(2): 263–90.

Panitch, L. and S. Gindin (2012). *The Making of Global Capitalism: The Political Economy of American Empire*, London: Verso.

Panizza, F. (2009). *Contemporary Latin America: Development and Democracy Beyond the Washington Consensus*, London: Zed Books.

Persaud, R. B. (2001). *Counter-Hegemony and Foreign Policy: The Dialectics of Marginalized and Global Forces in Jamaica*, Albany: State University of New York Press.

Petras, J. and H. Veltmeyer (2011). *Social Movements in Latin America: Neoliberalism and Popular Resistance*, New York: Palgrave.

Polanyi, K. (2001 [1944]). *The Great Transformation: The Political and Economic Origins of Our Time*, Boston: Beacon Press.

Purvis, T. and A. Hunt (1993). 'Discourse, Ideology, Discourse, Ideology, Discourse, Ideology . . .', *The British Journal of Sociology*, 44(3): 473–99.

Ramo, J. C. (2004). 'The Beijing Consensus', The Foreign Policy Centre, May.

Ray, R., K. Gallagher and R. Sarmiento (2016). 'China-Latin America Economic Bulletin 2016 Edition', Global Economic Governance Initiative, Boston University, March.

Roberts, K. (2008). 'The Mobilization of Opposition to Economic Liberalization', *Annual Review of Political Science*, 11: 327–49.

Robinson, W. I. (1996). *Promoting Polyarchy: Globalization, US Intervention, and Hegemony*, Cambridge: Cambridge University Press.

Robinson, W. I. (2002). 'Capitalist Globalization and the Transnationalization of the State', in *Historical Materialism and Globalization*, edited by M. Rupert and H. Smith, London: Routledge: 210–29.

Robinson, W. I. (2003). *Transnational Conflicts: Central America, Social Change, and Globalization*, London: Verso.

Robinson, W. I. (2004). *A Theory of Global Capitalism: Production, State and Class in a Transnational World*, Baltimore: Johns Hopkins University Press.

Robinson, W. I. (2006). 'Promoting Polyarchy in Latin America: The Oxymoron of "Market Democracy"', in *Latin America after Neoliberalism: Turning the Tide in the 21st Century*, edited by E. Hershberg and F. Rosen, New York: The New Press: 96–119.

Robinson, W. I. (2008). *Latin America and Global Capitalism: A Critical Globalization Perspective*, Baltimore: Johns Hopkins University Press.

Robinson, W. I. (2014). *Global Capitalism and the Crisis of Humanity*, Cambridge: Cambridge University Press.

Rodrik, D. (2006). 'Goodbye Washington Consensus, Hello Washington Confusion? A Review of the World Bank's "Economic Growth in the 1990s: Learning from a Decade of Reform"', *Journal of Economic Literature*, 44(4): 973–87.

Roett, R. and G. Paz (2008). 'Introduction: Assessing the Implications of China's Growing Presence in the Western Hemisphere', in *China's Expansion into the Western Hemisphere*, edited by R. Roett and G. Paz, Washington, DC: Brookings: 1–23.

Rupert, M. (1995). *Producing Hegemony: The Politics of Mass Production and American Global Power*, Cambridge: Cambridge University Press.

Rupert, M. (2003). 'Globalising Common Sense: A Marxian-Gramscian (Re-)Vision of the Politics of Governance/Resistance', *Review of International Studies*, 29(5): 181–98.

Rupert, M. (2005). 'Class Powers and the Politics of Global Governance', in *Power in Global Governance*, edited by M. Barnett and R. Duvall, Cambridge: Cambridge University Press: 205–28.

Rupert, M. and S. Solomon (2006). *Globalization and International Political Economy: The Politics of Alternative Futures*, Lanham: Rowman & Littlefield Publishers.

Serra, N., S. Spiegel and J. Stiglitz (2008). 'Introduction: From Washington Consensus towards a New Global Governance', in *The Washington Consensus Reconsidered: Towards a New Global Governance*, edited by N. Serra and J. Stiglitz, Oxford: Oxford University Press: 3–13.

Silva, E. (2009). *Challenging Neoliberalism in Latin America*, Cambridge: Cambridge University Press.

Stiglitz, J. (1998). 'More Instruments and Broader Goals: Moving Toward the Post-Washington Consensus', Annual WIDER Lecture, World Institute for Development Economics Research (WIDER), Helsinki, Finland, 7 January.

Stiglitz, J. (2008). 'Is There a Post-Washington Consensus Consensus?' in *The Washington Consensus Reconsidered: Towards a New Global Governance*, edited by N. Serra and J. Stiglitz, Oxford: Oxford University Press: 41–56.

Stokes, D. (2005). 'The Heart of Empire? Theorising US Empire in an Era of Transnational Capitalism', *Third World Quarterly*, 26(2): 217–36.

Strange, S. (1988). *States and Markets: An Introduction to International Political Economy*, London: Pinter Publishers.

Strange, S. (1996). *The Retreat of the State: The Diffusion of Power in the World Economy*, Cambridge: Cambridge University Press.

Thompson, J. A. (2015). *A Sense of Power: The Roots of America's Global Role*, Ithaca: Cornell University Press.

Tickell, A. and J. Peck (2003). 'Making Global Rules: Globalization or Neoliberalization?' in *Remaking the Global Economy*, edited by J. Peck and H. W. Yeung, London: Sage: 163–81.

Tokatlian, J. G. (2008). 'A View from Latin America', in *China's Expansion into the Western Hemisphere*, edited by R. Roett and G. Paz, Washington, DC: Brookings: 59–89.

The Washington Post (2009). 'A Conversation With John Williamson, Economist', 12 April. Avaliable online at www.washingtonpost.com/wp-dyn/content/article/2009/04/09/AR2009040903241.html (accessed 2 September 2015).

Webb, M. C. and S. D. Krasner (1989). 'Hegemonic Stability Theory: An Empirical Assessment', *Review of International Studies*, 15(2): 183–98.

Williams, R. (1988 [1976]). *Keywords*, London: Fontana Press.

Williamson, J. (2005). 'The Strange History of the Washington Consensus', *Journal of Post Keynesian Economics*, 27(2): 195–206.

Williamson, J. (2008). 'A Short History of the Washington Consensus', in *The Washington Consensus Reconsidered: Towards a New Global Governance*, edited by N. Serra and J. E. Stiglitz, Oxford: Oxford University Press: 14–30.

Williamson, J. (2012). 'Is the "Beijing Consensus" Now Dominant?', *Asia Policy*, 13: 1–16.

Wood, E. M. (2002). 'Global Capital, National States', in *Historical Materialism and Globalization*, edited by M. Rupert and H. Smith, London: Routledge: 17–39.

Zakaria, F. (2008). *The Post-American World*, New York: W. W. Norton & Company.

Zibechi, R. (2012). *Territories in Resistance: A Cartography of Latin American Social Movements*, Oakland: AK Press.

3 Reviving neoliberalism
US trade policy after the Washington Consensus

This chapter explores the role of US trade policy in reviving neoliberalism in the Americas. Building on the previous chapter's discussion of the relationship between the Washington Consensus, neoliberalism and US hegemony in Latin America, it traces US trade policy from the dawn of the NLL to the TPP. 'Free trade', a pillar of the Washington Consensus, remained a prominent part of the Post-Washington Consensus landscape. Formalised free trade regimes encompass much more than the reduction of tariffs and non-tariff barriers to the exchange of goods and services. They play a pivotal role in opening up markets to the penetration of foreign capital through processes of privatisation and deregulation (Rupert 2000; Rupert and Solomon 2006). In facilitating the neoliberalisation of the hemispheric political economy, FTAs between the United States and Latin American countries sit at the core of US structural power in the region. FTAs provide a means of 'locking in' processes of neoliberal restructuring, enhancing the mobility of transnational corporations and improving the conditions for foreign investment. This is done through the construction of legal regimes designed to protect 'free market' economic policies from the political backlash engendered by their effects in the social sphere.

Social structures assign agents the capacity to act. This constitutive form of power is, by definition, direct, as agents are enabled and constrained through the internal relations of pre-existing structures (Barnett and Duvall 2005). However, structures do not allocate social capacities in equal measure. Structures position actors in relation to one another, meaning they necessarily differentiate between agents. In other words, structural arrangements are hierarchical. They privilege actors in different ways, assigning competing interests to different actors in the process. Moreover, structural power shapes the subjectivities of differentiated actors. Ideologies thus emerge from the interests and imperatives of structural relationships, even if ideational phenomena cannot be wholly reduced to structures in the final analysis. As implied in the terminology, it is the structures themselves that take precedence. The work of Susan Strange highlights this point (1988: 43–134; Stopford and Strange 1991: 32–64). In much of her writing, changes in the international system are traced back to shifts in areas such as security, production, credit and knowledge. Structures give rise to economic imperatives that alter markets, patterns of production, financial flows and the international division of labour in ways that feed back into the structures themselves—through the mediation of agents. States, embedded in the structural milieu of the global economy, do have the (limited) capacity to shape existing structures through things like economic policymaking. Mann's notion of economic power is important here because it explicitly links the 'intensive mobilization of labor' with the 'extensive circuits of capital, trade, and production chains' found in markets (2012: 9).

Analyses of structural/economic power in IR/IPE are often associated with Marxian approaches. For historical materialists, economic production underpins all forms of power. To utilise coercive and institutional tools states must first possess the requisite material capabilities. Ultimately, in this view, it is the 'structure of global capitalism (that) determines the capacities and resources of actors' and 'shapes their ideology' (Barnett and Duvall 2005: 19). Following Cox (1996), neo-Gramscian scholars tend to link the structural bases of hegemony to dominant ideologies. The structural power of free trade regimes functions alongside other forms of power. Rupert writes of the 'dialectical interdependence of structural and ideological-discursive or productive forms of power, as well as their enactment in institutional contexts and exercises of compulsory power among concretely situated agents' (2005: 210). In this vein, it is worth reiterating that neoliberalism is both a model of capitalist political economy and the ideological expression of the policies used to shape this structural arrangement (Harvey 2005). To a degree, processes of neoliberal globalisation are contingent on institutional arrangements, including trade agreements.

Although structural power can operate as a kind of domination (as in master–slave relations), processes of structural (re)production are not set in stone. Theorising structural power does not negate agency because it does not imply that purposive action is reducible to structural domination. Analysis of structural power in international relations requires an accounting of the constitutive properties of pre-existing political-economic arrangements, including the differentiated ways in which these arrangements enable and constrain state actors. But such analyses must also account for the role of states in reinforcing and/or challenging those very same arrangements. In this sense, we can talk about the structural power of given states. This includes hegemons who, in accordance with their structurally allocated position, have a greater capacity to (re)shape structures than do other actors. Although neoliberal 'free trade' creates winners and losers within and across national economies, it has, on the whole, enabled the expansion of US firms, investors and capital in a way that feeds back into the structural power of the United States as an actor. In other words, it allocates material resources in a manner that reinforces US hegemony.

Economic integration against the Washington Consensus

The United States pursues free trade through several tracks: global, regional and bilateral. Following the Cold War, the United States utilised multilateral negotiations to transform the General Agreement on Tariffs and Trade (GATT) into the more comprehensive World Trade Organization (WTO). The Doha Round of WTO negotiations, initiated in 2001, stagnated over the following decade.[1] The United States was compelled to seek out other means of market liberalisation. Regional agreements, such as the FTAA and the Asia-Pacific Economic Cooperation (APEC), were seen as the next best option. Like the WTO talks, however, the agenda and scale of these proposed agreements presented problems. Negotiations for the hemispheric FTAA ground to a halt in the early 2000s. Turning to the sub-regional track, the United States finalised the CAFTA-DR in 2005 but was unsuccessful in establishing a similar agreement with South America's Andean countries. The bilateral track bore more fruit in Latin America, where the Bush and Obama administrations signed and implemented FTAs with Chile, Peru, Panama and Colombia. Finally, the United States also made use of a unilateral track: 'Under this approach, the United States threatens retaliation, usually in the form of restricting trade partners' access to the vast US market, in order to get the partner to open its markets to US exports or to cease other offensive commercial practices and policies' (Cooper 2014: 3).

The North American Free Trade Agreement (NAFTA), which went into effect on 1 January 1994, served as a model for future FTAs. Joining the United States, Canada and Mexico, NAFTA comprises the world's second-largest free trade zone, after the European Union (EU). Amongst policymakers in Washington, NAFTA was widely (if not universally) heralded as a success. Yet, years after entering into force, it remained controversial with the US public, precipitating a spirited defence of the agreement on the part of the Bush administration (Public Citizen 2008; USTR 2008). The unpopularity of NAFTA portended the growing opposition to free trade in general, which undercut support for FTAs in Congress. Likewise, free trade and other Washington Consensus policies fuelled intense opposition in Latin America. With the emergence of the NLL, this opposition gained expression in the region's electoral politics. In a few short years, the Washington Consensus on trade liberalisation gave way to a set of contentious negotiations across the various tracks of the United States' free trade push. This dissensus was most evident at the hemispheric level, as seen in the collapse of the FTAA, but it also found expression in alternate mechanisms of economic co-operation and integration, including existing institutions (like Mercosur) and newer groupings (such as ALBA).

With the election of NLL leaders in the early 2000s the landscape of inter-American trade relations changed considerably. In 2003, Brazil's Lula and Argentina's Kirchner signed 'the Buenos Aires Consensus'. The agreement formalised a budding alliance between the countries on matters of international economic policy. The twenty-point declaration consolidated a common approach on foreign debt, IMF negotiations, economic growth, trade, wealth redistribution, taxation, social policy and the strengthening of Mercosur. Though imprecise in its proposals, the declaration was a forceful rejoinder to the Washington Consensus (Smith 2003). Its anti-neoliberal tinge was evident in its insistence that the state play a more active role in encouraging equitable and sustainable economic growth. The most concrete impact of the alliance was in the countries' relations with the Bretton Woods institutions. In 2004, the leaders signed a follow-up agreement calling on the IMF to reform its 'rules of engagement' with debtor nations. Lula and

Kirchner wanted to ensure that the repayment of IMF loans did not jeopardise economic growth and infrastructure investment (Bretton Woods Project 2004: 3). At the time, the two countries' debt accounted for nearly 50 per cent of the IMF's loan portfolio. 'By joining forces', Brazil and Argentina were 'sending a message to the international community that, together, they have much leverage and are in a position to bargain with the international financial institutions' (Center for Strategic and International Studies 2004: 6).

The Lula–Kirchner agreement can be traced back to an earlier 'Buenos Aires Consensus', drawn up in 1998 by social democratic leaders and thinkers from across Latin America. Featuring the likes of Ricardo Lagos, who would become Chile's president, Jorge Castañeda and Lula himself, the 1998 meeting assessed Latin America's future 'after neoliberalism'. As stated by William Robinson, 'while the document called for "growth with equity" and a greater role for the state in assistance to the poor it was explicit that the logic of the market must not be challenged' (2008: 270). This was partly the product of Castañeda's strategising, in which leftists would win centrists away from the right on the basis of a post-neoliberal platform. An alliance-based approach was distinct from more radical or overtly anti-neoliberal paths, which threatened to alienate key sectors of the elite, thus spurring capital flight and/or outright reaction from more conservative elements (Ellner 2004: 11–15). The Lula–Kirchner alliance, built on the earlier Buenos Aires Consensus, represented a 'mildly reformist path for regional integration into global capitalism'. This was in contrast to ALBA, a more authentically counter-hegemonic project of regional economic development (Robinson 2008: 350–2).

There was little alarm amongst US policymakers over the Lula–Kirchner pact. Argentina was recovering from economic catastrophe, and Lula had proved to be a restrained and pragmatic figure in Washington's eyes. However, the Buenos Aires Consensus did indicate that even the more reformist agents of the NLL would prioritise South American integration over the discredited policies of the Washington Consensus. One could argue that the pact aided in the creation of new regional forums and institutions. After all, the Buenos Aires Consensus predated UNASUR, CELAC, the Bank of the South and even ALBA, which would be announced by Chávez the following year. Moreover, Brazil and Argentina sought the reinvigoration of Mercosur as a counterweight to the FTAA, and the Lula–Kirchner alliance provided much-needed momentum towards this objective. A more dynamic Mercosur would be realised, they hoped, through its expansion outside of the Southern Cone. Thus, Mercosur would come to include Venezuela as a full member, even as Chávez pursued his own project of regional integration. Together, the forums provided considerable space for co-ordinating opposition to the FTAA.

Mercosur: an FTAA roadblock

With the NLL in ascendancy, the dynamics of regional economic co-operation shifted. On one side sat the United States and its network of bilateral and sub-regional free trade regimes, collectively advancing the neoliberalisation of the

Washington Consensus. On the other side sat the Mercosur countries, governed mainly by centre-left parties, which united in one pact the majority of the Western hemisphere's opposition to the FTAA (Carranza 2004; Grinberg 2010). Politically, Mercosur was surpassed by the Bolivarian governments of ALBA, themselves closing ranks with the Mercosur nations. From Washington's perspective, economic integration had been overtaken by an 'ideological' turn. US trade policy, put on the defensive, sought to manage and deflect opposition to the FTAA. But Mercosur and ALBA offered more than a rejection of Washington's policies. They offered alternative paths of integration devoid of the asymmetry imposed by the inclusion of the United States in a hemispheric accord (even as they featured asymmetries associated with including larger economies like Brazil, Argentina and Venezuela alongside smaller countries).

Mercosur pre-dated the rise of the NLL. As South America's military dictatorships came to an end in the 1980s, the new democracies were presented with opportunities for closer co-operation. In 1991, Argentina, Brazil, Paraguay and Uruguay signed the Treaty of Asunción, formally creating the Common Market of the South. Inspired by the EU, Mercosur was a project of economic integration infused with political objectives, including the cessation of the traditional rivalry between Argentina and Brazil. With the import substitution industrialisation model seen as obsolete, Mercosur embraced 'open regionalism' aimed at 'globalising' South American economies. Inter-governmental rather than supranational, the customs union was an attempt to steer these processes towards economic development. Generally speaking, 'its objectives are to create a common market with free movement of goods, services and productive factors; adopt a common external policy; coordinate common positions in international forums; (and) coordinate sector and macroeconomic policies' (Baumann 2008: 3).

From a certain vantage, Mercosur's formation *contributed* to the structural power of the United States. Writing on the tenth anniversary of its founding, Cammack characterised Mercosur as an 'agent of discipline' in the construction of a more globalised capitalism. Much like other trade agreements, Mercosur fostered a market-led approach to development. And much like the IMF and World Bank, Cammack argued, Mercosur internalised the role of surveillance and enforcement of neoliberal macroeconomic reforms. This was done through, among other things, proposed limits on public spending, as well as IFI-related country assistance strategies, which facilitated new loans from the Bretton Woods institutions (Cammack 2002). Mercosur's supposed developmentalist project was undermined by its neoliberal limitations. Trade increased during its first decade, but so did poverty and inequality. Furthermore, Mercosur's institutional structure was shaky and uneven. The adoption of the common external tariff, for example, a core objective of the customs union, 'was imperfect, riddled with exemptions and lacking in transparency' (Mecham 2003: 378). However, partly a response to US-led globalisation, Mercosur was also a political initiative aimed at advancing co-operation in the Southern Cone. Whatever its failures as a development project, Mercosur would soon help consolidate the 'South American position' in global trade talks, playing a key role in obstructing the FTAA (Council on Foreign Relations 2012).

In an indirect manner, it was the FTAA that allowed for a 'reinvigoration of purpose' for Mercosur. The Brazilian and Argentinean crises of the 1990s and early 2000s had damaged the institution. By the time Lula and Kirchner had announced the Buenos Aires Consensus, a degree of post-crisis normalcy had returned to the Southern Cone, just as Washington sought to complete the FTAA. Under the stewardship of the PT and Peronist governments, Mercosur was presented as an alternative to the 'deep integration' proposed by the Bush administration. According to Sader (2011: 32–3), Lula's 'decision to prioritise the regional process of integration led Brazil to veto the FTAA, opening the space for Mercosur to be revived from its state of inactivity, and almost inexistence'. Argentina, for its part, was also invested in a more dynamic Mercosur, as was Venezuela, which sought full membership. Despite their differences, the leaders of South America's NLL governments were enthusiastic about Mercosur's possibilities. During the 2006 summit, they reiterated that Mercosur was a viable alternative to US-led free trade. In 2007, Chávez pushed further, calling for it to be 'decontaminated of neoliberalism' (Council on Foreign Relations 2012). The Lula and Kirchner governments were generally more muted, insisting that Mercosur's development need not threaten economic co-operation with the United States.

For Washington, Venezuela's inclusion in Mercosur threatened to further politicise the group. Facilitated by Argentina during its *pro tempore* presidency, the move demonstrated that Kirchner was prone to 'populism'. On occasion, Kirchner was staunchly opposed to US trade policy. A 2006 cable summarising his tenure criticised his foreign policy as 'erratic'. His focus on regional integration meant little more than the 'strengthening of relations with Venezuela and Brazil'. 'Kirchner's top officials', wrote the US embassy, 'have repeatedly told Embassy officials that the GOA's relationship with Venezuela is based on economics and Mercosur. Kirchner sees Venezuela as a solution for Argentina's energy and financing problems' (Wikileaks 2006a). The Venezuela–Argentina relationship hinged on Chávez's financing of Argentinean debt, which allowed Buenos Aires to sever ties with the IMF. Additionally, Argentina, Brazil and the other Mercosur countries offered political support for Chávez, even as Washington leaned on Argentina and Brazil to moderate his government.

How did the United States interpret Mercosur's evolution? A 2006 cable offers insight:

> Over the past couple of years, Mercosur has evolved from a benign trading bloc into a political union with a robust foreign policy agenda. More often than not, this agenda has clashed with some USG objectives—particularly since Venezuela became its fifth member. A prime example of Mercosur's politicization was manifested by its unflinching support for Venezuela's bid for a semi-permanent seat on the (UN Security Council). Earlier examples include Mercosur's anti-FTAA posture at the Summit of the Americas in Mar del Plata . . . The unpredictability of two Mercosur leaders (Argentina's Nestor Kirchner and Venezuela's Hugo Chavez) have further complicated Mercosur politics. There's been recent talk about bringing Bolivia into the bloc, adding the fiery Evo Morales into the Mercosur mix.
>
> (Wikileaks 2006b)

The cable also criticised Mercosur's broader trade agenda as 'little more than a failure'. Specifically, it highlighted uncertainties over the common external tariff and the group's inability to move forward on its process to negotiate a trade deal with the United States. 'In light of these developments', it read, 'a re-examination of our overall relationship with Mercosur may be warranted' (Wikileaks 2006b).

The expansion of Mercosur did not mean that South America had wholly embraced the Mercosur agenda. Regional fissures remained. Venezuela's departure from the Community of Andean Nations (CAN), another multilateral forum, left CAN weakened at a time when Washington was actively pursuing free trade deals with several of its members, including Peru and Colombia. The gradual movement of Bolivia and Ecuador away from CAN and towards Mercosur further reduced the relevancy of the Andean body, which had been open to the prospect of free trade with the United States.[2] Reflecting the political and economic tensions of the region, Mercosur was nevertheless consolidated as a major obstacle to the FTAA. A more direct challenge to US structural power would come in the form of the Bolivarian Alliance.

The Bolivarian alternative to the FTAA

Originally known as the 'Bolivarian *Alternative* for Our Americas', ALBA (meaning 'dawn' in Spanish, and later dubbed the Bolivarian Alliance for the Peoples of Our Americas) represented a multifaceted configuration of Latin America's leftist governments, with participation by a number of smaller Caribbean countries. In contrast to Mercosur, the Venezuelan-led group confronted US hegemony head-on. Beginning as an alliance between Venezuela and Cuba, it quickly became a regional project intended to compete directly with the neoliberal agenda (Hart-Landsberg 2010; Muhr 2013). 'Intended to be a counter-point to the FTAA', read a 2005 US cable, 'ALBA has yet to be more than a rallying theme for radical Latin American "socialists"'. From the outset Chávez insisted that ALBA 'must go beyond Cuba and Venezuela'. The forum's social mission, he surmised, would 'declare war . . . on misery, on sickness, on exclusion'. The US embassy in Venezuela concluded that the 'barely defined counter-proposal to the FTAA' was largely a means of funnelling subsidised oil to Cuba (Wikileaks 2005a).

ALBA promotes nonmarket-shaped structures through regional public enterprises and bilateral partnerships between existing state enterprises. Its initiatives have helped members strengthen planning capacity, modernise industrial and agricultural operations and provide much-needed social services, including the establishment of medical centres and literacy programmes. 'Moderate' NLL governments tended to distance themselves from ALBA, though Brazil and Argentina joined ALBA's Petrosur initiative, which facilitates co-operation amongst South America's state-run energy firms. The Petrocaribe programme, which has provided subsidised oil to over a dozen Caribbean and Central American countries, is co-ordinated through ALBA. Additionally, ALBA members created an integrated trade and currency zone backed by the Sucre, a new regional currency that exists largely as a virtual unit of account. The further institutionalisation of the Sucre could scale back the use of the US dollar for intra-Latin American trade (Hart-Landsberg 2010). Members also created an ALBA Bank to promote development (separate from the Bank of the South, a similar project associated with Mercosur), originally capitalised at $1 billion. Outside of these initiatives, much of ALBA's activity has been bilateral. This includes trade pacts that employ a kind of bartering system (e.g. Venezuelan oil traded for Cuban doctors and teachers).

ALBA has been financed almost entirely by Venezuela. Even prior to the oil boom of the mid-2000s, Chávez was candid about the use of petroleum as a foreign policy tool. Running for office in 1998, he called oil a 'geopolitical weapon' while criticising Venezuela's political class for neglecting the country's power as a major oil-producer (Kozloff 2006: 7). For its proponents, ALBA is about leveraging Venezuela's oil wealth into a counter-hegemonic project of transnational co-operation that extends beyond the energy sector itself. In addition to subsidised oil, for instance, Petrocaribe has financed aerial and maritime transport projects across the Caribbean basin. Robinson writes that 'ALBA envisions a regional economic development plan for Latin America and the Caribbean involving solidarity with the weakest national economies so that all can cooperate and benefit from regional exchange networks and development projects' (2008: 351–2). Petrocaribe also features a development component (the ALBA Caribe Fund), financed by PdVSA, Venezuela's state-run energy firm.

The institutionalisation of ALBA's economic agenda was facilitated by the pan-Latin discourse of Bolivarianism, which targeted the FTAA as an expression of US hegemony. An articulation of Venezuelan nationalism and 'Twenty-first Century Socialism', Bolivarianism gave ALBA a regional appeal. US policymakers were attuned to the broader ideological challenge it represented. ALBA, through its various summits, 'provided Hugo Chavez a platform to rail against capitalism and the United States' (Wikileaks 2008a). He used ALBA to criticise the World Bank and IMF, to link the IFIs to 'savage capitalism' and 'US imperialism', and to 'trumpet' ALBA's tangible projects, many of them funded by Venezuelan foreign aid (Wikileaks 2007a). At the intersection of structural and ideological forms of power, the United States would denigrate this as 'populism' to deflate the appeal of the Bolivarian model and bolster the prospects for US-led free trade (see Chapter 6).

A 2006 cable stated that Chávez was increasingly 'crafting his rhetoric of hate for international audiences', never failing to 'hawk his anti-imperialist diatribe in international fora'. One important 'cut of hate rhetoric', it said, was 'between imperialism and Bolivarianism . . . Chavez uses "Bolivarian" as a loose synonym for anti-imperialism. He paints his Bolivarian Alternative for the Americas . . . as the morally pure version of the FTAA', which is depicted as 'an attempt to colonize Venezuela' (Wikileaks 2006c). The US approach to this confrontational discourse generally involved ignoring provocative comments so as not to 'dignify them with a response' (Wikileaks 2007a). If the strategy denied Chávez the heated exchanges he relished, it also denied Washington the opportunity to respond to some of the challenges presented by ALBA's anti-imperialist message.

For smaller states, participation in ALBA presented a difficult balancing act regarding relations with the United States, as illustrated by an exchange between Orlando Gómez, a Sandinista diplomat, and the US embassy in Managua:

> Gomez expected ties with Venezuela and Bolivia and other ALBA states to deepen in the coming years. In part, this (was) because free trade, particularly CAFTA-DR, did not deliver the expected results for Nicaragua and new models were needed to expand social and economic development in the country. CAFTA-DR, he claimed, has not produced results in employment and the trade has only benefitted certain sectors, 'making only a few rich'. ALBA projects and trade, however, would create new sources of employment and generate other improvements in the productive bases of Nicaragua's economy. ALBA, however, should not be viewed as contradictory to or competitive with CAFTA-DR and US trade.
>
> (Wikileaks 2009a)

For Gomez, ALBA would help develop Nicaragua in ways that trade with the United States had not, but without damaging relations with the United States. For Washington, this 'skewed Sandinista worldview' seemed to be less threatening than mistaken (Wikileaks 2009a).

Indeed, Washington was of two minds on ALBA. On the one hand, the bloc was dismissed as irrelevant—its plans were 'grandiose', its projects 'incompetent' and 'muddled' (Wikileaks 2006d). There was the sense that, without greater participation from Mercosur members, it would fail to move beyond its status as a loose collection of 'anti-American' governments and smaller states seeking closer energy ties with Venezuela. Although, for the United States, ALBA may have played a role in galvanising opposition to the FTAA, it never had hemispheric potential. On the other hand, officials characterised ALBA as an 'increasingly vocal and coordinated grouping that demands attention in international fora, both inside and outside the Hemisphere' (Wikileaks 2010a). Some expressed concern that ALBA undermined the authority of the IFIs by offering alternative sources of funding. Trade between its members increased considerably as the bloc expanded (Muhr 2013). Although ALBA's long-term future remained an uncertainty, for Washington's trade agenda the damage had been done. Alongside Mercosur's opposition, ALBA's co-ordination of the region's anti-neoliberal governments played an important part in stunting momentum for the FTAA.

The collapse of the Free Trade Area of the Americas

As of January 2015, the official website of the FTAA was fully functional. A message noted that the website was last updated on 21 June 2006, but active links provided the inquisitive visitor with an abundance of official documents and contact points for all thirty-four of its prospective member states.[3] The immense scope of the FTAA was evident in its cornucopia of drafts and declarations, even as the dense, official discourse of the treaty process hid its relationship to neoliberal restructuring behind a wall of jargon. The FTAA was widely—and accurately—attributed to the hegemonic designs of the United States; as an attempt by Washington to extend NAFTA to the entire hemisphere (Katz 2002; Nelson 2015). Its breakdown denoted the collapse of the Washington Consensus at the regional level, diverting Washington's free trade ambitions to bilateral and sub-regional tracks.

The FTAA's phantasmal online presence was eerily apropos. Even in 2008, several years after the cessation of formal talks, the CRS claimed the United States was committed to finding a solution to the impasse. The CRS stated that 'getting the FTAA back on track (was) one of the major challenges to US-Latin America trade policy', but it acknowledged that 'recent political realignments in Latin America suggest that this task (would) only become more difficult' (Hornbeck 2008: 5–6). The ascendency of NLL governments complicated the FTAA nego-tiations. President Lula's election in 2002 was a turning point, and Brazil's unease with the FTAA process proved to be its greatest hurdle. Additionally, following the collapse of Argentina's economy in 2001–2, the Kirchner government moved the country decisively away from Washington's trade agenda. In the Andes, Venezuela's steadfast opposition to US-backed trade deals would soon be shared by Bolivia and Ecuador.

From the start, the FTAA was unquestionably a US project. The idea of a hemi-spheric free trade area extending from Alaska to the Tierra del Fuego originated during the Reagan presidency. In 1990, the incipient plan was given a name by the George H. W. Bush administration: the Enterprise for the Americas Initiative. It was Bill Clinton who would make the free trade vision a reality, and his imple-mentation of NAFTA fuelled momentum for the wider hemispheric pact. In 1994, the newly christened FTAA was placed on the regional agenda during the inau-gural Summit of the Americas. The heads of state signed an action plan designed to position the FTAA process alongside existing GATT/WTO talks. It pledged to 'maximize market openness' in a wide range of areas: 'tariffs and non-tariff barriers affecting trade in goods and services; agriculture; subsidies; investment; intellectual property rights; government procurement; technical barriers to trade; safeguards; rules of origin; antidumping and countervailing duties; sanitary and phytosanitary standards and procedures; dispute resolution; and competition policy'. The action plan called for the liberalisation and progressive integration of capital markets, and for an increased role for the multilateral development banks (First Summit of the Americas 1994). These proposals were fleshed-out at subse-quent summits. Committees and working groups were set up along the NAFTA model, with the goal of privatising and deregulating key sectors. Beyond 'tradi-tional' trade issues, the United States aimed to foster an integrative process to deepen neoliberalisation (Carranza 2004; Katz 2002; Nelson 2015), reinforcing US structural power in hemispheric relations.

In the common metaphor, 'by "locking in" open access to markets, free trade pacts help reduce uncertainty about the future course of trade and regulatory policies and thus facilitate business planning and investment'. According to its proponents, then, the FTAA, seen as 'the most ambitious free trade initiative of the postwar trading system', would have deadbolted 'the conduct of overall economic policy in and economic relations among the participating countries', thus yielding 'both economic and foreign policy benefits' (Schott 2005: 1–7). The FTAA was thus partly geopolitical. Indeed, the Bush administration—a more enthusiastic set of 'free traders' than even the Clinton team—went so far as to link trade to the US security agenda, arguing that, as a manifestation of 'freedom' itself, 'free trade' would help combat terrorism. In its 2002 National Security Strategy, the White House reiterated its commitment to finalising the FTAA by 2005 (Bush 2002: 17–20).

For the FTAA to come to fruition, all parties would have to agree to the entire set of requirements in the final text. The sheer scope of the agreement made this exceedingly difficult (Hornbeck 2008). In 2003, the United States and Brazil steered the talks towards a two-tier framework comprised of (1) a set of 'common rights and obligations' for all participating countries, and (2) a set of plurilateral arrangements related to voluntary commitments. Called the 'FTAA-lite' (an outcome of the 'Miami compromise', named for the site of the 2003 summit), the move sparked widespread debate over the direction of the broader process (Wikileaks 2005b). Did the changes give Latin American countries the policy space they desired? Was the new structure a step towards a final agreement, or a step back from Washington's goal of a more thoroughly neoliberalised hemisphere? In effect, the two-tier framework provided individual countries (including the United States) the option of withdrawing from certain commitments, allowing them to protect chosen industries/sectors. As delegates debated the merits of the two-tier system behind closed doors, the streets of Miami witnessed raucous demonstrations. The protests were more monumental two years later, when a chorus of politicians and activists led by Hugo Chávez ceremoniously 'buried' the FTAA at a 'People's Summit' held alongside the 2005 Summit of the Americas in Mar del Plata, Argentina. By that point, the talks had ground to halt. Bush's visit to Argentina provoked an outpouring of opposition. In the streets and boardrooms, it was obvious that the two-tier framework had yielded neither consensus nor a way forward (Wikileaks 2005b).

Brazil's wariness was fuelled by the perception that the FTAA was an attempt to co-opt Mercosur, an important component of Brazil's gambit for increased international influence. Brazil pivoted to a '3-track' proposal on trade policy: disaggregating the Mercosur, FTAA and WTO negotiations (Wikileaks 2003a). Lula, who downplayed his anti-neoliberalism from 2002 onward, had staked his presidency on the PT's social agenda. The country's social movements, which backed Lula's candidacy, continued to resist the FTAA talks, but the PT gradually toned down its anti-FTAA rhetoric and moved towards orthodox macroeconomic policies. The PT did retain a level of commitment to its traditional socialist platform, elements of which it tried to incorporate into the FTAA—a nonstarter for the Bush administration (Wikileaks 2003b). Additionally, Lula's efforts at replacing the FTAA process with one based on bilateral and/or sub-regional commitments (i.e. Mercosur) were rebuffed by the United States, which pushed for a comprehensive treaty by attempting to reassure Brazilian officials that Washington was 'not afraid of the PT and its social agenda', in the words of Otto Reich (Wikileaks 2002). Brazil clearly saw the FTAA as involving much more than trade. For the PT, the agreement had the potential to seriously compromise its social, environmental and technological policies (Wikileaks 2003a). US officials lamented that the PT's political goals, namely its social agenda and regional leadership role, clashed with the prevailing economic orthodoxy (Wikileaks 2003c).

Why would the centre-left government of South America's largest economy entertain the notion of a trade pact with the United States? In the context of transnational capitalism, and in the logic of structural power, Brazil was compelled to join the FTAA process to gain favourable access to the massive US market. With its exports in mind, it consistently pushed for a beneficial outcome in the 'common set' element of the FTAA's two-tier structure. 'For Brazil', one cable read, 'the bottom line is improved access to the US market for its agricultural and industrial goods, not regional rules for attracting foreign direct investment' (Wikileaks 2003c). Agriculture proved to be a major issue. Brazil unsuccessfully campaigned against US farm/agribusiness subsidies in the negotiations. Meanwhile, the United States was unable to persuade Brazil to discuss the liberalisation of its services sector. Lula himself stated that the United States 'only want(ed) to negotiate on matters that serve its interests, such as services', and not on matters important to Brazil, such as agriculture (Wikileaks 2005c).

US officials were pleased that Lula's team remained at least nominally committed to the FTAA. 'Despite campaign rhetoric asserting that the FTAA would result in Brazil's "annexation" to the United States', Lula 'quickly committed to continuing negotiations in good faith', even as 'radicals' within his party pushed for a public referendum on the free trade proposal (Wikileaks 2003d). Washington maintained a relatively optimistic attitude following the 2003 compromise. To sustain momentum, the United States sought to carefully 'massage' Brazil's status as the leader of the South American bloc. One cable written just before the 2003 ministerial concluded:

> Whatever construct the USG decides to pursue for the negotiations in Miami, it would be wise to orchestrate it in a way that amicably leaves the door open for greater participation of Brazil in the future; not only to enable the USG to continue to strive for the larger goal of a totally integrated hemisphere, but also to minimize the opportunity for anti-FTAA factions within Brazil to lay the blame for 'failure' . . . at the feet of the USG. A consistent message from other countries in the region that their interests do not coincide with Brazil's will be key to helping with the latter.
>
> (Wikileaks 2003e)

By 2004, it was clear that the gulf was in fact widening in the wake of the Miami compromise. The Bush administration began entertaining the possibility of advancing a hemispheric free trade area through an 'alternate process' (outside of existing declarations). US officials viewed the FTAA process as 'fraught with uncertainty' due to Lula's wavering. It didn't help that Brazil's commercial lobby failed to overcome the 'ideological hurdles' of the PT government, which ensured that the FTAA was (correctly) seen as a 'US-led initiative' (Wikileaks 2004a). As Brasilia clarified that Brazil viewed the FTAA as 'desirable' but 'not essential', the United States chaffed at the PT's prioritisation of its 'geopolitical partnerships' over trade (Wikileaks 2005d). A 2005 cable stated that, 'because the GOB looks at the world through an outdated third world . . . lens', US–Brazil relations were 'often difficult'. As US officials encouraged Brazil to 'stay the course with its orthodox economic program', they fretted over Lula's budding alliance with Chávez (Wikileaks 2005b). Brazil's commitment to Mercosur grew more apparent. As the FTAA process stalled, Mercosur expanded its trade ties with those South American countries outside of its existing customs zone—namely Colombia, Venezuela, Ecuador, Peru, Chile and Bolivia.

Ultimately, the FTAA went the way of the WTO's Doha Round, where talks withered amidst the conflicting interests of the North–South divide. In South America, however, opposition appeared more 'ideological'. The rise of the NLL peaked just as FTAA negotiations reached a head. By the time that Chávez could taunt Bush at Mar del Plata, the broader regional trend had been set. If, in 1994, there had been an elite consensus regarding the desirability of 'free trade' as defined by the United States, by 2005 it had largely evaporated. Washington would doggedly push for neoliberalisation amidst this new regional dissensus.

Competitive liberalisation: promoting 'free trade' amidst regional dissensus

The breakdown of the FTAA coincided with the breakdown of the Doha Development Round (DDR). Despite the setbacks, the United States' goals in the international economy remained firmly in place. With the hemispheric process in tatters, US trade policy jumped to alternate tracks. In constructing agreements with Latin American nations outside of the FTAA framework the USTR explained that it would 'pursue all available multilateral, regional and bilateral opportunities to lower trade barriers and promote international commerce' (Wikileaks 2006e). This was the cornerstone of the Bush administration's doctrine of 'competitive liberalisation', which updated the long-standing objectives of US trade policy for the post-Doha environment. Competitive liberalisation had three purposes: opening up national economies to US goods and capital; fostering the adoption of laws and regulations to accommodate US-based businesses; and building support around wider (non-trade related) US foreign policies (Evenett and Meier 2008). In Latin America, this meant the pursuit of sub-regional and bilateral agreements.

The Central American Free Trade Agreement

Signed in 2004, the Central American Free Trade Agreement (CAFTA[-DR], which includes the Dominican Republic) was passed by the US House of Representatives by a razor-thin margin of 217 to 215 in July 2005. The Bush White House had to fight to get the deal done. The US public had grown increasingly sceptical of free trade. Meanwhile, Latin America's left turn had deepened, and the geopolitical arguments for CAFTA were brought to the forefront of the debate. Although the economic stakes were low, wrote *The Economist* (2005), 'the politics were intense. Turn your backs on this agreement', the administration warned lawmakers, 'and your country's Central American allies might opt instead for the "Bolivarian alternative"'. Proponents hoped it would kick-start the FTAA. This proved farfetched, however. CAFTA was comprised of small countries with far less bargaining power than Brazil or Argentina. In the end, it was less a stepping stone in the direction of the FTAA than a (temporary) step back in Washington's hemispheric designs. CAFTA was a 'consolation prize' on the way to a more limited agenda, albeit one firmly focused on neoliberalising the hemispheric political economy.

Although popular opposition to the accord was strong in many parts of Central America, CAFTA was eventually ratified by all seven countries, entering into force for the United States, El Salvador, Guatemala, Honduras and Nicaragua in 2006, for the Dominican Republic in 2007, and for Costa Rica on 1 January 2009. Together, the CAFTA-DR countries represent the third largest US export market in Latin America (behind Mexico and Brazil). From 2006 to 2010, US exports to the CAFTA countries grew by 43 per cent, compared to 25 per cent growth during the five years (2001–5) before the agreement (Export.gov 2012a).

Although US exporters stood to benefit from reduced barriers, and while the Central Americans were aiming for duty-free access to the US market, CAFTA's rules were about much more than trade. Indeed, while the agreement lowered some trade barriers, it strengthened others, such as those on patented pharmaceutical drugs. 'Equally important for the United States were enhanced rules covering multiple disciplines', including services, intellectual property rights, government procurement and labour and environmental regulations (Hornbeck 2012: 2). Though the impact of CAFTA would vary from country to country, the pattern was unquestionably one of liberalisation, privatisation and deregulation, with the goal of 'opening up' Central American economies to the free movement of transnational capital. By deepening existing processes of economic neoliberalisation, CAFTA bolstered the structural power of the United States, even though post-agreement trends in trade were mixed. The United States remained the region's dominant trade partner, but its share of total trade began to decline over the 2000s, replaced by intra-Central American trade and growing links with China and Mexico (Hornbeck 2012).

The desire to attract new inflows of foreign investment was a key objective for Central America's neoliberal governments. However, CAFTA's investment provisions restricted 'the ability of signatory countries to require that foreign firms adhere to performance requirements, such as local content standards and technology transfer requirements'. What is more, CAFTA set 'broad rules regarding what constitutes an expropriation, as well as the compensation due to investors if expropriation does indeed occur' (Gallagher 2005). The agreement created the possibility that ad hoc investment tribunals would interpret social and environmental regulations as a kind of 'indirect expropriation' in certain cases. Despite these measures, the level of foreign investment coveted by the Central American states was far from certain; FTAs have not always led to increased foreign investment, and investment trends after CAFTA were uneven (Gallagher 2005; Hornbeck 2012: 14–15).

On the US side, domestic interest groups weighed in on CAFTA's rules and regulations. Although some US industries (e.g. sugar, cotton) opposed the agreement, the American business lobby as a whole supported it with vigour. With the FTAA, APEC and WTO talks floundering, CAFTA took on added importance. The Chamber of Commerce spearheaded advocacy on behalf of CAFTA. Support from US apparel manufacturers was also crucial to its passage. The business lobby was opposed by labour unions, environmentalists and human rights groups. UNITE HERE, a union representing workers in the textile and apparel industry, lobbied against CAFTA, as did the larger AFL-CIO federation. The rules of the agreement, labour argued, were designed to facilitate and protect foreign investment by multinational corporations. CAFTA would effectively enable corporations to be more mobile and thus less accountable to local communities, 'dramatically shifting the balance of power' away from elected governments towards private firms, 'increasing the bargaining power of employers vis-à-vis their workers' (Gelb 2005: 6). According to the AFL-CIO (2005), CAFTA allowed the 'enormous legal obstacles' confronting Central American workers to 'remain in place, making it nearly impossible for workers in the region to win a real voice at work and bargain for fair wages and decent working conditions'. A Human Rights Watch report condemned CAFTA's labour provisions for, among other things, their lack of enforceability (2004).

Central American opposition to CAFTA reflected a related set of concerns. Across the region, criticism came from unions, environmentalists, indigenous and peasant groups and the Catholic Church. As written, its opponents alleged, CAFTA had woefully inadequate labour and environmental provisions. They maintained that CAFTA would unfairly pit subsidised US agricultural interests against subsistence farmers. Examining the legacy of NAFTA, critics charged that the agreement would exacerbate socio-economic inequality, that it would limit access to much-needed generic drugs and that certain provisions would hasten the privatisation of state-run programmes (Ribando 2005). Violent protests against CAFTA flared up in El Salvador, Honduras and Guatemala in 2004 and 2005. In Nicaragua, the Sandinista party galvanised opposition. Political and grassroots opposition to CAFTA was monitored by US embassies, which, on at least one occasion, contributed resources to the policing of anti-CAFTA demonstrations (Wikileaks 2007b). In general, US officials were dismissive of the criticism of the accord by labour unions, human rights monitors and legislators (Wikileaks 2005e). Politically, however, the antagonism needed to be addressed to smooth the completion of the accord.

In Costa Rica, opponents nearly defeated CAFTA in a public referendum, delaying its ratification. Activists expressed concerns that its rules would gut the country's highly regarded environmental laws and force the privatisation of its telecommunications system (Ribando 2005: 3). In the end, however, 51.6 per cent of Costa Rican voters endorsed CAFTA, a victory for Washington. A leaked memo from the Costa Rican government showed that the pro-CAFTA administration of Óscar Arias had contemplated a public relations strategy linking the 'No' campaign to Hugo Chávez and Fidel Castro. The leaked memo forced the resignation of its author, vice president Kevin Casas-Zamora. 'A month after the memo scandal', wrote one observer, 'the Bush administration threatened to eliminate Costa Rica's (existing) trade preferences in textiles, tuna, and other sectors if its voters rejected CAFTA' (Beeton 2008: 47–8).

The ratification of CAFTA was not the end of the story. The implementation of its regulations remained a major undertaking. Embassy cables demonstrate how US officials were active in attending to CAFTA's implementation in Central America. Of particular concern to the United States were the agreement's investment rules; regulations on intellectual property; and the countries' adherence to CAFTA's arbitration mechanism (Wikileaks 2008b, 2009b). Where CAFTA was approved without difficulty (as in the Dominican Republic), the United States hoped the ease of its legislative victory would facilitate implementation at the national level. Elsewhere, as in Costa Rica, Washington needed to actively press for its finalisation. This included putting 'pressure on the GOCR to move CAFTA-DR forward expeditiously', in the words of one cable (Wikileaks 2005f). Meanwhile, in El Salvador, the US Agency for International Development (USAID) financed an implementation programme 'long before CAFTA-DR ratification' (Wikileaks 2005g).

For Washington, CAFTA had been jeopardised by political trends in the region, though, in hindsight, its implementation was never seriously threatened. Latin America's left turn would soon make its presence felt in Central America, with the election of Ortega in Nicaragua, Colom in Guatemala and Funes in El Salvador. Additionally, Honduran president Zelaya, elected in 2005, transformed himself from a free trader into a 'Bolivarian'. In March 2006 Assistant Secretary of State Thomas Shannon met with the US ambassadors to El Salvador, Honduras, Costa Rica, Guatemala, Nicaragua, Belize and Panama to discuss regional integration and other pressing issues. Shannon expressed concerns regarding the perception of US trade policy. He noted that the United States experienced 'difficulty in packaging what we do'. While governmental support for CAFTA was stable, 'populism' appeared to be on the rise. The ambassadorial group concluded that it needed to better co-ordinate its outreach on CAFTA implementation, including through the sharing of best practices (Wikileaks 2006f). As was the case in the pre-ratification period, much of the Bush administration's work on CAFTA was in public relations. Its messaging was geared towards 'countering the myth that "CAFTA-DR" is bad for Central America', to quote one document (Wikileaks 2005h).

Had the national votes on CAFTA been a few years later, it is possible the agreement would have gone the way of the FTAA. Once it was in place, though, both the 'populists' and moderates in Central America could do little to challenge it. Colom and Funes supported CAFTA, the latter with some reservations and in a conscious attempt to bolster his 'pragmatism', thus putting his government on better footing with the United States. In conversations with

US officials, representatives of Funes' party (the majority of which opposed the deal) stated that they wanted to make 'adjustments' to the agreement, 'but backed away when (the US) suggested how difficult that would be' (Wikileaks 2008c). Ortega, on the other hand, seemed to relish blasting CAFTA in speeches, calling it an unfair manifestation of Yankee imperialism. Ortega's government faced a dilemma. It needed to attract capital investment, but wanted simultaneously to curb Nicaragua's economic dependence on the United States and the IFIs. Hoping to 'revisit' certain elements of the agreement, Ortega would eventually call for a 'comprehensive renegotiation' (Wikileaks 2008d). From Washington's view, CAFTA was a macroeconomic success, boosting Nicaragua's exports to the United States, fostering a competitive investment environment and opening up key sectors (including telecommunications) to privatisation. For the Sandinista government, however, CAFTA's rules had restricted its manoeuvrability in a host of areas, from minimum wage laws to its ability to impose liability on foreign companies who manufactured or used chemical pesticides in the country. The accord was never renegotiated.

Given this closure of policy space, why would a government led by former Marxist revolutionaries remain wedded to Washington's free trade accord—one that was signed into law by a rival party? The true value of CAFTA for its proponents was that Nicaragua, like other countries, remained 'locked in' to its neoliberal strictures. Ortega could use the agreement as a rhetorical punching bag, but withdrawing from CAFTA outright would create interminable legal, financial and economic problems for a country with a GDP equivalent to a moderately sized US city. Even with the 'Bolivarian alternative' up and running, the costs of leaving CAFTA would simply be too great. And, like the Nicaraguans, Honduran policymakers found themselves wedded to a less-than-desirable set of 'trade' rules. Following ratification, Washington used CAFTA to persuade Honduras to pass and enforce a new telecoms law aimed at opening the industry to private competition (Wikileaks 2007c). As his term progressed, Honduran president Zelaya was hamstrung by CAFTA, particularly in regards to food security and fuel imports. His efforts to circumvent CAFTA's rules in these areas signalled a shift in the ideological orientation of his government, one that would culminate in a *coup d'état*.

Zelaya began his term as an advocate of free trade and IMF lending policies. The United States saw him as a partner but was suspicious of his 'populist' advisors. In 2008, Zelaya enacted a consumer protection law to fix prices for essential goods (including food) via emergency declaration (to circumvent CAFTA rules on price fixing). The move was condemned as 'statist' by the United States, reflecting 'a distrust of markets' (Wikileaks 2008e). Honduras' decision to 'nationalise' its fuel imports also caused alarm, in part because it was facilitated via Venezuela's Petrocaribe initiative. In a leaked cable, the embassy in Tegucigalpa wrote: 'Our aggressive public and private interventions have significantly reduced the chances that this process will result in a political and economic alliance of GOH with Venezuela under a Petrocaribe arrangement.' US officials asserted that Zelaya's energy policies were non-compliant with CAFTA (Wikileaks 2006g). Less than two years later, Zelaya announced that Honduras would join ALBA. Citing US farm subsidies and regional free trade policies, he criticised the United States over Honduras's food crisis. In response, the United States endeavoured to 'remain out of the public fray', no doubt aware that condemnation could stoke nationalist sentiments. However, the embassy emphasised that it expected Honduras 'to honor its obligations under CAFTA, which, unlike ALBA, has a formal legal text, has been approved by both . . . legislatures and contains clear rules, rights, obligations and procedures for resolving disputes' (Wikileaks 2008f). When Zelaya was deposed, he and other regional leaders suggested that Honduras be suspended from CAFTA as part of a broader sanctions regime. Evidently, this was never on the table. Washington was full-steam-ahead on free trade, its attention squarely on a series of bilateral agreements with key regional partners.

The bilateral path: Chile, Colombia, Panama, Peru

In 2003 and 2004, with the FTAA talks deteriorating, the Bush administration launched formal negotiations for bilateral free trade agreements (FTAs, also called trade promotion agreements [TPAs]) with Bolivia, Colombia, the Dominican Republic, Ecuador, Panama and Peru. Under Bush's competitive liberalisation strategy, these would be pursued alongside CAFTA, FTAA and WTO talks, and would be modelled largely on the US–Chile FTA, which was completed in June 2003. The election of NLL governments (and future ALBA members) in Bolivia and Ecuador effectively ended US trade discussions with those countries, but the proposed FTAs with Colombia, Panama and Peru would eventually come to fruition (the Dominican Republic was brought into CAFTA-DR).

There was a political pattern to the bilateral agenda, but it wasn't as clear-cut as one might suppose. Colombia's right-wing government, the United States' closest ally in South America, was 'rewarded' with an FTA, but the United States was also able to negotiate an FTA with the socialist government of Chile, its first in Latin America. The United States also flirted with an FTA with the centre-left government of Uruguay. In Peru, US efforts to secure an FTA were jeopardised during the country's 2006 presidential election, when both leftist candidate Ollanta Humala and centrist candidate Alan García campaigned against the agreement, which was signed by outgoing president Alejandro Toledo in June 2006, just before García's inauguration. Soon thereafter, García reconsidered his position, and he entered office a backer of the FTA. That Humala (in a more moderate guise) would win Peru's presidency in 2011 demonstrated the value of the accord for its proponents: in 2006, Humala panned the FTA, but by 2011 it had entered into force, and his administration was obliged to accept it. Partly a political move to appeal to moderate voters, Humala's about-face was also aimed at curbing capital flight and preventing a drop in foreign investment if/ when he assumed office.

The situation confronting Humala was similar to that confronting the Ortega and Funes governments in regards to CAFTA. Bilateral FTAs, like their multilateral counterparts, lock-in neoliberal reforms by increasing the costs associated with dismantling those policies most likely to engender political opposition. The move towards bilateral FTAs was largely strategic, in that it did not signal any changes in the goals of Washington's foreign economic policy. As noted above, the United States would continue to use 'all available opportunities' to revive the neoliberalism challenged by the NLL. In the absence of broader agreements, 'smaller FTAs accomplish the goal of liberalization and the expansion of markets for US goods', providing a 'better climate for US investors' (Council on Foreign Relations 2006). With the FTAA moribund, and with the Andes undergoing a profound political transformation, the bilateral path, though not ideal, was increasingly vital.

The Bush administration had planned for a CAFTA-style agreement for the Andean region. In 2003, Robert Zoellick, the US Trade Representative, stated that Latin American countries would be in danger of losing access to the US market should they withdraw from FTA talks. Previously, trade between the United States and the Andean region had been conducted under the framework of unilateral trade preferences in the Andean Trade Preference Act. Zoellick said that, while the Act had been a '"positive force" in creating jobs and opportunity in the region, the negotiation of a US free trade agreement with the Andean nations (was) the next logical step in securing market access on a "more mutual and more permanent basis"' (US Department of State 2003). The rise of Evo Morales and Rafael Correa made this step increasingly improbable. Closer to home, the White House's difficulties in marshalling CAFTA through Congress translated into a loss of flexibility in the Andean talks (Wikileaks 2005i). Nonetheless, the United States would leverage the discussion over the Andean FTA into bilateral agreements with Peru and Colombia (Wikileaks 2005j).

Chile was the first country in South America to sign an FTA with the United States. For the Bush administration, the finalisation of an agreement with a centre-left government showed it could work with ideological adversaries, though Chile's ruling Concertación coalition, led by the Socialist Party, had shed whatever leftist inclinations it once shared with Salvador Allende's experiment. US officials were critical of Chile's implementation of the agreement, including in regards to intellectual property rights and pharmaceutical patents. US officials saw the need to 'keep up the pressure' on Chile to follow through with the full implementation of the agreement (Wikileaks 2008g). Chile was even placed on the Special 301 Priority Watch List, a designation by the USTR that can result in retaliatory sanctions. Like the multilateral agreements, then, the bilateral FTA provided the United States with a legal framework to press for the interests of US corporations, enhancing US structural power.

Peru was next up. The politics were stark in the Peruvian case, particularly because Ollanta Humala, a nationalist military officer, was then viewed as a protégé of Chávez. Under the Toledo and García governments, Lima remained receptive to the FTA, even as polls and protests suggested dwindling public support (Wikileaks 2005k). Opposition to the FTA was tied to the bogey of Chávez. The US embassy sought to 'emphasize to Peruvian officials that they need to address the dichotomy between their desire for FTAs with the United States and the EU on the one hand, and Venezuela's approach to regional development' on the other (Wikileaks 2005k). The reputed link with Chávez likely cost Humala the 2006 election. For his part, García, who stated that he wanted to 'revise' the FTA during the campaign, privately pushed for it to be approved as soon as possible. According to US officials, García said explicitly that he wanted 'the FTA signed, sealed and delivered before he (took) office', and that he knew he would not be able to renegotiate the deal (Wikileaks 2006h). US officials were integral to the finalisation of the FTA text (Public Citizen 2010). The embassy described itself a 'very active' in the process, promoting the agreement throughout the country and helping to secure its passage by the Peruvian Congress while maintaining 'an open door policy for US businesses' (Wikileaks 2006i). The embassy hosted training programmes in compliance, monitoring and standards, while also sending Peruvian officials to training conferences in the United States.

The next spate of FTAs would be overseen by Obama, who finalised the agreements with Panama, Colombia and South Korea in October 2011. The US–Panama Trade Promotion Agreement went into effect in October 2012. Benefits highlighted by the US government included access to Panama's $20.6 billion services market, namely its financial and telecommunications sectors. The agreement created significant opportunities for US businesses in Panama's major infrastructure projects, such as the ongoing $5.25 billion Panama Canal expansion (Export.gov 2012b). For Panamanian officials, the agreement was 'about investment, not trade'. In consultation with the United States, they 'touted the FTA for its positive effects on procurement and contracting as the main lever to get foreign financing for (the) Canal expansion', the largest infrastructure project in the Americas (Wikileaks 2004b). In the context of CAFTA, the Panamanian government was concerned the country would 'lose out' to its neighbours on investment. The FTA was a vehicle to 'lock in the status quo or better . . . improve market access for Panama in niche areas (e.g., banking, maritime, and sugar), and most importantly to attract "good US investment"'. It would 'mitigate against future leftist-populist tendencies' while improving relations with the United States. It would also ensure Panama remained competitive with CAFTA's 'low wage' countries (Wikileaks 2004c).

The Colombia FTA was the most controversial of the United States' bilateral agreements in Latin America. Human rights abuses associated with Colombia's decades-old internal conflict made it a harder sell. Nevertheless, right-wing president Uribe was a key ideological ally of the United States, and although opposition to the FTA existed in both countries, pro-free traders used a range of arguments to press for its implementation. A confidential 2007 cable reads: 'Uribe considers FTA ratification essential for Colombia to receive long-term investment, increase economic growth, create jobs, and boost government revenues.' At the time, Uribe was concerned that the US Congress would force a renegotiation of the text. The document stated that 'US failure to approve the FTA soon would be a major domestic and regional political blow to Uribe. It would also boost Venezuelan President Chavez' alternative Bolivarian economic model' (Wikileaks 2007d). With the deal languishing two years later, then-Vice President Santos warned the United States that its failure to pass the FTA before

Colombia's 2010 election would 'send the wrong message at a critical time that it was not worth working with the United States'. He argued that Washington's inaction was 'isolating' Colombia and steering investment away from the country (Wikileaks 2009c).

In part, the slow pace of the ratification of the Panama and Colombia agreements was attributable to the eroding consensus on trade in the US Congress. Additionally, however, the logistics of constructing a network of FTAs began to wear on US policymakers. Instead of one accord, Washington had to negotiate agreements on a case-by-case basis. Assistant Secretary of State Shannon told Colombian officials in 2007 that the United States was 'considering establishing a forum of countries that had FTAs with the US that would promote broader economic integration among interested countries'. This idea was welcomed by Colombia, which had a 'vision of a Latin Pacific coast network of free trade agreements'. The forum would include all of Latin America's 'FTA-aspirant' countries, including Caribbean states (Wikileaks 2007e). This idea would be formalised as the Arc of the Pacific Initiative, the creation of which would 'counteract the isolation that Peru and Colombia face as moderate, centrist governments in a region susceptible to populism'. The forum attracted interest from Mexico, Chile, Canada and the United States, with the 'eventual goal of creating a "free trade area"' (Wikileaks 2008h). The Arc of the Pacific Initiative held several ministerial meetings in 2007 and 2008 before evolving into the Pacific Alliance, made up of Chile, Colombia, Peru and Mexico. The burgeoning 'Pacific' orientation of these governments portended Latin American interest in the TPP, which brought together a similar grouping of states in a US-led and Asia-centric initiative. Beyond the limits of bilateral free trade, then, a more expansive process of neoliberal integration appeared back on the hemispheric agenda.

Renewing consensus? The Americas in the Trans-Pacific Partnership

Despite the passage of CAFTA and the bilateral FTAs, the George W. Bush years were deleterious to the United States' free trade goals. Not only did the FTAA unravel on Bush's watch, so too did the WTO's Doha Round. By the end of his administration, free trade advocates in Washington were lamenting the collapse of the traditional bipartisan consensus on trade liberalisation (Cato Institute 2009: 611–23; Ikenson and Lincicome 2009). The 2008 financial crisis cast a shadow over Washington's seemingly boundless enthusiasm for 'free markets'. Mired in a severe recession, US economic policy turned inward, towards bailouts and fiscal stimulus. In the context of economic contraction, growing trade deficits and the persistent loss of manufacturing jobs, free traders found themselves on the defensive. The collapse of Washington Consensus on trade was even more pronounced in Latin America. Of those Latin American countries without FTAs with the United States, none were open to the prospect. From the perspective of inter-American relations, the antimonies of neoliberal capitalism had (further) destabilised US structural power, already challenged by the NLL.

Although Obama campaigned against free trade, he later reversed course, finalising Bush-era FTAs with Panama, Colombia and South Korea. Still, the pro-free-trade consensus of previous decades remained elusive. The bilateral route allowed the United States to press for 'competitive liberalisation', but bilateral FTAs can act as roadblocks to more comprehensive regimes (Bhagwati 2008). The Western hemisphere saw the emergence of an 'expansive system of disparate bilateral and plurilateral agreements', which was 'widely understood to be a second best solution for reaping the benefits of trade liberalization' (Hornbeck 2011: ii). In this context, US trade policy aimed for convergence; for a way of harmonising the overlapping layers of trade agreements completed in recent decades (Estevadeordal 2012: 27; Hornbeck 2011). A reconstitution of Washington's free trade consensus would entail a reinvigorated commitment to neoliberalisation, but in a manner that tied up the loose strands of existing agreements to give the 'spaghetti bowl' of overlapping rules a more coherent shape.

The original Trans-Pacific Strategic Economic Partnership Agreement was signed by Brunei, Chile, New Zealand and Singapore in 2005 as a means of supporting APEC's wider liberalisation push. The outgoing Bush administration committed the United States to an expanded version of the TPP in 2008 as a pathway to a Free Trade Area of the Asia-Pacific. Obama's backing the following year brought with it some support from the Democratic Party, which endorsed the TPP in its 2012 platform (Democratic National Committee 2012). Obama won trade promotion authority (known as 'fast track') in June 2015 after a drawn-out legislative battle, in which lawmakers from his own party criticised the TPP as a continuation of the discredited NAFTA model. Opponents had suggested that if the TPP failed to break with past agreements (in regards to its investment provisions, for example) it would risk generating a public backlash (Gordon 2012; Sanchez and Miller 2010). Although fast track is not required for trade negotiations, it signifies legislative support for specific agreements, as it allows the executive the flexibility to negotiate trade deals without interference from Congress. With fast track in place, Obama hoped to finalise the deal before the end of his presidency. (As of this writing, the accord has yet to be ratified, and its status remains in doubt. Donald Trump campaigned against the TPP, which was supported by much of the Republican Party establishment.)

A new model?

The TPP stands to be the world's largest free trade area. Together, the TPP's twelve countries (Australia, Brunei, Canada, Chile, Japan, Malaysia, Mexico, New Zealand, Peru, Singapore the United States and Vietnam) account for 40 per cent of global output. Although, for Washington, the TPP is mainly about the large East Asian economies, its value lies in its ability to connect East and West while reinvigorating the global trade agenda (Biegon in press). Analysts have called it the 'most comprehensive agreement in terms of breadth and depth of commitments undertaken by the United States' (Fergusson *et al.* 2014: 49). Importantly, it gives Washington an architectural role in the harmonisation of existing trade rules. The Obama administration's slogan for the TPP, unveiled as part of a public relations campaign, was telling: 'Made in America' (USTR 2015).

During the TPP negotiations 'cross-cutting issues emerged as high-priority areas, including supply-chain management, competitiveness, transparency, regulatory coherence, labor and the environment, development, and small and medium businesses'. Put on the agenda by Washington, these rules, 'largely aimed at behind-the-border regulatory barriers, became the basis for proclaiming that the TPP would become the new model for a twenty-first-century FTA' (Barfield 2011: 2). The rules dealt with a number concerns for US and transnational capital, including intellectual property rights, pharmaceuticals, government procurement and e-commerce (Public Citizen 2015; USTR 2015). In Washington's view, the TPP would need to address 'the proliferation of regulatory and non-tariff barriers, which have become a major hurdle for businesses gaining access to foreign markets' (Fergusson *et al.* 2014: 41). Like previous agreements, then, the TPP is driven to facilitate capital accumulation by breaking down select barriers, blending liberalisation with protectionism to reinforce the structural advantages in the composition and relative sophistication of the US economy. Moreover, as a so-called 'living agreement', the TPP is designed to deal with new trade, commercial and investment issues as they emerge. Planners hoped it would have 'intangible effects of renewed momentum toward global economic integration', creating a 'convergence toward market economics' similar to previous 'waves of liberalization' (Petri and Plummer 2012: 8).

The TPP's liberalisation regime is similar to the rules found in NAFTA, though, in some respects, the TPP goes further. Its investor–state dispute procedures were reportedly among the most contentious in the negotiations (Schott *et al.* 2013: 34). Critics asserted that these rules threatened existing health and environmental regulations. According to Stiglitz (2014), the TPP would allow 'corporations to seek restitution in an international tribunal, not only for unjust expropriation, but also for alleged diminution of their potential profits as a result of regulation'. The text all but eliminates capital controls (USTR 2015). It handcuffs fiscal policy through the construction of new rules on government procurement. Unlike previous FTAs, the TPP effectively empowers financial firms to 'use extrajudicial tribunals to challenge financial stability measures that do not conform to their expectations'. Despite the centrality of so-called 'toxic derivatives' to the global financial crisis of the late 2000s and subsequent Great Recession, 'the TPP would impose obligations on TPP countries to allow new financial products and services to enter their economies if permitted in other TPP countries' (Public Citizen 2015: 6).

The TPP's more protectionist elements are broadly consistent with the United States' existing structural-economic advantages. For instance, its rules go beyond the protections provided in the WTO Trade Related Aspects of Intellectual Property agreement to include the application of protections to digital media (Fergusson *et al.* 2014: 29; Public Citizen 2015: 11–12). It holds stringent enforcement mechanisms to protect copyrights and punish trademark counterfeiting, including online, with major ramifications for internet governance. The United States pushed for enhanced protections for pharmaceutical patents. This may limit access to generic medicines in developing countries. Additionally, the United States pushed for 'language to improve the protections for trade secrets' in response to the 'concerns of US business that governments have pressured them to reveal trade secrets or transfer technology to further a country's "indigenous innovation" policies' (Fergusson *et al.* 2014: 33). In the e-commerce discipline, the framework adjusts and synchronises various impediments to e-trade, including customs duties, the digital environment, authentication of electronic transactions, and localisation requirements. The rules here operate to 'ensure that services distributed electronically benefit from the same protections as services distributed by other means' (Fergusson *et al.* 2014: 40).

Furthermore, at the behest of US negotiators, the TPP included rules on state-owned enterprises (SOEs), which have generally been excluded from previous free trade agreements (Public Citizen 2015: 20–1; USTR 2015). These provisions are designed to regulate the subsidies, low-cost credit and preferential access to government procurement enjoyed by state-backed firms (Fergusson *et al.* 2014: 42–4). Widely understood as targeting China should the country eventually seek to sign up to the accord, the rules on SOEs may undercut the development strategies of participating countries in the Global South. The ostensible goal is competitive neutrality; in practice, however, the application of the provisions on SOEs favours US business interests. As with most trade deals, 'the US position on SOEs (sought) to balance both US defensive and offensive interests', meaning the rules were devised in a way that allowed for government support for market-oriented products and services within the United States (Fergusson *et al.* 2014: 43).

The TPP and Latin America in Obama's pivot to Asia

American officials were forthright about the TPP's connection to Obama's 'pivot' to Asia, the realignment of strategic priorities and resources announced in 2011 (Donilon 2014; Ross 2012). Later dubbed the 'rebalance', the pivot, as outlined by then-Secretary of State Hillary Clinton (2011), blended security and economic concerns amidst a general recalibration of US power in global affairs. While the Obama administration argued that the pivot was not about China per se, most observers saw it in this light; likewise for the TPP, an agreement that excludes China. The Asia-Pacific has seen the emergence of a 'contest of templates' (Gordon 2012; Petri and Plummer 2012), with the United States and China competing to construct regimes that improve the terms of trade for their strongest sectors. (In 2012, China launched the Regional Comprehensive Economic Partnership, advancing a goods-based template for economic integration to rival the TPP.) There is debate over the degree to which the TPP 'targets' China, and the Obama administration has sent mixed messages in this regard (Song and Yuan 2012). China's potential inclusion in the free trade zone would have to garner the support of existing TPP members. It would also depend on Beijing's willingness to participate in a comprehensive, US-led regime.

Even if China's rise provided much of the impetus, the TPP, as part of the strategic rebalance, has implications extending well beyond Sino-US relations, especially in the Western hemisphere (Biegon in press). China's drive to build economic linkages with Latin America adds weight to the TPP's geo-economic logic. Beijing's activity in Latin America has increased considerably since the early 2000s (Ellis 2009; Gallagher *et al.* 2012; Jenkins 2010). Chinese exports to Central and South America have boomed across a number of sectors, as has Chinese investment. Latin American exports to China, as noted in the previous chapter, also grew sharply, namely in key commodities like copper, crude oil, soybeans and iron ore. Between 2000 and 2009, for example, with commodity prices rising, total trade between China and Latin America increased by over 1,000 per cent. China became the largest trading partner for a host of South American countries, including Brazil. Chinese President Xi Jinping visited Mexico, Costa Rica and several Caribbean countries in 2013 in a high-profile riposte to Obama's pivot. At the 2015 China–CELAC summit Xi pledged $250 billion in investment over a ten-year period (Rajagopalan 2015). Chinese lending to Latin America outpaced loans made by the IMF and World Bank, and with fewer policy conditionalities to boot (Gallagher *et al.* 2012). The emergent triangular dynamic led some analysts to speculate that China could counterbalance US hegemony (Ellis 2009; Jenkins 2010). In this context, the extension of the TPP to Latin America was more than an afterthought for Washington, but partly a response to China's burgeoning role in the hemisphere.

For the Obama administration, the TPP provides an opportunity for the United States to 'remake its economic relationship with Latin America' by 'deeply (engaging) with nations intent on becoming more important global players' (Inter-American Dialogue 2012: 14). It creates a mechanism for Washington to consolidate the Pacific-oriented bloc of governments in the Americas under new commercial and juridical disciplines not covered in previous trade agreements. This process would be expedited by the TPP's integration of existing rules. And through the building of structural links to Asian markets, the TPP provides additional incentives for those countries that may be 'on the fence' regarding the procurement of an FTA with the United States. As an open, 'living' agreement, the TPP responds to the geopolitical realities of an NLL-led Latin America. It is designed to bring additional countries into the fold if and when political conditions allow. With this in mind, some observers deemed the TPP as a replacement for the failed hemispheric pact, an 'FTAA of the willing' (Estevadeordal 2012: 28; Hidalgo 2012).

The TPP talks brought together several of Washington's most important partners in the Americas. The Chilean government, one of the signatories to the original accord, saw value in the TPP's ability to harmonise existing FTAs. If implemented properly, it had the capacity to 'return order to the "spaghetti bowl"', according to Chilean officials (Wikileaks 2009d). Records show that Peru was more hesitant to join the TPP, with officials basing their decision on the accession of other countries, and in consultation with the United States (Wikileaks 2008i). With the announcement that Mexico was entering the talks, the USTR (2012) stated: 'Mexico has assured the United States that it is prepared to conclude a high-standard agreement that will include issues that were not covered in the North American Free Trade Agreement.' Mexico's inclusion in the TPP expanded the call for a renewed free trade consensus in the Western hemisphere, intimating increased co-operation among 'like-minded globalizing countries' to benefit from, and compete with, a 'rising Asia' (O'Neil 2014: 14).

Proponents of the TPP called for the United States to 'strengthen' the regime 'by supporting broader Latin American participation' (Kotschwar and Schott 2013). As negotiations advanced, officials were directed to 'continue talks with other trans-Pacific partners that have expressed interest in joining the TPP in order to facilitate their future participation' (White House 2011). In the LAC region, interest was driven by the appeal of deepening networks and expanding markets in East Asia, even if 'short-term market access gains appear(ed) very modest' (Herreros 2012: 275). Colombia's leaders expressed considerable interest (Wikileaks 2010b). Costa Rica and Panama are also seen as possible future members. As new countries are brought into the fray, the TPP would deepen divisions between the Pacific Alliance countries and the Atlanticist cohort, including Mercosur members Brazil and Argentina alongside the Bolivarian cohort, namely Venezuela, Bolivia and Ecuador (Herreros 2012: 275–6; Kotschwar and Schott 2013). This weakens efforts to construct mechanisms to unite the region through institutions that exclude US participation, from economic groups like Mercosur and ALBA to diplomatic bodies, such as CELAC. In contrast to these organisations, the rules and provisions of the TPP were written with a great deal of input from US negotiators and formal stakeholders, including corporations. From an (inter)regional perspective, then, the TPP consolidates the US-led neoliberal position on trade integration against models associated with ALBA and Mercosur, globalising the hemispheric political economy in a manner that reinforces US structural power.

Conclusion

At first blush, by focusing on US trade policy, this chapter may suggest a more agential—rather than structural—account. Ultimately, however, structures 'are (re)produced or transformed only through the mediation of historically concrete agency' (Rupert 2005: 209). It is in this sense that we can assess the structural power of particular states. The United States' leadership role in the creation of free trade regimes is an outcome of its historically-allocated, structurally-determined position in the political economy of the Americas. As the largest economy in the Western hemisphere by a wide margin, the United States enjoys considerable structural leverage over other states. Washington has used multi-track trade negotiations to push for greater mobility for transnational capital, safer opportunities for US investors and a general opening of markets through privatisation and deregulation. In an era of burgeoning post-neoliberalism, the Bush and Obama administrations doubled down on (Post-)Washington Consensus policies, extending the NAFTA model. Where the FTAA failed, the United States carried forward neoliberalisation using bilateral and sub-regional accords. The TPP is the latest manifestation of this project, and the agreement holds the potential to expand over time, in terms of membership and its rules and provisions.

The structural power of US trade policy is interwoven with other forms of hegemonic power, including, importantly, institutional power. Even if they are not wholly dependent on institutional mechanisms, structural relationships are often readjusted through formal arrangements like FTAs, which codify and shape economic practices and outcomes in relation to production, investment and exchange. Similarly, much of the opposition to the US free trade model was co-ordinated via regional institutions, namely Mercosur and ALBA. Additionally, structural power is inexorably interlinked with the ideas and representations that help to constitute the United States and its Latin American partners (and adversaries) as particular kinds of actors in the global economy. As seen in Bolivarian anti-imperialism and the Buenos Aires Consensus, ideological/discursive challenges to US trade policy have helped to consolidate and redirect these institutional projects, undermining the 'common sense' purchase of the Washington Consensus.

In the preceding analysis, and as highlighted in the previous chapter, the distinct forms of US hegemonic power are mutually imbricated. Further, the shifting 'balance' between the various elements of US hegemony is shaped by the concomitant powers of the NLL's counter-hegemonic agents. This dialectical relationship is evident across Washington's ongoing foreign policy efforts in the hemisphere. The ability of US hegemony to internalise ideological opposition to free trade is the subject of Chapter 6, which examines the construction of 'populism' in US discourse. As illustrated in Chapter 5, the NLL also challenged the institutional power of the United States in the OAS, the hemisphere's oldest inter-governmental body. And, as examined in the next chapter, NLL governments sought to combat the manoeuvrability of the US military in the region, with implications for Washington's coercive reach—the traditional 'armour' of its hegemonic supremacy.

Notes

1 The Doha Round, launched in Doha, Qatar in November 2001, is also referred to as the Doha Development Agenda. The Doha Round was dealt a severe blow during the 2003 ministerial, held in Cancún, Mexico, when talks failed to produce a comprehensive agreement. This setback had echoes of the WTO's failed 1999 conference. Famously dubbed the 'Battle in Seattle', the 1999 negotiations collapsed amidst protests by unions, environmentalists and 'anti-globalisation' groups, which brought considerable public attention to trade issues in the United States and elsewhere. Efforts to revive the Doha Round have, as of this writing, proved unsuccessful.

2 Following the Central American Free Trade Agreement, the United States planned on negotiating a sub-regional FTA for the Andean region, to include Bolivia, Colombia, Ecuador and Peru, but excluding Venezuela. The negotiations process was facilitated through the Community of Andean Nations (CAN). The talks did not result in an Andean FTA, though the United States would later finalise bilateral agreements with Peru and Colombia.

3 The official website of the Free Trade Area of the Americas is www.ftaa-alca.org/alca_e. asp (accessed 6 January 2015). In Spanish, the agreement is known as the *Área de Libre Comercio de las Américas* (ALCA). All the countries of the Western hemisphere except for Cuba were included in the FTAA talks.

References

AFL-CIO (2005). 'Statement of AFL-CIO President John Sweeney on Bush Administration CAFTA and Labor Proposal', 10 June. Available online at www.aflcio.org/Press-Room/Press-Releases/Statement-of-AFL-CIO-President-John-Sweeney-on-Bus (accessed 23 July 2013).

Barfield, C. (2011). 'The Trans-Pacific Partnership: A Model for Twenty-First Century Trade Agreements', International Economic Outlook No. 2, American Enterprise Institute, June.

Barnett, M. and R. Duvall (2005). 'Power in Global Governance', in *Power in Global Governance*, edited by M. Barnett and R. Duvall, Cambridge: Cambridge University Press: 1–32.

Baumann, R. (2008). 'Integration in Latin America—Trends and Challenges', Economic Commission for Latin America and the Caribbean, January.

Beeton, D. (2008). 'The Media Need More TLC in CAFTA Reporting', *NACLA Report on the Americas*, March/April: 47–8.

Bhagwati, J. (2008). *Termites in the Trading System: How Preferential Agreements Undermine Free Trade*, Oxford: Oxford University Press.

Biegon, R. (In press). 'The US and Latin America in the Trans-Pacific Partnership: Renewing Hegemony in a Post-Washington Consensus Hemisphere?' *Latin American Perspectives*.

Bretton Woods Project (2004). 'Lula and Kirchner Want IMF to Relax Grip', *The Bretton Woods Update*, 40, May/June.

Bush, G. W. (2002). National Security Strategy of the United States of America, September.

Cammack, P. (2002). 'Dependent and Disciplinary Regionalism', in *Ten Years of Mercosur*, edited by P. van Dijck and M. Wieisbron, Amsterdam: Centre for Latin American Research and Documentation: 85–96.

Carranza, M. E. (2004). 'Mercosur and the End Game of the FTAA Negotiations: Challenges and Prospects after the Argentine Crisis', *Third World Quarterly*, 25(2): 319–37.

Cato Institute (2009). *Cato Handbook for Policymakers*, seventh edition, Washington, DC: Cato Institute.

Center for Strategic and International Studies (2004). *Hemisphere Highlights: Americas Program*, 3(4), April.

Clinton, H. (2011). 'America's Pacific Century', *Foreign Policy*, November.

Cooper, W. H. (2014). 'Free Trade Agreements: Impact on US Trade and Implications for US Trade Policy', Congressional Research Service, 26 February.

Council on Foreign Relations (2006). 'The Rise in Bilateral Free Trade Agreements', 13 June. Available online at www.cfr.org/trade/rise-bilateral-free-trade-agreements/p10890 (accessed 23 July 2013).

Council on Foreign Relations (2012). 'Mercosur: South America's Fractious Trade Bloc', 31 July. Available online at www.cfr.org/trade/mercosur-south-americas-fractious-trade-bloc/p12762 (accessed 23 July 2013).

Cox, R. W. (1996). *Approaches to World Order*, Cambridge: Cambridge University Press.

Democratic National Committee (2012). 'Moving America Forward', Democratic National Platform. Available online at http://assets.dstatic.org/dnc-platform/2012-National-Platform.pdf (accessed 23 July 2013).

Donilon, T. (2014). 'Obama is on the Right Course with the Pivot to Asia', *Washington Post*, 20 April. Available online at www.washingtonpost.com/opinions/obama-is-on-the-right-course-with-the-pivot-to-asia/2014/04/20/ed719108-c73c-11e3-9f37-7ce307c56815_story.html (accessed 7 November 2015).

The Economist (2005). 'A Small Victory for Free Trade as CAFTA Passes', 28 July. Available online at www.economist.com/node/4221299 (accessed 18 October 2015).

Ellis, R. E. (2009). *China in Latin America: The Whats and Wherefores*, Boulder: Lynne Rienner.

Ellner, S. (2004). 'Leftist Goals and the Debate over Anti-Neoliberal Strategy in Latin America', *Science & Society*, 68(1): 10–32.

Estevadeordal, A. (2012). 'Economic Integration in the Americas: An Unfinished Agenda', in *The Road to Hemispheric Cooperation: Beyond the Cartagena Summit of the Americas*, Brookings Institution, Washington: 22–30.

Evenett, S. J. and M. Meier (2008). 'An Interim Assessment of the US Trade Policy of "Competitive Liberalization"', *The World Economy*, 31(1): 31–66.

Export.gov (2012a). 'Dominican Republic-Central America-United States Free Trade Agreement (CAFTA-DR)'. Available online at http://export.gov/FTA/cafta-dr/index.asp (accessed 18 December 2012).

Export.gov (2012b). 'The U.S.—Panama Trade Promotion Agreement'. Available online at http://export.gov/fta/panama/index.asp (accessed 16 December 2012).

Fergusson, I. F., M. A. McMinimy and B. R. Williams (2014). 'The Trans-Pacific Partnership: Negotiations and Issues for Congress', Congressional Research Service, 19 November.

First Summit of the Americas (1994). Summit of the Americas Plan of Action, December.

Gallagher, K. (2005). 'CAFTA', Center for International Policy, Americas Program, 26 September. Available online at www.cipamericas.org/archives/1355 (accessed 24 October 2015).

Gallagher, K., A. Irwin and K. Koleski (2012). 'The New Banks in Town: Chinese Finance in Latin America', Inter-American Dialogue, February.

Gelb, B. A. (2005). 'DR-CAFTA, Textiles, and Apparel', Congressional Research Service, 20 May.

Gordon, B. K. (2012). 'Trading Up in Asia', *Foreign Affairs*, 91(4): 17–22.

Grinberg, N. (2010). 'Where is Latin America Going? FTAA or "Twenty-first-Century Socialism"?' *Latin American Perspectives*, 30(1): 185–202.

Hart-Landsberg, M. (2010). 'ALBA and the Promise of Cooperative Development', *Monthly Review*, 62(7): 1–17.

Harvey, D. (2005). *A Brief History of Neoliberalism*, Oxford: Oxford University Press.

Herreros, S. (2012). 'Coping with Multiple Uncertainties: Latin America in the TPP Negotiations', in *The Trans-Pacific Partnership: A Quest for a Twenty-First Century Agreement*, edited by C. L. Lim, D. K. Elms and P. Low, Cambridge: Cambridge University Press: 260–78.

Hidalgo, J. C. (2012). 'Building a Free Trade Area of Most of the Americas', Cato Institute, 31 October. Available online at www.cato.org/blog/building-free-trade-area-most-americas (accessed 24 July 2013).

Hornbeck, J. F. (2008). 'A Free Trade Area of the Americas: Major Policy Issues and Status of Negotiations', Congressional Research Service, 15 July.

Hornbeck, J. F. (2011). 'US-Latin America Trade: Recent Trends and Policy Issues', Congressional Research Service, 8 February.

Hornbeck, J. F. (2012). 'The Dominican Republic-Central American Free Trade Agreement (CAFTA-DR)', Congressional Research Service, 2 April.

Human Rights Watch (2004). 'CAFTA's Weak Labor Rights Protections: Why the Present Accord Should be Opposed', March.

Ikenson, D. and S. Lincicome (2009). 'Audaciously Hopeful: How President Obama Can Help Restore the Pro-Trade Consensus', Cato Institute, April.

Inter-American Dialogue (2012). 'Remaking the Relationship: The United States and Latin America', April.

Jenkins, R. (2010). 'China's Global Expansion and Latin America', *Journal of Latin American Studies*, 42(4): 809–37.

Katz, C. (2002). 'Free Trade Area of the Americas: NAFTA Marches South', *NACLA Report on the Americas*, 35(4): 27–45.

Kotschwar, B. and J. J. Schott (2013). 'The Next Big Thing? The Trans-Pacific Partnership and Latin America', *Americas Quarterly*, Spring. Available online at www.americas quarterly.org/next-big-thing-trans-pacific-partnership (accessed 8 November 2015).

Kozloff, N. (2006). *Hugo Chávez: Oil, Politics, and the Challenge to the US*, New York: Palgrave.

Mann, M. (2012). *The Sources of Social Power Volume 3: Global Empires and Revolution*, Cambridge: Cambridge University Press.

Mecham, M. (2003). 'Mercosur: A Failing Development Project?' *International Affairs*, 79(2): 369–87.

Muhr, T. (2013). 'Introduction: The Enigma of Socialism', in *Counter-Globalization and Socialism in the 21st Century: The Bolivarian Alliance for the Peoples of Our America*, edited by T. Muhr, London: Routledge: 1–30.

Nelson, M. (2015). *A History of the FTAA: From Hegemony to Fragmentation in the Americas*, New York: Palgrave.

O'Neil, S. K. (2014). 'Mexico: Viva las Reforms', *Foreign Affairs*, 93(1): 11–16.

Petri, P. A. and M. G. Plummer (2012). 'The Trans-Pacific Partnership and Asia-Pacific Integration: Policy Implications', Peterson Institute for International Economics.

Public Citizen (2008). 'Debunking USTR Claims in Defense of NAFTA: The Real NAFTA Score 2008'.

Public Citizen (2010). 'A Year after Implementation of Peru Free Trade Agreement, US and Peru Left with Broken Promises and No New Trade Model', 1 February.

Public Citizen (2015). 'Initial Analyses of Key TPP Chapters', November.

Rajagopalan, M. (2015). 'China's Xi Woos Latin America with $250 Bln Investments', *Reuters*, 8 January. Available online at http://in.reuters.com/article/2015/01/08/china-latam-idINKBN0KH0BC20150108 (accessed 7 November 2015).

Ribando, C. (2005). 'DR-CAFTA: Regional Issues', Congressional Research Service, 8 July.

Robinson, W. I. (2008). *Latin America and Global Capitalism*, Baltimore: Johns Hopkins University Press.

Ross, R. S. (2012). 'The Problem with the Pivot', *Foreign Affairs*, 91(6): 70–82.

Rupert, M. (2000). *Ideologies of Globalization: Contending Visions of a New World Order*, New York: Routledge.

Rupert, M. (2005). 'Class Powers and the Politics of Global Governance', in *Power in Global Governance*, edited by M. Barnett and R. Duvall, Cambridge: Cambridge University Press: 205–28.

Rupert, M. and S. Solomon (2006). *Globalization and International Political Economy: The Politics of Alternative Futures*, Lanham: Rowman & Littlefield Publishers.

Sader, E. (2011). 'The Lula Government's Foreign Policy: An Interview with Emir Sader', *NACLA Report on the Americas*, March/April: 32–3.

Sanchez, L. and G. Miller (2010). 'Obama's Trade Opportunity', *The Hill*, 15 June. Available online at http://thehill.com/blogs/congress-blog/economy-a-budget/103281-obamas-trade-opportunity-rep-linda-sanchez-and-rep-george-miller (accessed 24 July 2013).

Schott, J. J. (2005). 'Does the FTAA Have a Future?' Institute for International Economics, November.

Schott, J. J., B. Kotschwar and J. Muir (2013). *Understanding the Trans-Pacific Partnership*, Washington, DC: Peterson Institute for International Economics.

Smith, T. (2003). 'Argentina and Brazil Align to Fight US Trade Policy', *The New York Times*, 21 October.

Song, G. and W. J. Yuan (2012). 'China's Free Trade Agreement Strategies', *Washington Quarterly*, 35(4): 107–19.

Stiglitz, J. (2014). 'On the Wrong Side of Globalization', *The New York Times*, 15 March. Available online at http://opinionator.blogs.nytimes.com/2014/03/15/on-the-wrong-side-of-globalization/?_php=true&_type=blogs&_r=0 (accessed 5 November 2015).

Stopford, J. M. and S. Strange (1991). *Rival States, Rival Firms: Competition for World Market Shares*, Cambridge: Cambridge University Press.

Strange, S. (1988). *States and Markets: An Introduction to International Political Economy*, London: Pinter Publishers.

US Department of State (2003). 'USTR Announces Intent to Initiate FTA Talks with Andean Nations', 18 November. Available online at www.america.gov/st/washfile-english/2003/November/20031118153511rellims0.867428.html (accessed 23 July 2013).

US Trade Representative (USTR) (2008). 'NAFTA – Myths vs. Facts', March.

US Trade Representative (USTR) (2012). 'US Trade Representative Kirk Welcomes Mexico as a New Trans-Pacific Partnership Negotiating Partner', 18 June. Available online at www.ustr.gov/about-us/press-office/press-releases/2012/june/ustr-mexico-new-tpp-partner (accessed 24 July 2013).

US Trade Representative (USTR) (2015). Text of the Trans-Pacific Partnership. Available online at https://medium.com/the-trans-pacific-partnership (accessed 9 November 2015).

White House (2011). 'Trans-Pacific Partnership Leaders Statement', 12 November. Available online at www.whitehouse.gov/the-press-office/2011/11/12/trans-pacific-partnership-leaders-statement (accessed 9 November 2015).

Wikileaks (2002). 'A/S Reich's Meeting with Lula', 22 November. Reference ID: 02BRASILIA4227.

Wikileaks (2003a). 'No Public Sign of Retreat from FTAA Proposal', 28 July. Reference ID: 03BRASILIA2364

Wikileaks (2003b). 'Brazilian FTAA Coordinator on a Social Agenda for the Negotiations', 3 April. Reference ID: 03BRASILIA1066.

Wikileaks (2003c). 'What's Behind Brazil's FTAA Policy', 18 July. Reference ID: 03BRASILIA2233.

Wikileaks (2003d). 'Brazil Continues to Debate Trade Policy on Eve of USTR Zoellick's Visit', 20 May. Reference ID: 03BRASILIA1321.

Wikileaks (2003e). 'Can ITAMRATY'S Stranglehold on FTAA Policy be Broken?' 27 October. Reference ID: 03BRASILIA3459.

Wikileaks (2004a). 'Scenesetter: The Secretary's Visit to Brazil, 4–6 October 2004', 29 September. Reference ID: 04BRASILIA2468.

Wikileaks (2004b). 'Panama: Who is President-Elect Martin Torrijos and How Will He Govern?' 3 May. Reference ID: 04PANAMA1015

Wikileaks (2004c). 'U.S.-Panama FTA Negotiations – Thoughts on Timing and Issues', 19 March. Reference ID: 04PANAMA648.

Wikileaks (2005a). 'Chavez Visit to Havana Leaves Plethora of Economic Agreements', 4 May. Reference ID: 05CARACAS1359.

Wikileaks (2005b). 'Scenesetter Cable for Visit of Secretary Snow', 22 July. Reference ID: 05BRASILIA1974.

Wikileaks (2005c). 'Presidential Chief of Staff of Dirceu on FTAA and Potential Compulsory Licensing of Pharmaceuticals', 20 April. Reference ID: 05BRASILIA1067.

Wikileaks (2005d). 'Brazil's 2005 Trade Agenda: More of the Same', 24 January. Reference ID: 05BRASILIA212.

Wikileaks (2005e). 'Honduran Labor Leaders' Opposition to CAFTA: More Ideological than Informed', 14 February. Reference ID: 05TEGUCIGALPA364.

Wikileaks (2005f). 'Jan. 1, 2006 Entry into Force Helps CAFTA-DR in Costa Rica', 15 November. Reference ID: 05SANJOSE2664.

Wikileaks (2005g). 'CAFTA Brings Hope to Sluggish Salvadoran Economy', 13 September. Reference ID: 05SANSALVADOR2541.

Wikileaks (2005h). 'Congressional Staffers Visit Honduras, Question CAFTA-DR's Impact on the Poor', 8 April. Reference ID: 05TEGUCIGALPA765.

Wikileaks (2005i). 'Visit of Peruvian Ministers to Discuss the FTA', 17 June. Reference ID: 05LIMA2720.

Wikileaks (2005j). 'The Toledo-Uribe Meeting and Peru's Game Plan for US-Andean FTA', 8 September. Reference ID: 05LIMA3888.

Wikileaks (2005k). 'Countering Chavez in Peru', 22 November. Reference ID: 05LIMA4983.

Wikileaks (2006a). 'Argentina: Kirchner at Three Years', 18 July. Reference ID: 06BUENOSAIRES1594.

Wikileaks (2006b). 'How Mercosur Has Changed', 16 November. Reference ID: 06MONTEVIDEO1097.

Wikileaks (2006c). 'Chavez and the Rhetoric of Hate', 19 June. Reference ID: 06CARACAS1789

Wikileaks (2006d). 'Update on Petrocaribe', 12 June. Reference ID: 06CARACAS1712.

Wikileaks (2006e). 'AUSTR Eissenstat Visit to Argentina', 12 October. Reference ID: 06BUENOSAIRES2292.

Wikileaks (2006f). 'US Ambassadors Outline Agenda for Central America', 11 April. Reference ID: 06SANSALVADOR963.

Wikileaks (2006g). '(S) Honduras Under CAFTA: After Six Months, Little to Show', 4 October. Reference ID: 06TEGUCIGALPA1881.

Wikileaks (2006h). 'President-Elect Garcia Wants the US-Peru FTA', 9 June. Reference ID: 06LIMA2323.

Wikileaks (2006i). 'Post's Active Trade Agreement Compliance Efforts', 26 September. Reference ID: 06LIMA3804.

Wikileaks (2007a). 'Likely Chavez Rants in Argentina and Bolivia', 2 March. Reference ID: 07CARACAS444.

Wikileaks (2007b). 'Costa Rica: Next Anti-CAFTA Protest on 26 Feb', 23 February. Reference ID: 07SANJOSE361.

Wikileaks (2007c). 'Honduras: "Lizzie Law" Falls Victim to Corruption', 8 August. Reference ID: 07TEGUCIGALPA1337.

Wikileaks (2007d). 'Scenesetter Checklist for Visit of President Bush to Colombia', 5 March. Reference ID: 07BOGOTA1472.

Wikileaks (2007e). 'WHA A/S Shannon and FM Araujo Discuss Plan Colombia, Human Rights, Free Trade, and Ecuador', 31 January. Reference ID: 07BOGOTA670.

Wikileaks (2008a). 'Not Much Substance at the VI ALBA Summit', 30 January. Reference ID: 08CARACAS118.

Wikileaks (2008b). 'Guatemala's Telecoms CAFTA Dispute', 13 August. Reference ID: 08GUATEMALA1036

Wikileaks (2008c). 'FMLN Pushes Pragmatism', 31 July. Reference ID: 08SANSAL VADOR915.

Wikileaks (2008d). 'Nicaragua: Rhetoric Aside, Exports are Booming', 28 October. Reference ID: 08MANAGUA1317.

Wikileaks (2008e). 'Consumer Protection Law Reflects Statist Mentality', 4 August. Reference ID: 08TEGUCIGALPA722.

Wikileaks (2008f). 'Zelaya Announces at Petrofood Summit he is Joining ALBA', 31 July. Reference ID: 08TEGUCIGALPA718.

Wikileaks (2008g). 'Chile: Post Recommends Chile Remain on Priority Watch List', 21 February. Reference ID: 08SANTIAGO167.

Wikileaks (2008h). '"Arc of the Pacific" Initiative Quietly Progresses', 2 April. Reference ID: 08LIMA564.

Wikileaks (2008i). 'Peru on Trans-Pacific Partnership (TPP) Agreement', 3 October. Reference ID: 08LIMA1606.

Wikileaks (2009a). 'Nicaragua's Foreign Ministry – Patience Running Out for Obama Administration', 22 May. Reference ID: 09MANAGUA520.

Wikileaks (2009b). 'El Salvador: 2009 Special 310 Input', 20 February. Reference ID: 09SANSALVADOR158.

Wikileaks (2009c). 'Vice President Santos Pitches FTA Passage', 17 August. Reference ID: 09BOGOTA2585.

Wikileaks (2009d). 'Chilean Reaction to President Obama's Announcement on TPP', 10 December. Reference ID: 09SANTIAGO1198.

Wikileaks (2010a). 'Ortega and the US: New-found True Love or Another Still-born Charm Offensive', 25 February. Reference ID: 10MANAGUA115.

Wikileaks (2010b). 'FTA with US is Blocking Colombia's Global Trade Policy', 11 February. Reference ID: 10BOGOTA217.

4   Redirecting force

US coercive power and the New Latin Left

Compared to other forms of US hegemonic power, coercive power is more direct, making it more intuitive. Borrowing from Dahl's famous formulation (1957), it asks: How does actor A (e.g. the United States) get actor B (another state) to do something it otherwise wouldn't? The immediacy here implies some degree of conflict. It also suggests that, to get other actors to oblige, the United States must develop specific frameworks to deploy its foreign policy as a tool of 'statecraft'. In the geopolitical realm, coercive power rests on the deployment of material resources to elicit a certain response, change a given behaviour, realise a specific outcome and/or gain leverage over another actor. This is similar to Barnett and Duvall's concept of compulsory power, which involves the interactions of fully constituted agents. In contrast to Barnett and Duvall, however, who argue that compulsory power 'need not hinge on intentionality' (2005: 14), my notion of coercive power does depend on the expressed objectives of the actor. There must be a deliberate attempt to change behaviour or outcomes in some way for it to be coercive. Strategy matters, as decision-makers weigh up means and ends in pursuit of the US 'national interest'.

My conceptualisation of coercive power is not restricted to the use of military force. That said, the 'hard power' of military action may be the purest expression of the command logic at work here. Borrowing from Mann's concept of military power (2012), as the concentrated ability to inflict lethal violence, this form of power conjures the beastly side of Machiavelli's centaur, as well as Gramsci's related maxim that consent is typically protected by the 'armour of coercion' (1971: 169–70, 263). Ultimately, military force doesn't have to be exercised to have a tangible impact. Because all power is social, for state A to reap the benefits of its advantage in military resources—for it to enjoy the *leverage* provided by its ability to project its physical capacity to compel—state B only need be aware of state's A advantage. This allows state A to transform its strategic resources into desired outcomes without resorting to violent confrontation. The *ability* to inflict lethal violence is often enough. Even so, maintaining this ability means holding the requisite resources, deliberately positioned in a way to give the dominant state its greatest coercive reach.

The United States enjoys a tremendous advantage in military resources, not only in the Western hemisphere, but worldwide. Seeking to remain the global 'security partner of choice', the Obama administration committed the United

States to continued military primacy (US Department of Defense 2012a). Historically, US–Latin American relations have been fashioned by the former's military might, which made possible the profusion of interventions carried out by Washington during the twentieth century. 'Speak softly', cracked Teddy Roosevelt, the most imperialist of American presidents, 'and carry a Big Stick'. As the famous quote suggests, the coercive power of military force is always deployed against a broader political backdrop. The Big Stick's clout was not limited to the invasions and incursions of the US military, important though they were. It was integral to various facets of US regional hegemony, including both security and economic issues, and was expressed diplomatically, institutionally and ideologically, reflecting the core belief that US superiority was natural and preordained (Schoultz 1998: xiii–xvii).

The use of military resources remained central to Washington's foreign policy agenda after the Cold War. However, in the era of the NLL, US coercive power grew more contested. Both anti-neoliberal and reformist NLL governments demonstrated deep scepticism (if not open hostility) towards the United States' continuing military presence in the region. This chapter investigates US efforts to redirect its coercive power in Latin America amidst intensifying opposition. After outlining the transition from Bush's War on Terror to Obama's 'smart power' approach, I analyse the shifting deployment of coercive resources through the US Southern Command (Southcom), the Pentagon's unified command structure for Latin America. Specifically, I look at the reconstitution of a navy fleet for the region and changes to Southcom's basing posture. Finally, I examine the US response to the 2009 military coup in Honduras, which deposed the 'populist' government of Mel Zelaya and consolidated the country's position as a vital outpost of US military capacity in Central America.

From the 'War on Terror' to 'smart power'

George W. Bush entered office pledging to place Latin America at the centre of his foreign policy agenda. Following the 9/11 attacks, however, the 'backyard' was put on the backburner. From a certain vantage, the de-prioritisation of Latin America actually contributed to the militarisation of US policy in the region, which quickly came under the influence of the new 'War on Terror'. Colombia's guerrilla groups became 'narco-terrorists'. The 'ungoverned spaces' of South America were securitised as potential incubators of Islamist extremism. For several years, considerable attention was given to the remote and supposedly 'lawless' tri-border region between Brazil, Argentina and Paraguay, home to a large community of Muslim émigrés. Perhaps most importantly, however, both the White House and Congress ceded much of their traditional responsibility over the direction of US policy to the Pentagon. The DoD had the capacity to act as the main interlocutor with the region at a time when the United States' geostrategic focus was elsewhere. In other words, US policy was channelled increasingly through its immense and unrivalled military. This 'hardening' occurred as the region was beginning to assert greater autonomy from Washington.

The US military was no stranger to Latin America. The War on Drugs ensured that, even after the Cold War, Washington was committed to maintaining a robust military presence in the region (Isacson *et al.* 2007; LeoGrande 2006). The Bush presidency witnessed the heightened militarisation of US policy. This was seen in, among other things, the changing make-up of US foreign aid in the late 1990s/ early 2000s. There was a tilt away from development and humanitarian aid towards military and police assistance. In 1997, US economic and development aid to Latin America and the Caribbean equalled more than twice the amount of military and police aid (with approximately $589 million in economic and social assistance set against $269 million in military and police aid for that fiscal year). By 2007, however, that gap had narrowed substantially, with economic assistance outpacing military aid by approximately one-third, with $1.196 billion in total economic and social aid contrasted with $794 million in military and police assistance (Isacson *et al.* 2007: 2–3). The overall uptick in foreign aid from 1997 to 2007 demonstrates that, contrary to some, the Bush administration did not simply 'ignore' Latin America after 9/11.

This militarisation trend was reflected in the training and equipping of Latin American military forces, which has a long and sordid history, especially in relation to the Cold War-era School of the Americas facility (Blakeley 2006). More recently, the State Department oversaw key training programmes. Under George W. Bush, however, the DoD was given greater control over training procedures, blurring the lines between military and civilian forces (Isacson *et al.* 2007; Withers *et al.* 2008). Resources and responsibilities shifted from the State Department to the Pentagon, increasing the import of Southcom. The Pentagon viewed State's security assistance programmes as 'too slow and cumbersome' (Serafino 2008: 1). In response, Section 1206 of the 2006 National Defense and Authorization Act provided the DoD with the authority to train and equip foreign military forces through funds appropriated for two purposes: counterterrorism operations, and support for 'military and stability operations in which US armed forces participate' (Serafino 2008: 1). Because there is greater congressional oversight of State than DoD, Section 1206 strengthened the military's flexibility in this key policy area.

The Pentagon had been 'gradually increasing its control over military training and equipping programs' for years, 'spanning Democratic and Republican administrations' (Withers *et al.* 2008: 1). It may be unsurprising, then, that a strong emphasis on military power continued under the Obama administration, despite Obama's early overtures to reform, punctuated by his pledge at the 2009 Summit of the Americas that the United States would seek an equal partnership with the region. The continuity with the Bush White House was seen in Obama's (attempted) military base agreement with Colombia and his administration's ambiguous response to the coup in Honduras, addressed below. In 2012 Southcom announced it was acquiring remotely piloted aircraft (drones) no longer needed in the Afghan theatre. That year the DoD released a policy statement specifically for the Americas, stating it would strive to be the 'security partner of choice' through an 'innovative, low-cost, and small-footprint' approach (2012b: ii).

In concert with the Obama administration's broader foreign policy re-set, it outlined a 'smarter' direction for US strategy. This was seen in its emphasis on synergy, partnership and multilateral co-operation.

'Smart power' in Latin America

Set against broader continuities in US objectives, the Obama administration did make adjustments to Washington's geostrategic approach. Whereas the Bush years were dominated by the War on Terror, the Obama administration framed its foreign policy around 'smart power'. Though it wasn't formulated specifically for the Americas, this framework fit the hemispheric context as a response to the emergence of the NLL. In a touchstone report on smart power by the Center for Strategic and International Studies (CSIS), the authors noted that, in Latin America, US leadership was under duress from 'a new generation of populist leaders . . . tapping into old threads of anti-Americanism' to challenge US-led economic globalisation (Armitage and Nye 2007: 22). Under the leadership of Admiral James Stavridis, Southcom thoroughly embraced the smart power framework. In the main, the idea was to better fuse hard and soft power. On the surface, then, it represented a 'softening' of US policy through a greater reliance on multilateralism, economising, cost-sharing and the deliberate legitimation of US actions and objectives. But, despite being packaged in a soft shell, it most definitely had a hard core. Washington did not lose sight of the leverage of its asymmetric advantage in military resources. Hegemonic renewal would require the 'smarter' use of coercive power.

As a strategic framework, 'smart power' was developed to redress concerns over the legitimacy of US hegemony in the wake of Bush's neoconservative unilateralism. It originates in the work of Joseph Nye, an IR scholar with sway in US foreign policy circles. Nye famously differentiates between hard and soft power. The former has military and economic manifestations involving inducements and/or threats, whereas soft power 'arises from the attractiveness of a country's culture, political ideals, and policies', and has much to do with the legitimation of a state's behaviour 'in the eyes of others' (Nye 2004: x). The importance of soft power for Nye is that it can reduce the costs associated with 'carrots' and 'sticks', the tools over which states have more direct control. He is careful to remind his readers of its limits. Nye stresses that international leadership is not 'synonymous with the soft power of attraction'. Rather, 'effective leadership requires a mixture of soft and hard skills', which he dubs 'smart power' (Nye 2008: x). Under Obama, the concept migrated from beltway think tanks to the heart of the executive branch. In her confirmation hearing, Secretary of State Clinton (2009a) said the Obama administration would be guided by smart power, which she defined as the United States using 'the full range of tools at (its) disposal—diplomatic, economic, military, political, legal, and cultural—picking the right tool, or combination of tools, for each situation'.

Conceptually, smart power is banal. Clinton referred to it as 'old-fashioned common sense' (2009b). When wouldn't a country use its full range of foreign policy tools? But smart power thinking did impact the regenerative efforts behind

US hegemony. Under Obama, it represented a means of retooling Washington's coercive capabilities, but in a more image-conscious way. In contrast to the heavy-handedness of the War on Terror, the new framework signalled a more considerate foreign policy, one that—contrary to the 'dumbness' of the Bush years—would feature pragmatic restraint when necessary, thus responding to declinist anxieties (Armitage and Nye 2007: 3, 17; Clinton 2009a, 2009b). In Latin America, the Bush administration's abrasive style had seemingly aggravated the policy concerns fuelling the rise of the new left. Smart power discourse went hand-in-hand with Obama's pledge for a 'new era' of 'true partnership'. To the degree that this 'new' approach masked a reconstituted military presence in Latin America, however, the 'hard core' of US power remained a source of consternation among NLL governments. This was shown in the controversies that erupted over the positioning of US military resources, as addressed below.

According to Clinton, smart power translated into concrete policy formation through co-operation with partners; principled engagement with those who disagree with US policy; the notion of development as a core pillar of US power; the integration of civilian and military action; and the leveraging of multiple sources of American power (2009b). Based on the wider smart power discourse, as well as the ways in which it was utilised, I maintain that the framework's impact was concentrated in four overlapping thematic areas: partnership, image, integration and leverage.

Partnership: Co-operation was part and parcel of the smart power approach (Clinton 2009a, 2009b). This entailed the cultivation of US allies as more active participants in the pursuit of joint objectives. Partnership is crucial as a means of buttressing US soft power while at the same time conserving hard power resources. It implied a more enduring form of co-operation in place of alliances built solely on expediency or short-term gain. Thus, smart power called for a greater emphasis on diplomacy and multilateralism.

Image: Smart power is highly attentive to the image(s) of US policy, as seen in the creation of new public diplomacy initiatives (Armitage and Nye 2007: 47). This involves augmenting the attractiveness of US policy through the judicious management of messaging, including through case-specific narratives appropriate to multilateral hard power missions. The image of an active US foreign policy (backed by an outwardly 'engaged' military) fortifies the image of American leadership. In this vein, US military documents emphasised the need for 'strategic communication' (US Department of Defense 2010).

Integration: The smart power strategy calls for the integration of hard and soft power into a unified whole (Armitage and Nye 2007: 65; Nye 2008). Not only should separate governmental agencies work with one another, there should be a level of inter-institutional integration that allows them to synergistically leverage the resources of their partners. For example, the 2010 Quadrennial Defense Review made multiple references to 'integrating all elements of national power' (US Department of Defense 2010: iv–v, 9).

Leverage: The notion of leverage has a straightforward meaning in the broader strategic vision. 'Maintaining US military power is paramount to any smart power approach' (Armitage and Nye 2007: 62). What smart power adds to the equation is the idea that leverage can be augmented if Washington uses its coercive apparatus in a more image-conscious way, and with the backing of partners. The smart power approach has heightened the focus on the flexibility, agility and manoeuvrability of US forces and their partners (US Department of Defense 2010: x–19), often referred to as 'lift' in strategic jargon.

The Pentagon and the New Latin Left

In 1963, the Pentagon created the US Southern Command (Southcom) out of the Caribbean Defense Command, which oversaw US military missions in the Caribbean basin during the Second World War. The name-change reflected Southcom's expanding role, which grew even more in the 1980s with conflicts raging in Central America. Following the Cold War, Southcom shifted its focus to counter-narcotics operations and humanitarian missions. The emergence of the NLL and the rise of 'radical populism' gave Southcom new threats to contemplate, as Latin American countries expanded ties with China, Russia and Iran (Barry 2005; Ellis 2011; LeoGrande 2006; Stavridis 2010). In 2008, Southcom reframed its command strategy around the theme of partnership. Under the stated goal of ensuring hemispheric security and stability (which included maintaining the ability to operate from the global commons onto the Western hemisphere), the document read: 'Partnerships are critical to the success of (our) mission, the US, and the nations of South and Central America and the Caribbean. As a result, every command activity, event, and task must focus on developing and strengthening enduring partnerships' (Southcom 2008: 11). This rhetoric was consistent in the Pentagon's wider approach to the hemisphere (US Department of Defense 2010: 68–9; 2012b: 4–5).

The goal was nothing less than a new regional image. In an interview titled 'US smart power in Latin America', James Stavridis, Southcom's director from 2006 to 2009, challenged its characterisation as a 'proconsul to the empire'. He stated that, rather than launching missiles, Southcom was responsible for 'launching ideas' related to international co-operation, interagency co-ordination and the provision of humanitarian services (Stavridis 2008). Southcom, he wrote, needs 'to be relentless in searching for and developing new vehicles and methods of delivery to communicate our strategic message—*we care about you*' (Stavridis 2010: 202–3). Its efforts were attuned to improving the perception of US policy; officials were well-aware of the worsening views of the United States in Latin American opinion polls. Southcom's soft side was apparent in the humanitarian missions of the naval ship *Comfort*, a medical vessel that treated thousands of individuals in the region, and in the organisation of baseball tournaments, among other initiatives (Stavridis 2010: xix, 218). Ultimately, Southcom's 'smart' strategy redirected the command functions that define coercive power through a softer package.

Behind the partnership discourse sat a well-defined hard power rationale. Closer co-operation with allies enhanced the Pentagon's ability to 'work through politico-military and diplomatic channels to enhance US military freedom of movement throughout the Western Hemisphere' (Southcom 2008: 12). Southcom remained fundamentally 'a military organization conducting military operations . . . in order to achieve US strategic objectives' (Stavridis 2010: 175). According to its 'Command Strategy 2020' plan:

> We will continue to focus on synchronizing words and actions, ensuring deeds mirror thoughts, and doing so across all elements of national power. The way we tell our story needs to be viewed as a vital extension of national policy, and that this story is never ending and always changing . . . To facilitate and perpetuate this environment of collaboration and teamwork, we need to better communicate, to our various audiences not only what we are doing, but also why we are doing it.
>
> (Southcom 2010: 9)

Southcom highlighted the interagency component of its evolving mission: 'We envision a future organization that has a regional focus seen through an interagency lens. This organization would have the capability to reach across traditional government stovepipes and help create interagency partnerships to develop holistic solutions.' It aimed to 'improve synchronization of operations and activities between Southcom and other US government organizations . . . to create a collaborative, effective, and efficient command' (Southcom 2008: 15). Southcom's efforts to utilise 'all instruments of national capability'—including military, diplomatic, economic, informational, financial, intelligence and legal resources—would reputedly have a 'synergistic effect' on the protection of security and stability in the hemisphere (Southcom 2008: 13–14). It thus embraced smart power even before the transition to Obama. This proved opportune mainly because, under Bush, Southcom was given an increasingly important role in the formation of Washington's overall approach to the region, as noted above. Of course, the ability of the United States to deploy coercive power (via Southcom's geographic access and manoeuvrability) depended on receptiveness to US forces. The contextual conditions shifted with the rise of the NLL.

Re-engaging the region: a new naval fleet

At the tail end of the Bush administration, the Pentagon announced that it was formally re-establishing the Fourth Fleet to co-ordinate all US Navy ships, aircraft and submarines operating in the Caribbean and in South American waters. Dormant since 1950, when it was decommissioned after patrolling the Atlantic during the Second World War, the fleet was re-established 'to address the increased role of maritime forces in the US Southern Command area of operations, and to demonstrate US commitment to regional partners' (US Department of Defense 2008). Largely an organisational move, one Southcom official stated that the re-establishment of the fleet would send a message to the entire region, and not just prominent adversaries like Venezuela (Bloomberg 2008).

In a 2009 report on the Fourth Fleet, CSIS referred to it as a tool of US engagement in the Americas, linking it directly to Southcom's smart power approach.

The 'smarter' aspects of the fleet were manifest in its interagency co-ordination function and in the recognition that co-operation 'cannot be surged' because it takes 'long-term engagement' (Maclay *et al.* 2009: 8). In its recommendations for hemispheric strategy, the report stated:

> The Fourth Fleet can contribute to the pursuit of a smart power strategy for the United States. It brings together the training and skill of the US Navy to provide a wide range of security activities in the Western Hemisphere while also serving as a complement to US civilian support for humanitarian activities throughout the Caribbean and South America. Coordination among agencies—the Department of State, Homeland Security, and Defense—over integrated missions of the Fourth Fleet will ensure that this military asset fulfils its stated missions.
>
> (Maclay *et al.* 2009: 13)

Partly a rebranding exercise, the reactivation of the fleet was opposed by many in Latin America, eliciting a great deal of suspicion (Wikileaks 2008a, 2008b). Not only did the news attract negative attention from a number of leaders, it also 'provided part of the rationale for the creation of a South American Defense Council under the leadership of Brazil' (Maclay *et al.* 2009: 3). The CSIS report repeatedly emphasised the need for a public diplomacy campaign specific to the Fourth Fleet, to dispel unease amongst Latin Americans wary of military diplomacy. If the creation of the fleet was a redirection of coercive power resources, it seemed to be aimed squarely at 'the rise of populist governments . . . antagonistic to US policies', including Venezuela, which had developed closer military ties with Russia (Maclay *et al.* 2009: 1).

Brazilian President Lula, for example, warned that the recreation of the fleet might be geared towards the country's newly discovered offshore oil reserves. This represented a genuine concern of Brazilian military officials. Other leaders were much more forceful in their condemnation of the fleet's re-establishment, including Chávez, who responded by underscoring Venezuela's co-operation with Brazil on the new South American Defense Council, and Morales, who dubbed it 'the Fourth Fleet of intervention' (Kozloff 2008). It is unclear if this level of disapproval was anticipated by US policymakers, though it seemed to counteract the smart power brand. Devised with hindsight, CSIS's call for a public diplomacy campaign specific to the Fourth Fleet appeared trivial. In the context of the United States' historical advantage in (and use of) coercive power, any reorganisation of US forces was likely to be interpreted as a flexing of military muscle, sending a message that the Pentagon desired a more streamlined approach to the 'backyard'.

Re-engaging the region: a new basing posture

Projecting coercive power means having the requisite territorial architecture, and the focus on a sleeker, smarter approach was also seen in the United States' basing posture. More than symbolic outposts of US influence, bases are crucial to the physical deployment of military force. As noted by Lutz, bases are 'normalized through a commonly circulating rhetoric that suggests that their presence is natural and even gift-like rather than the outcomes of policy choices made in keeping with the aim of pursuing a certain imperial vision of US self-interest' (2009: 20–1). And yet, naturalised as a military necessity, bases can become a political liability. As seen in Ecuador and Colombia (detailed below), bases have the potential to generate political blowback that can hamper the ability of the United States to realise its advantage in coercive reach. Southcom's basing posture would need adjustment in an era of NLL ascendancy.

After the Second World War, the United States quickly developed a global 'empire of bases', with the total number in the several hundred (at least) for most of the second half of the twentieth century (Johnson 2004; Lutz 2009; Vine 2015). This period witnessed the further development of basing infrastructure in the United States' overseas and neo-colonial possessions in Latin America (including Cuba and Panama). As the Cold War came to a close, political pressures emerged in Washington to reform the United States' military garrisons—to save money and to address the political and diplomatic controversies that swirled around many of the larger bases; oftentimes, the mere presence of these facilities stimulated nationalist and anti-imperialist opposition within host countries, movements that generally grew more pronounced during periods of high-profile conflict, as with the wars in Vietnam and Iraq (Enloe 2000; Lutz 2009; Sandars 2000: 303–31). In the post-Iraq War context, the Bush administration reformed its military basing strategy to reflect new geopolitical realities (Rumsfeld 2004).[1] Under its smart power framework, the Obama administration reinforced the turn to a more flexible, 'small-footprint' posture (US Department of Defense 2012a: 3).

Commensurate with its evolution as a hemispheric hegemon, the history of US military bases in Latin America goes back many decades. The now-notorious base at Guantánamo Bay, Cuba, for example, dates to a 1903 lease agreement (still contested by the Cuban government), and continues to be one of the United States' most prominent overseas military complexes (Lindsay-Poland 2009; Sandars 2000: 142–5; Vine 2015). Of particular importance to inter-American relations were outposts in Panama and Puerto Rico, as they were operationally critical to the numerous interventions carried out by US forces following the acquisition of Spain's imperial vestiges in the war of 1898. As the twentieth century came to a close, the facilities in Panama and Vieques (Puerto Rico) proved too problematic to maintain, setting in motion a series of twists and turns that defined US basing strategy in the region (Lindsay-Poland 2009).[2] The rise of the NLL upset the status quo in regards to the Pentagon's Latin American outposts. This resulted in a greater strategic reliance on Colombia. It also facilitated the turn to a more flexible basing strategy—one in which the footprint of US coercion was less visible.

John Lindsay-Poland (2009: 73–4) has identified nine purposes served by US military bases in Latin America: 'police interventions; tropical sanitation; Panama Canal defense, which was interpreted liberally; troop training; tests of weapons and other materiel; environmental engineering, particularly of the tropical environment; counter-insurgency warfare; counter-drug operations; and intelligence and communication tasks'. As of fiscal year 2012, the US military's property portfolio numbered 666 sites in non-US territory in addition to ninety-four sites in overseas (but nominally 'US') territories, including sixty-three sites in Latin America and the Caribbean directly controlled by the DoD, forty-one of which were located in US territories in Puerto Rico and the Virgin Islands (US Department of Defense 2011). These numbers have come down slightly in recent years through a 'freeze the footprint' initiative (announced in 2012) to reduce the department's spending on infrastructure. However, the totals do not include bases outside of the Pentagon's 'real property inventory', meaning that the number of overseas bases/sites to which the US military has access (through defence co-operation agreements, joint task force agreements or other arrangements) is substantially larger. Analysts continue to put the number of overseas US military bases at close to 800 (Vine 2015).

Considering the scale of the DoD's basing infrastructure, it is dynamic, regardless of whether it owns or manages a site or property. Major adjustments are sometimes necessary. In 1999, for instance, as a response to the closure of its military bases in Panama, the United States formalised an agreement with Ecuador giving Southcom access to an Ecuadorian air force base outside the coastal city of Manta. Covering a ten-year span, the agreement was to strengthen co-operation for aerial detection and control of illegal narcotics trafficking and activity. The Forward Operating Location (FOL) was widely seen as one of the United States' most valuable military assets in Latin America. However, the Manta FOL grew increasingly controversial with the Ecuadorian public as it became apparent that the US military presence had the potential to draw the country into the conflict in neighbouring Colombia (Edwards 2007; Lindsay-Poland 2009: 85). Additionally, Washington paid no rent to the Ecuadorian government for use of the base (though the DoD invested tens of millions of dollars in various improvements to the facility over the years).

Campaigning in 2006, Rafael Correa came out strongly against US military presence in Ecuador, helping propel him to victory. The US lease on the Manta airbase ended in 2009. The Correa government chose not to renew the lease, and the base was formally closed as an FOL. Ecuador's foreign minister remarked that the closure marked a 'moment of deep transformation and Latin American vision' (Lindsay-Poland 2010: 22). Correa did not actually 'eject' the United States from the base; he merely demurred on renewing the agreement which would have allowed US forces to stay. Opposition to the arrangement reflected a strong current of opinion in Ecuador, based largely on concerns over sovereignty, transparency and the potential overreach of US interdiction efforts (Edwards 2007). As the United States moved out of Manta, Venezuelan and Chinese capital moved into the city to invest in the area and develop its port facility (Partlow 2008).

Southcom's eviction from Ecuador was taken as proof of the increasingly 'anti-American' features of Latin America's new left (Edwards 2007; Partlow 2008). Much was made of Correa's oft-repeated quip that he would consider renewing the agreement if the United States gave Ecuador a base in Miami. Washington was attuned to the political controversies surrounding the base, but there is little doubt that Southcom would have preferred to maintain access to the FOL had it been able to persuade the Ecuadorians to extend the lease. US officials devised a 'strategic plan to influence Ecuadorian public and political opinion to create an environment more favorable to the possibility of negotiations to renew the FOL agreement' (Wikileaks 2007). DoD officials continued to negotiate with their counterparts after Correa came to power (Lindsay-Poland 2009: 89). Unable to override Correa's campaign commitments, the Obama administration was forced look elsewhere—to neighbouring Colombia.

In 2009, Washington signed an agreement with right-wing Álvaro Uribe, giving the United States access to seven bases in Colombian territory. The deal was nullified by Colombia's Constitutional Court in 2010 because it hadn't been legislated in Congress. Juan Manuel Santos, Uribe's successor, initially supported the deal, but subsequently declined to pursue the agreement, which, much like the renewal of the Fourth Fleet, had become highly controversial in the region (Forero 2009). Nevertheless, reports indicated that the United States was already using most of the facilities covered by the deal through previous agreements. The Pentagon continued to pour millions of dollars into Colombia to upgrade the base facilities even after the court's verdict. Negotiated through a Defense Cooperation Agreement (DCA), the language of the accord highlighted the bilateral nature of the partnership, consistent with the smart power approach. According to the United States, the DCA aimed to 'facilitate effective bilateral cooperation on security matters in Colombia, including narcotics production and trafficking, terrorism, illicit smuggling of all types, and humanitarian and natural disasters' (US Department of State 2009a). The United States leaned on Brazilian President Lula to dampen down the furore unleashed by the agreement amongst NLL governments (Wikileaks 2009a).

Although officials insisted that operations stemming from the bases would be limited to Colombian territory, documents acknowledged that the Palenquero Air Base (the largest of the seven) was regional in scope. The budget estimate for Palenquero referenced its importance to 'full spectrum operations throughout South America', which was 'under constant threat from narcotics funded terrorist insurgencies, anti-US governments, endemic poverty and recurring natural disasters' (US Department of the Air Force 2009). 'Nowhere in the agreement (did) it actually state that US military operations launched from the Colombian bases (were) to be restricted to Colombia' (Leech 2009). Cables illustrated the degree to which officials wanted to 'sell the agreement to the Colombian public and the region' as an extension of ongoing efforts, 'rather than as a major escalation in US engagement'. Officials said the agreement should 'avoid the use of the word "base"' (Wikileaks 2008c).

That the United States would use Colombian facilities rather than establish its own base(s) reflected reforms initiated in 2004, when President Bush announced the Integrated Global Presence and Basing Strategy. The outcome of the Overseas Basing Commission, this was the most significant realignment of overseas forces since the 1950s. It conformed to the needs of a 'more agile and more flexible force'. Between 60,000 and 70,000 troops were brought back from Europe and

Asia, with thousands more redeployed to newer sites to better handle 'emerging' and 'uncertain' threats. Washington stressed the budgetary savings as it consolidated and closed outmoded bases (US Department of State 2004). The shift was seen in a revamped discourse, with new names suggesting that 'a military base is less significant or permanent or externally controlled than a base is typically assumed to be' (Lutz 2009: 19). The Commission concluded that 'forward operating locations' and 'cooperative security locations' would help strengthen alliances and preserve a global presence. In contrast to larger, more traditional bases, newer expeditionary outposts meant greater mobility and flexibility, enhancing 'strategic lift' (Commission on Review of the Overseas Military Facility Structure of the United States 2005: 30). Colloquially known as 'lily pads', these facilities conjure images of US troops hopping effortlessly from point-to-point to access inauspicious platforms of strategic penetration.

As alternatives 'to large, expense, and politically vulnerable fixed bases', lily pads 'provide the US military the capacity to expand its presence on short notice, should a "contingency" arise requiring mobilization' (Lindsay-Poland 2010: 26). They require—and reinforce—a deeper level of partnership. A certain degree of control must be ceded to non-US personnel, but because they are less conspicuous, lily pads are politically less risky. For Southcom, lily pads were part and parcel of its streamlined, small-footprint approach (2012: 4), their flexibility wrapped up in the smart power framework. As discussed in the following section, the construction of new forward bases in Honduras demonstrates the US military's penchant for a lighter, 'smarter' approach to 'emerging threats' (such as the changing routes of narco-traffickers, uncertainties associated with 'radical populist' governments, and so on).

Notwithstanding the limited transparency surrounding the creation of these bases, reports indicate that the United States has sought to create or upgrade forward operating sites across the region, from Central to South America. In 2012, Southcom gained access to a site in the Chilean city of Concón through negotiations with the conservative Piñera government (Kozloff 2012). However, similar arrangements were rejected by the (NLL) governments of Paraguay and Argentina (Vine 2012). Southcom's increased presence in Guatemala (which includes access to at least one Pacific-coast base) came under controversy in 2012 when reports surfaced of renewed human rights abuses by Guatemalan forces, including the fatal shooting of several indigenous demonstrators (Archibold 2012). The US military's presence in Honduras has also been cause for controversy.

Similar to the agreements for forward sites, Southcom maintains a joint task force agreement with Honduras for the Palmerola Air Base (also known as the Soto Cano Air Base). The headquarters of the Honduran Air Force and Naval Academy, Palmerola hosts between 500 and 600 US military personnel. It was central to US counter-insurgency efforts in Central America in the 1980s (including covert operations). In the late 2000s, the Honduran government of Manuel Zelaya set in motion a plan to convert Palmerola into a civilian airport with Venezuelan funding (Kozloff 2009). President Zelaya was deposed in a *coup d'état* before the end of his term, however, sparking a diplomatic firestorm in Latin America. Despite the protests of his supporters and the efforts of Latin American governments (led by Brazil), he was not returned to power. The post-coup government emerged as a major strategic ally of the United States, with the DoD investing in several new 'lily pad' bases there. Washington's ambivalent response to the coup represents an enlightening case study of the diplomatic component of US coercive power in Latin America, and its relationship to military force in the era of the NLL.

Diplomacy and coercive power: Washington and the 2009 Honduran coup

During the Cold War, the United States leveraged its coercive power in Latin America through military interventions, covert operations, counter-insurgency practices, proxy armies and support for highly repressive anti-communist governments, many of which engaged in state-directed terrorism to quash guerrillas and political opponents. Force remained vital to US policy after the Cold War as well, as displayed in interventions in Panama and Haiti; in support for allied governments in the Wars on Drugs and Terror; and in US military outposts in the region. There is a diplomatic element to coercive power, which ultimately rests on military resources. US policy towards the extra-judicial overthrow of elected presidents, for instance, is related to coercion whether or not US actions are among the proximate causes of such coups. Diplomatic or financial support from Washington can enable extra-legal actions, or allow for the consolidation of post-coup regimes, with or without an explicit quid pro quo.

The NLL reinforced existing processes of democratisation. Administrations of the left and centre-left sought institutional reforms, in some cases through constitutional referenda, but all were chosen through open and contested elections. Several of these governments faced illegal or extra-legal challenges, including military coups. In 2002, an alliance between the opposition and elements of the Venezuelan military deposed Hugo Chávez for two days before he was returned to office by supporters and pro-Chávez military officials. The coup was enthusiastically endorsed by the Bush administration. Similarly, in 2004, Haitian President Aristide was driven from office by paramilitary groups comprised of former military officials (Aristide had disbanded the Haitian military, which initially ousted him in a 1991 coup). Washington welcomed Aristide's violent overthrow, quickly recognising the forces that drove him from office.

Although several neoliberal, 'pro-Washington' presidents were forced from office in recent decades amidst violent social upheaval,[3] it is notable that those heads of state toppled by extra-legal methods since 2000 were members of the NLL. Paraguayan President Lugo's removal in 2012 was viewed by some as an impeachment, though Lugo maintained it was a 'parliamentary coup'. The ouster of the Rousseff government in Brazil in 2016 echoed Lugo's ordeal. In contrast, the overthrow of Zelaya in Honduras was a more conventional *coup d'état*, but even in the Honduran case, the *golpistas* ('coupsters') presented a legal rationale for his forced dismissal. Zelaya was removed by the military after aligning his government with the NLL's anti-neoliberal, 'pro-Chávez' bloc, and for subsequently calling for constitutional reform. In analysing the role of the United States in the Honduran crisis, I do not aim to downplay the agency of local actors or the power of Latin American states, as is clear from the following discussion. Washington was responding to events as much as driving them.

Manuel 'Mel' Zelaya was elected president in 2005 as a candidate of the Liberal Party, one of Honduras' two dominant political parties. Seen early on as a relatively traditional politician, Zelaya's campaign focused on enhancing citizen involvement, building transparency in government and modestly strengthening existing social programmes. Over the course of his truncated presidency Zelaya moved to the left, costing him support from members of his own party, which encompassed both progressive and centre-right elements (Meyer 2009; Ruhl 2010). Though he came from a wealthy landowning family, Zelaya railed against the country's oligarchy. His positions became increasingly, if mildly, anti-neoliberal. A supporter of CAFTA during the campaign, Zelaya gradually aligned himself with the country's labour unions while bringing more left-leaning Liberal Party officials into his cabinet.

The political crisis that precipitated his ouster began when Zelaya issued a degree for a popular referendum on convening a constitutional assembly (Ruhl 2010). Although it was non-binding, the referendum was opposed by much of the country's political elite, with the opposition arguing that Zelaya would use it to run for re-election. Following months of legal wrangling, the military arrested Zelaya and flew him into exile in Costa Rica. Although officials from the newly installed government of Roberto Micheletti claimed Zelaya's removal was consistent with constitutional procedure, it was widely condemned as a *coup d'état*. The OAS unanimously voted to suspend the country for an interruption of the democratic order in accordance with its Inter-American Democratic Charter (Meyer 2009: 6). In the immediate aftermath of the coup the UN, the EU and a number of other regional bodies (such as CARICOM [Caribbean Community] and UNASUR [Union of South American Nations]) sought to isolate the Micheletti government by applying diplomatic and financial pressure. In this context, Washington's approach to the crisis, as discussed below, struck a discordant note. Its nominal commitment to democracy and the rule of law was blunted by a deep ambivalence toward Zelaya's 'populism'.

The coup elicited spirited protests from unions, peasant groups and civil society organisations in Honduras, fuelling international condemnation. 'After the coup, security forces committed serious human rights violations, killing some protesters, repeatedly using excessive force against demonstrators, and arbitrarily detaining thousands of coup opponents.' To consolidate its rule, the de facto government 'imposed unreasonable and illegitimate restrictions on the rights to freedom of expression and assembly' (Human Rights Watch 2010: 1; Frank 2012). These violations persisted after the January 2010 inauguration of Porfirio Lobo, Micheletti's successor. The Inter-American Commission on Human Rights (2010) expressed 'deep concern' over ongoing violations in the context of the post-coup environment, undermining claims by Honduran officials (and Washington) that the situation had returned to normal.

In contrast to the firm condemnation of the coup in Latin America, the response of the Obama administration was ambiguous. Whereas Latin American leaders were uniform in their insistence on Zelaya's return, Washington was evasive on the matter. There was some criticism of Zelaya's removal, which was (eventually) backed up by bilateral action, including the suspension of tens of millions of dollars in foreign assistance. Crucially, however, the Obama administration never labelled the action a military coup, which would have triggered the termination of a much greater portion of the funds. Classified cables released via Wikileaks (2009b) demonstrate that, contrary to the administration's public equivocations, US policymakers had no doubts as to the illegality of the coup itself. Although the State Department backed negotiations that would have returned Zelaya to office, it quickly undercut the agreement by stating that Washington would recognise the new government regardless of whether Zelaya's reinstatement was implemented (Casas-Zamora 2011: 123). The timing of the administration's actions proved decisive. The United States 'waited more than two months before imposing effective sanctions—including freezing the visas of military and political actors—to press the de facto government to restore democratic rule' (Human Rights Watch 2010: 11). Washington's calculated foot-dragging ensured that Zelaya would not be returned to power before the next presidential election.

Washington was isolated in recognising the legitimacy of the post-coup elections, which were boycotted by Zelaya's supporters and by most international observers. The United States went to great lengths to normalise Honduras' foreign relations. Lobo, welcomed to the White House in October 2011, became a key US ally; an embassy cable summarising his inauguration speech concluded that it 'could have been written by us' (Wikileaks 2010). Although several Latin American countries followed the United States' lead in re-establishing ties with Honduras, Washington's overall approach to the crisis struck many in Latin America as unilateralist, weakening Obama's claims to a new partnership with the region. There was 'uneasiness with the idea of having a close ally of Hugo Chávez . . . as the direct beneficiary of US sanctions'. This explains why sanctions were weak 'when compared with those genuinely feared in Tegucigalpa: the freezing of Honduran bank accounts in the United States and the imposition of commercial sanctions against the country' (Casas-Zamora 2011: 122). The (apparent) inconsistency masked a persistent desire to see the crisis resolved in a way that prevented Zelaya's return, depriving Chávez of an ally while undercutting 'populism'.

Domestic politics played a key role in shaping the White House's views on Honduras. Obama was challenged by conservative Republicans in Congress who were quick to link Zelaya to Chávez. In response to Obama's tepid 'support' for Zelaya, Republicans in the Senate temporarily blocked the administration's nominees for Assistant Secretary of State for Western Hemisphere Affairs (Arturo Valenzuela) and Ambassador to Brazil (Thomas Shannon). Although US policy was largely set by the Hillary Clinton-led State Department, the debate was impacted by the Cuban American contingent in Congress, which has long enjoyed incredible clout within Republican foreign policy circles. Knowing the political landscape in Washington, the Honduran backers of the coup lobbied intensely to persuade members of both the executive and legislative branches that Zelaya's removal from office was legal. The Business Council of Latin America, a right-wing lobby group, hired prominent lawyer Lanny Davis to conduct a campaign against Zelaya's reinstatement. Davis, previously an aide to the Clintons, later accepted a position lobbying on behalf of the Lobo government (Grandin 2009; *The Hill* 2010).

There is scant evidence that the Obama administration was an instigator of the coup in Honduras, despite reports that US policymakers met with Honduran military officials in the weeks leading up to Zelaya's ouster (Ruhl 2010: 101; US Department of State 2009b). Although the coup called to mind infamous covert interventions of previous eras, only the loosest of comparisons can be made with Guatemala in 1954 or Chile in 1973. His defenders even argued that Obama's sensitivity to the history of American interventionism prevented him from taking a harder line in calling for Zelaya's reinstatement. But there is no doubt that his position was at odds with the consensus in Latin America. The 'whitewashing' of the coup heightened tensions with NLL governments (not just the likes of Venezuela and Bolivia, but also Brazil and Argentina) while corroding the image of Obama as an agent of change.

Geopolitics and the Obama administration's response to the Honduran coup

Why should events in a small Central American country have such an outsized impact on inter-American relations? And, given that Washington did not appear to be directly responsible for the coup, what did it have to do with US power in the region? This section addresses US diplomacy towards the Honduran coup in the context of Washington's wider geopolitical approach to Latin America and the NLL.

On the surface, the controversy surrounding the coup swirled around the figure of Zelaya himself. At a deeper level, of course, were the policy implications of his political shift to the left. As a moderate turned 'populist', Zelaya's overtures to the NLL (as encapsulated by his decision to bring Honduras into ALBA) implied that the United States was in the process of 'losing' Honduras to the 'pro-Chávez' camp. Cables indicate that, prior to the coup, US officials identified Zelaya as inimical to US interests. According to Charles Ford, the US ambassador, Zelaya had a 'sinister' side, as evidenced by his advisors' ties to Venezuela, Cuba and organised crime. He was a 'caudillo' who acted like a 'rebellious teenager'. He harboured nationalist and anti-American views and opposed the US military's presence at the Soto Cano Air Force Base (Wikileaks 2008d). Some observers speculated that US officials were worried that the constitutional reform process put in motion by Zelaya could have outlawed the presence of foreign troops in the country. He had set in motion plans to convert Soto Cano into an exclusively civilian airport. In other words, the United States' coercive power in Central America was put at risk by Zelaya's 'transformation'.

Similar to its position in the 1980s, Honduras (re-)emerged as the geographic fulcrum of the United States' militarised counter-narcotics strategy in Central America, partly as a function of Zelaya's overthrow. In 2011, Honduras received more than $50 million in Pentagon contracts, which represented 62 per cent of all DoD funds slated for Central America for that fiscal year. This included $24 million for improvements to the Soto Cano base (Frank 2012). Additionally, the United States built three new forward bases in Honduras, one of which features an airstrip used by the CIA during the 1980s (Shanker 2012). As part of the 'small footprint' strategy that seeks to expand the Pentagon's assets 'under the radar' of public notice, the creation of these bases necessitated close co-operation with the country's post-coup governments. The interagency mix of programmes needed to construct and maintain these 'lily pads' was supported by approximately 200 US Special Forces soldiers who, among other duties, were actively training their Honduran counterparts (Shanker 2012).

The United States did not directly force Zelaya from office. Once he was gone, however, the Obama administration used a mix of tools to augment its coercive reach in the region. Economic sanctions were applied to the post-coup government, but in a manner that would ensure their 'ineffectiveness' in restoring the ousted president. Diplomacy was geared towards diffusing the crisis without rectifying the illegality of the coup or its social or political consequences. Rhetorically, Washington sought to have it both ways. It criticised Zelaya's removal as undemocratic, but it refused to label it a military coup. At times, the United States appeared to support the regional and multilateral consensus on Honduras, as when it voted to temporarily expel the country from the OAS. In fact, the United States consistently undermined this very same consensus, to the consternation of Brazil, the ALBA countries and leaders from across Latin America. To highlight one example, the State Department recognised the elections administered by the de facto government while the OAS did not. Although the vote was carried out under highly-repressive conditions, the United States maintained that the election allowed Honduras to 'turn the page' and re-join the hemispheric community of democracies.

As noted by one analyst, Honduras acted as a proving ground for Obama's smart power approach, where it provided 'a way to disguise Washington's unilateralism as multilateralism' (Golinger 2009). Had Obama backed the new regime unambiguously, it could have been highly deleterious to the United States' image in Latin America, particularly given past US support for military coups. But the multilateral disguise wasn't entirely plausible. The administration hoped it could retain this superficial posture while transforming Honduras into a veritable garrison of US 'hard power' in Central America. The OAS, meanwhile, had staked out a very different approach. By signifying a tolerance for putschist measures against 'populist' governments, Washington's acceptance of the coup may have served to put other NLL politicians 'on notice'. This is consistent with the logic of coercive power. At the same time, the actions of the OAS, so historically central to US influence in the region, were ineffectual; it was unable to return Zelaya to office. In the end, the episode strengthened efforts to build alternative mechanisms of regional co-operation that excluded the United States. Although the Honduran crisis benefitted the hegemon's coercive power, then, it damaged its institutional power, the subject of Chapter 5.

Conclusion

This chapter examined US military strategy towards Latin America in the age of the NLL. The post-Cold War hegemony of the United States developed from earlier waves of imperialism, which rested heavily on force and interventionism, as described in Chapter 1. In effect, the lasting coercive capability of the United States—evident in its overwhelming military advantages—undergirded the asymmetries of the Washington Consensus era, even though the ideational dimension of this consensus was more than a mere reflection of the unevenness in military force. From the standpoint of much IR theory, the logic of coercive power is fairly intuitive. That said, even this most 'traditional' form of power is clearly bound up with other forms of power in the international relations of the Americas. For starters, the ability of Washington to compel other actors—to get them to do something they otherwise wouldn't—depends on disproportionate material (and, in particular, military) resources, connecting us to the structural power discussed in the previous chapter. Moreover, coercive power is always deployed within broader geopolitical contexts (which it helps to shape). If used 'smartly', in the discourse of the Obama administration, it can allow a hegemon to gain leverage over subordinates, or realise an outcome at odds with the interests/motives of others, without resorting to actual kinetic force. But the directness of this interaction, brought out by the implicit conflict between actors, suggests coercion all the same.

Strategically, amidst broader continuities in the goals of its foreign policy, Washington shifted tack, attempting to protect and, where possible, augment its military access and manoeuvrability in Latin America, albeit in a 'softer' way. This was seen in the reconstitution of the US Navy's Fourth Fleet; in the changes to Southcom's basing posture; and in the consolidation of the post-coup government in Honduras. In the wake of the Bush administration's War on Terror, the Obama administration (re-)focused on the image of the US military via its 'smart power' framework. As illustrated in Pentagon documents, and in the continued search for military partners and bases, the rise of the NLL did not lead to strategic retrenchment by the United States; on the contrary, the United States remained committed to its 'hard power' capabilities in Latin America, repositioning its military resources to adjust to new hemispheric realities. This had complex implications for inter-American relations. The redirection of coercive power adversely impacted its institutional power. As explored in the following chapter, Latin American countries moved away from the OAS to address important security issues. Changes to the institutional make-up of inter-American relations impacted the structural power of the United States as it sought to shore up the Post-Washington Consensus trade regime, as analysed in Chapter 3. And Washington's shifting strategy was related to the threat of 'radical populism', the meaning of which was closely connected to US ideological power, as scrutinised in Chapter 6. I do not want to suggest that this was a linear process. These forms of power overlap and interact, and they must be examined together. However intuitive from an IR standpoint, coercive power is but one component of a deeper, more expansive hegemony.

Notes

1 In announcing changes to the US military's global posture in 2004, then-Defense Secretary Donald Rumsfeld stated that US troops 'should be located in places where they are wanted, welcomed, and needed', noting the problems caused when 'the presence and activities of (US) forces grate on local populations and . . . become an irritant for host governments'. Citing the need to make US forces more 'agile', Rumsfeld also stated that 'American troops should be located in environments that are hospitable to their movements' (Rumsfeld 2004).
2 The United States was compelled to give up its military bases in Panama at the behest of nationalist Panamanian politicians and citizens, many of whom had opposed US control of the Panama Canal Zone, which was returned to Panama by the United States in a 1979 treaty. The United States left the Zone (and its bases) in 1999. A similar dynamic was witnessed in regards to the US base on the Puerto Rican island of Vieques, which became a flashpoint for Puerto Rican social movements in the 1990s–2000s. The US Navy pulled out of Vieques in 2003. Puerto Rico itself, which is officially part of the United States, though not a state, continues to be an important site of US military activity.
3 This includes Ecuador's Jamil Mahuad, ousted in 2000 via a popular rebellion and subsequent coup, and Bolivia's Gonzalo Sánchez de Lozada, who resigned amidst widespread protests in 2003. Argentina's 2001–2 crises witnessed multiple presidential resignations amidst rioting and social upheaval.

References

Archibold, R. C. (2012). 'Guatemala Shooting Raises Concerns about Military's Expanded Role', *The New York Times*, 20 October: A9.
Armitage, R. L. and J. S. Nye (2007). 'CSIS Commission on Smart Power: A Smarter, More Secure America', Center for Strategic and International Studies.
Barnett, M. and R. Duvall (2005). 'Power in Global Governance', in *Power in Global Governance*, edited by M. Barnett and R. Duvall, Cambridge: Cambridge University Press: 1–32.
Barry, T. (2005). '"Mission Creep" in Latin America—US Southern Command's New Security Strategy', International Relations Center (IRC), July.
Blakeley, R. (2006). 'Still Training to Torture? US Training of Military Forces from Latin America', *Third World Quarterly*, 27(8): 1439–61.
Bloomberg (2008). 'US Navy Reviving Fleet for Latin America, Caribbean', 24 April. Available online at www.bloomberg.com/apps/news?pid=newsarchive&sid=a094x7Q a8Qeo (accessed 20 July 2013).
Casas-Zamora, K. (2011). 'The Honduran Crisis and the Obama Administration', in *Shifting the Balance: Obama and the Americas*, edited by A. F. Lowenthal, T. J. Piccone and L. Whitehead, Washington, DC: Brookings Institution: 114–31.
Clinton, H. R. (2009a). 'Nomination Hearing to Be Secretary of State', US Department of State, 13 January. Available online at www.state.gov/secretary/20092013clinton/ rm/2009a/01/115196.htm (accessed 10 December 2015).

Clinton, H. R. (2009b). 'Foreign Policy Address at the Council on Foreign Relations', 15 July. Available online at www.state.gov/secretary/20092013clinton/rm/2009a/july/126071.htm (accessed 10 December 2015).

Commission on Review of the Overseas Military Facility Structure of the United States (2005). May.

Dahl, R. (1957). 'The Concept of Power', *Behavioral Science*, 2(3): 201–15.

Edwards, S. (2007). 'The US Forward Operating Location in Manta: The Ecuadorian Perspective', Washington Office on Latin America, 30 March.

Ellis, R. E. (2011). 'China-Latin American Military Engagement: Good Will, Good Business, and Strategic Position', Strategic Studies Institute, August.

Enloe, C. (2000). *Bananas, Beaches and Bases: Making Feminist Sense of International Politics*, Berkeley: University of California Press.

Forero, J. (2009). 'South American Leaders Assail US Access to Colombian Military Bases', *Washington Post*, 29 August.

Frank, D. (2012). 'Honduras: Which Side is the US On?' *The Nation*, 11 June.

Golinger, E. (2009). 'Honduras: A Victory for "Smart Power"', Global Research, 3 November. Available online at www.globalresearch.ca/honduras-a-victory-for-smart-power/ (accessed 20 July 2013).

Gramsci, A. (1971). *Selections from the Prison Notebooks*, New York: International Publishers.

Grandin, G. (2009). 'Battle for Honduras—and the Region', *The Nation*, 31 August/7 September: 22–4.

The Hill (2010). 'Former Clinton Aide Hired by Honduran Government', 2 December. Available online at http://thehill.com/blogs/blog-briefing-room/news/131579-former-clinton-aide-hired-by-honduran-government (accessed 22 September 2016).

Human Rights Watch (2010). 'After the Coup: Ongoing Violence, Intimidation, and Impunity in Honduras', December.

Inter-American Commission on Human Rights (2010). 'Preliminary Observations of the Inter-American Commission on Human Rights on its Visit to Honduras, May 15–18, 2010', 3 June.

Isacson, A., J. Olson and L. Haugaard (2007). 'Below the Radar: US Military Programs with Latin America, 1997–2007', Center for International Policy, Latin America Working Group Education Fund and the Washington Office on Latin America, March.

Johnson, C. (2004). *The Sorrows of Empire: Militarism, Secrecy, and the End of the Republic*, New York: Owl Books.

Kozloff, N. (2008). 'US Fourth Fleet in Venezuelan Waters', Counterpunch, May. Available online at www.counterpunch.org/2008/05/24/u-s-fourth-fleet-in-venezuelan-waters/ (accessed 20 July 2013).

Kozloff, N. (2009). 'The Coup and the US Airbase in Honduras', Counterpunch, 22 July. Available online at www.counterpunch.org/2009/07/22/the-coup-and-the-u-s-airbase-in-honduras/ (accessed 20 July 2013).

Kozloff, N. (2012). 'What's Behind Obama's New Military Base in Chile?' Al-Jazeera, 2 June. Available online at www.aljazeera.com/indepth/opinion/2012/05/2012526163512636123.htm (accessed 21 July 2013).

Leech, G. (2009). 'US Military Documents Show Colombia Base Agreement Poses Threat to Region', Colombia Journal, 6 November. Available online at http://colombiajournal.org/u-s-military-documents-show-colombia-base-agreement-poses-threat-to-region.htm (accessed 20 July 2013).

LeoGrande, W. M. (2006). 'From Red Menace to Radical Populism: US Insecurity in Latin America', *World Policy Journal*, 22(4): 25–35.

Lindsay-Poland, J. (2009). 'US Military Bases in Latin America and the Caribbean', in *The Bases of Empire: The Global Struggle against US Military Posts*, edited by C. Lutz, London: Pluto Press: 71–95.

Lindsay-Poland, J. (2010). 'Retreat to Colombia: The Pentagon Adapts its Latin America Strategy', *NACLA Reports*, 43(1): 22–6.

Lutz, C. (2009). 'Introduction: Bases, Empire, and Global Response', in *The Bases of Empire: The Global Struggle against US Military Posts*, edited by C. Lutz, London: Pluto Press: 1–44.

Maclay, J. D., M. Potter, R. R. Scott and M. W. Sibley (2009). 'The Fourth Fleet: A Tool of Engagement in the Americas', Center for Strategic and International Studies, February.

Mann, M. (2012). *The Sources of Social Power Volume 3: Global Empires and Revolution*, Cambridge: Cambridge University Press.

Meyer, P. J. (2009). 'Honduran-US Relations', Congressional Research Service, 23 November.

Nye, J. S. (2004). *Soft Power: The Means to Success in World Politics*, New York: Public Affairs.

Nye, J. S. (2008). *The Powers to Lead*, Oxford: Oxford University Press.

Partlow, J. (2008). 'Ecuador Giving US Air Base the Boot', *Washington Post*, 4 September.

Ruhl, J. M. (2010). 'Honduras Unravels', *Journal of Democracy*, 21(2): 93–107.

Rumsfeld, D. (2004). 'Positioning America's Forces for the 21st Century', US Department of Defense, September. Available online at www.defense.gov/home/articles/2004-09/a092304b.html (accessed 20 July 2013).

Sandars, C. T. (2000). *America's Overseas Garrisons: The Leasehold Empire*, Oxford: Oxford University Press.

Schoultz, L. (1998). *Beneath the United States: A History of US Policy toward Latin America*, Cambridge, MA: Harvard University Press.

Serafino, N. M. (2008). 'CRS Report for Congress: Section 1206 of the National Defense Authorization Act for Fiscal Year 2006: A Fact Sheet on DoD Authority to Train and Equip Foreign Military Forces', Congressional Research Service, 9 April.

Shanker, T. (2012). 'A US Drug War Inside Honduras, Waged Iraq-Style', *The New York Times*, 6 May: A1.

Southcom (2008). 'United States Southern Command 2018: Partnership for the Americas', December.

Southcom (2010). 'Command Strategy 2020', July.

Southcom (2012). 'Posture Statement of General Douglas M. Fraser, United States Southern Command', 6 March.

Stavridis, J. G. (2008). 'US Smart Power in Latin America: An Interview with James G. Stavridis', *The Fletcher Forum of World Affairs*, 32(2): 45–52.

Stavridis, J. G. (2010). *Partnership for the Americas: Western Hemisphere Strategy and US Southern Command*, Washington, DC: National Defense University.

US Department of Defense (2008). 'Navy Re-Establishes US Fourth Fleet', 24 April. Available online at www.defense.gov/releases/release.aspx?releaseid=11862 (accessed 20 July 2013).

US Department of Defense (2010). 'Quadrennial Defense Review Report', February.

US Department of Defense (2011). 'Base Structure Report: Fiscal Year 2012 Baseline', September.

US Department of Defense (2012a). 'Sustaining US Global Leadership: Priorities for 21st Century Defense', January.

US Department of Defense (2012b). 'Western Hemisphere Defense Policy Statement', October.

US Department of State (2004). 'Bush Announces Largest US Force Restructuring in 50 Years: Troops to Move to Strategic Locations with 70,000 Fewer Overseas', 16 August. Available online at www.america.gov/st/washfile-english/2004/August/200408161747 27frllehctim0.490597.html (accessed 20 July 2013).

US Department of State (2009a). 'US-Colombia Defense Cooperation Agreement', Fact Sheet, 18 August. Available online at www.state.gov/r/pa/prs/ps/2009/aug/128021.htm (accessed 20 July 2013).

US Department of State (2009b). 'Background Briefing on the Situation in Honduras', 1 July. Available online at www.state.gov/r/pa/prs/ps/2009/july/125564.htm (accessed 20 July 2013).

US Department of the Air Force (2009). 'Military Construction Program, Fiscal Year (FY) 2010 Budget Estimates', May.

Vine, D. (2012). 'The Lily-Pad Strategy', Tom Dispatch, 15 July. Available online at www.tomdispatch.com/blog/175568/ (accessed 10 December 2015).

Vine, D. (2015). *Base Nation: How US Military Bases Abroad Harm America and the World*, New York: Metropolitan Books.

Wikileaks (2007). 'Manta FOL: Request for DOS and DOD Financial Support for Media Outreach and COMREL Activities', 20 March. Reference ID: 07QUITO642.

Wikileaks (2008a). 'A/S Shannon Engages with GOA Officials at U.S.-Argentine Bilateral Consultations', 4 August. Reference ID: 08BUENOSAIRES1068.

Wikileaks (2008b). 'Scenesetter for the November 20 Bilateral Defense Working Group', 14 November. Reference ID: 08BRASILIA1487.

Wikileaks (2008c). 'Colombian Counterproposal to US Defense Cooperation Agreement', 12 November. Reference ID: 08BOGOTA4083.

Wikileaks (2008d). 'President Jose Manuel Zelaya Rosales: Personal', 15 May. Reference ID: 08TEGUCIGALPA459.

Wikileaks (2009a). 'Brazil's Thinking on Colombia-US Defense Cooperation Agreement', 20 August. Reference ID: 09BRASILIA1041.

Wikileaks (2009b). 'TFHO1: Open and Shut: The Case of the Honduran Coup', 24 July. Reference ID: 09TEGUCIGALPA645.

Wikileaks (2010). 'President Lobo Urges National Reconciliation and Pledges Improved Quality of Life', 29 January. Reference ID: 10TEGUCIGALPA92.

Withers, G., A. Isacson, L. Haugaard, J. Olson and J. Fyke (2008). 'Ready, Aim, Foreign Policy', Center for International Policy, Latin America Working Group Education Fund and the Washington Office on Latin America, March.

5 Reforming institutional power

The OAS in the new regional landscape

Institutional power is less direct than structural and coercive power. In international relations, formal institutions mediate between actors, their limited autonomy putting 'distance' between member states. Institutional power is 'in effect when . . . states design international institutions in ways that work to their long-term advantage and to the disadvantage of others' (Barnett and Duvall 2005: 3). IOs build consensus while reflecting the 'frozen configurations of privilege and bias' of their architects (Barnett and Duvall 2005: 16). If coercive power is fundamentally about force, institutional power is about the organisational rules, norms and procedures that refract the interests and actions of participating agents. The logic of institutional power means that states use institutions to guide, steer and/or constrain other actors. IOs privilege their architects in a number of ways, including through processes of agenda-setting, self-insulation and self-restraint (Barnett and Duvall 2005; Hurrell 2005).

In other words, institutions are sites of both co-operative and competitive behaviour. States work through their rules and strictures in pursuit of their interests. My conceptualisation of institutional power borrows from Mann's understanding of political power, which he distinguishes from military force. Although Mann begins with the territorial state as the source of political power, he acknowledges that, in the geopolitics of inter-state relations, diplomacy comprises an 'important form of political-power organization' (1986: 27). Political power is institutionalised by definition, producing a regulatory 'centre' of rule-making that fosters 'peaceful but stratified' international networks (Mann 1986: 11). Like military power, political power can be projected outward, including through international organisations (Mann 2012: 15).

The OAS, created in 1948 and based in Washington, is the Western hemisphere's leading inter-governmental body, facilitating co-operation amongst the countries of North, Central and South America and the Caribbean on a range of issues. The United States was indispensable to the creation of the OAS, which has long been viewed as an instrument of its deep hegemony in the Americas. For Alberto Lleras Camargo, its first Secretary General, the organisation was 'what the member governments want(ed) it to be and nothing else' (Meyer 2014: 28). In reality, however, the OAS was what the United States wanted it to be, and little else. In the 2000s, however, Washington's influence within the institution was challenged by the reformist and counter-hegemonic currents of the NLL. At the same time, new forums and initiatives appeared on the scene, undermining the OAS's status as the centre of international co-operation in the Western hemisphere.

This chapter analyses Washington's efforts to reconstitute its institutional power in Latin America. After providing background on the relationship between the United States and the OAS, I examine the impact of the NLL on the inter-American system. This includes a section detailing Latin America's new regionalism, as expressed in three forums: ALBA, the economic bloc discussed in Chapter 3; UNASUR, a diplomatic body that features the South American Defense Council introduced in Chapter 4; and CELAC, created out of the Rio Group, envisioned by some as a potential replacement for the OAS. Collectively, these new forums undermined the OAS's importance in the institutional landscape. The chapter details US efforts to shore up the status of the OAS in concert with wider processes of hegemonic renewal, including through reforms to the organisation itself. Obama's rapprochement with Cuba is illustrative of this dynamic, as Cuba's exclusion from the OAS symbolised its ossification in the eyes of many in Latin America. Cuba was brought into the OAS-sponsored Summit of the Americas in 2015 to protect the viability of the Summit moving forwards.

Institutions can serve to legitimate the deployment of other forms of power in international affairs, helping to foster a Gramscian consensus in favour of an existing—and dynamic—hegemonic order. Although IOs are more than 'tools' of dominant states, hegemons often use them to pursue discrete foreign policy objectives. This instrumentalist side of institutional power co-exists with the interdependence that is implicit in these arrangements, as states bind themselves to one another through a formal, rules-based agreement. Often, states employ institutions to promote co-operation—to realise outcomes that benefit their collective well-being. But this too is an uneven process. States with greater resources have a disproportionate say in shaping collective goals and in defining the mechanisms at the heart of institutional action. Even under conditions of co-operation there are 'winners' and 'losers' (Barnett and Duvall 2005: 17). The United States may be 'winning' in the OAS less frequently than it used to. Nevertheless, the organisation remains vital to its hegemony in the Americas.

The OAS and US foreign policy

That the OAS could present challenges to Washington is a novel idea. It was the fear of communist encroachment in the hemisphere that provided much of the impetus for the organisation's formation. During the Cold War, when the region was dominated by rightist governments allied with the United States, the OAS generally acted as a 'rubber stamp' for the actions of its most powerful member. The unanimous expulsion of the Cuban government in 1962 epitomised its subservience to Washington's geopolitical interests. For decades, the OAS was an almost perfect reflection of US priorities, with few notable exceptions.

The OAS of the early twenty-first century appeared altogether different. The political environment surrounding the OAS shifted, impacting the operation of the institution. According to the CRS:

> Since the organization's foundation, the United States has sought to utilize the OAS to advance critical economic, political, and security objectives in the Western Hemisphere. Although OAS actions frequently reflected US policy during the 20th Century, this has changed to a certain extent over the past decade as Latin American and Caribbean governments have adopted more independent foreign policies. While the organization's goals and day-to-day activities are still generally consistent with US policy toward the region, the United States' ability to advance its policy initiatives within the OAS has declined.
>
> (Meyer 2014: 2)

In summarising recent debates, the congressional report revealed a strain of thinking that viewed the OAS not as an anachronistic obstacle to hemispheric consensus, but as an institution that was actively undermining Washington's objectives. The 'anti-OAS' camp grew more strident following the Republican victory in the 2010 midterm elections, which saw prominent conservatives take control of several committees in the US House of Representatives.

In actuality, the OAS sits at the core of US institutional power in Latin America. Created out of the aegis of the Pan-American Union following the Second World War, it is the centrepiece of the inter-American system formalised by the 1947 Rio Treaty. Its Charter, signed in 1948, pledged to 'strengthen the peace and security of the continent' and 'promote and consolidate representative democracy' in the region (Organization of American States 2016). The new organisation was head-quartered in Washington, just blocks from the White House. It was designed to subsume pre-existing regional inter-state institutions, some of which dated to the 1880s, allowing the OAS to bill itself as 'the world's oldest regional organization'. Founded by the United States and twenty Latin American countries, it expanded to include Canada and the Commonwealth countries of the Caribbean. Its remit spans four areas: democracy, human rights, security and development (Organization of American States 2016).

Ernesto 'Che' Guevara famously derided the OAS as the United States' 'Ministry of Colonies'. In an address to the UN General Assembly, Guevara condemned the use of the OAS to justify co-ordinated acts of aggression against Cuba, including an economic embargo. The OAS had expelled Cuba in 1962, proclaiming Marxism-Leninism to be incompatible with the democratic principles of the inter-American system. The irony that Latin America was bloated with US-backed dictatorships was not lost on Guevara, who called for the liberation of the region 'from the colonial yoke of the United States' (Guevara 1964). Cuba's expulsion from the OAS led most of its members to cut ties with the country, isolating the island from trading partners and hastening its alliance with the Soviet Union. As Latin America descended deeper into the Cold War morass,

Cuban officials routinely lambasted the OAS as a puppet of the United States, a charge levied against the institution more recently by Chávez (Council on Foreign Relations 2015). Even Cuba's recent rapprochement with the regional body could do little to temper Fidel Castro's disdain for the organisation. He called the OAS 'vile', saying it had produced '60 years of betrayal of the people of Latin America' (Reuters 2009).

Notwithstanding the hyperbole of Guevara, Castro and Chávez, the basic characterisation of the OAS as a facilitator of US hegemony is well-founded. The notion that it reflected the United States' geopolitical dominance is uncontroversial, despite the fact that the OAS always enjoyed some autonomy from its most powerful patron. On occasion, the OAS mediated against US interests. For instance, the OAS sided with Argentina during its 1982 conflict with Great Britain over the status of the Falklands/Malvinas islands. In the Nicaraguan conflict of the late 1970s, the United States was unable to win agreement for a US-led 'peacekeeping force', widely seen as an attempt to pre-empt the Sandinista revolution (Shaw 2004: 121–9). A unified Latin America also rebuffed the United States in 1960, when the organisation condemned the dictatorship of Rafael Trujillo, an ally of the United States, following a conflict with Venezuela in which Trujillo's forces violated Venezuelan sovereignty. The OAS even implemented sanctions against the Dominican Republic despite Washington's opposition (Shaw 2004: 116–21).

In 1965, however, when the United States invaded the Dominican Republic to prevent the potential emergence of a 'Castroist' government there, it was able to secure the backing of the OAS, even though the military occupation was in blatant violation of its founding principles of non-invention, a fairly routine transgression during the Cold War (Atkins 1999: 227; Shaw 2004: 103–11). In cases in which the United States was unable to obtain OAS approval the organisation was virtually powerless to prevent or protest Washington's imperious behaviour. That the United States sought but was denied a clear OAS mandate for its 1954 overthrow of the Árbenz government in Guatemala was evidence of this. Tellingly, Árbenz, a reformer whom the United States accused of communism, wanted to move the multilateral discussion of US interference in Guatemala to the UN Security Council. Washington insisted that the dispute be handled in the OAS, where it held more sway (Shaw 2004: 78–80). From the 1950s through the 1980s, the OAS's security agenda centred on the communist bogey, a concern that united Washington and regional elites. Once Cuba was expunged from the OAS, the United States used the organisation to tighten sanctions against the country in the mid-1960s.

Washington's dominance of the OAS has ebbed and flowed, the early Cold War years representing its apogee (Atkins 1999: 47–9; Shaw 2004: 95–132). This dominance was not owed to the rules or structure of the inter-American system. Historically, Washington's influence within the organisation had more to do with broader geopolitical trends than it did with the make-up of the institution itself. The consensus mechanism at the core of OAS decision-making can be a hindrance to US influence as much as an enabler. Moreover, the principle of non-intervention enshrined in the OAS Charter was included at the behest of Latin American states wary of their northern neighbour. All members are granted the same status under its procedures. The United States was the major force behind its formation, and it has traditionally provided the bulk of the OAS's funding, including through voluntary contributions which allowed it considerable influence on the implementation of specific OAS decisions (Meyer 2014: 28; Shaw 2004: 30). However, it never fully 'possessed' the institution. This is perfectly consistent with the logic of institutional power. The OAS functions to guide and constrain the actions of member states, but not in equal measure.

With the rise of the NLL, the OAS was increasingly seen as neglected and/or damaged by political divisions. According to the Council on Foreign Relations (2015):

> while the organization has been recognized for its value in providing information and serving as a forum for high-level discussion, it has also come under fire for the weakness of its political power, ineffectiveness in decision-making, and inconsistency in applying its democratic principles to states.

Additionally, 'ideological polarization and mistrust of the OAS have prompted doubts over its relevance in the region, spurring the creation of alternative platforms for regional integration'. The sense was that the United States had 'lost control' of the organisation; that it had been captured by those elements who wished to directly challenge US hegemony or, at the very least, de-link themselves from US power.

And yet, the OAS, as the most established venue for multilateral co-operation in the hemisphere, remained crucial to US foreign policy. The Obama years saw the United States recommit itself to the organisation, even as some conservative Republicans assailed it. As Hillary Clinton (2010) explained to the OAS General Assembly, the United States wanted 'a stronger, more vibrant OAS', but there was 'serious work to be done to bolster the institution'. Priorities included: regional agenda-setting through the Summit of the Americas; promoting representative democracy; addressing security concerns; and protecting human rights (Clinton 2010; Meyer 2014). This expansive agenda hints at the ways in which US institutional power overlaps other forms of hegemonic power in the Americas, from security issues (closely tied to coercive power) to economic issues (structural power, detailed in Chapter 3). Insofar as the OAS was utilised to damp down 'populism' in the region, it is bound up with US ideological power, as well. Perhaps most importantly, it has featured widely in Washington's efforts to reinforce polyarchic governance in the Americas.

Democracy, the OAS and Washington's hemispheric agenda

During the Cold War, security concerns dominated US policy in the inter-American system. In the post-Cold War era, greater emphasis was placed on democracy promotion, illustrated by the signing of the Inter-American Democratic Charter by all

OAS members in 2001. As argued by William Robinson (1996), however, and as discussed in Chapter 2, the US democracy agenda was best conceptualised as the promotion of polyarchy—elite-led representative democracy amenable to socio-economic neoliberalisation. This remained the case during the backlash against the Washington Consensus, which saw anti-neoliberal forces make inroads across the region. It was evident in Washington's efforts to protect the status quo in the OAS's human rights and democratisation regimes. As the NLL was consolidated in the mid- to late 2000s, the United States continued to view the OAS as playing an important (if diminished) role in maintaining the integrity of (neo)liberal democracy.

Ideologically, the OAS became a means of criticising the reputedly 'authoritarian' tendencies that Washington saw as an ingredient of the populism of Chávez, Morales, Correa and others. Election monitoring programmes and human rights reporting could help check illiberal practices. Generally speaking, when electoral outcomes went the way of Washington's favoured candidate, OAS election oversight was deemed useful. Where 'populist' politicians won, however, the organisation's monitoring was often seen as ineffectual, rendering the organisation 'weak' on democracy. This amplified calls from US officials to strengthen the Inter-American Democratic Charter, as discussed below.

Regarding Venezuela, US officials developed a somewhat schizophrenic position on OAS election monitoring. They clearly valued the oversight provided by observers. More prominently, though, they criticised these efforts as inadequate, with the implication that this weakness benefited Chávez's Bolivarian movement. There was the sense that the OAS did not commit sufficient resources to guarantee effective election observations missions in Venezuela (Wikileaks 2006a). Cables around the time of the 2006 election, in which Chávez won a large majority, show American officials supportive of OAS challenges to 'violations of campaign regulations' (specifically those regulations prohibiting the use of government funds and employees to indirectly campaign for pro-government candidates). However, US officials were deeply sceptical of the OAS's capacity to combat the supposed bias of the country's National Electoral Council (Wikileaks 2006b). One document concluded that the lack of OAS criticism of Venezuela's electoral council suggested 'the OAS (was) more concerned about sparking (Chávez's) ire than providing a fully accurate and useful report'. It continued: 'The OAS' feeble performance in this instance must be factored into a decision on whether to support future OAS observation missions in Venezuela' (Wikileaks 2006c). The United States was also critical of the OAS for not addressing Venezuela's alleged attempt to influence elections in Peru, Mexico and Nicaragua.

This contradictory position extended to OAS oversight of elections involving other 'populist' governments/candidates. In Peru, the United States viewed the OAS as playing an important role in the 2006 election, which saw the defeat of Ollanta Humala, the 'pro-Chávez' candidate. At the same time, however, US officials described the observers as 'ineffectual' (Wikileaks 2006d). In Ecuador, the United States supported OAS oversight of the 2006 election with the understanding that monitors would preserve the credibility of the results should Correa lose and then claim fraud (Wikileaks 2006e). A comparable situation emerged in Nicaragua, where the United States robustly supported observation missions to discourage the possibility that Sandinista leader Daniel Ortega would manipulate events in his favour (Wikileaks 2006f). In Ecuador, Bolivia and elsewhere, cables show that the United States assumed authorities were either unwilling or unable to enforce campaign laws. This uncertainty gave increased importance to multilateral efforts to oversee the vote. New organisations like UNASUR would occasionally take on this role, traditionally played by the OAS.

The United States had a similarly mixed relationship with the OAS human rights regime, which grew increasingly contested as new left governments attempted to expand the human rights agenda to include social and economic rights. The Bolivarian governments in particular were suspicious of OAS human rights bodies, which, on occasion, levelled criticisms against the status of civil and political rights in Venezuela, Bolivia, Ecuador and Nicaragua. These tensions came to a head during the 2012 General Assembly meeting, when the ALBA countries called for an overhaul of the Inter-American Human Rights Commission and Inter-American Human Rights Court. They threatened to abandon the OAS system if reforms were not met (Wyss 2012). Although the effort was led by the ALBA bloc, representatives from Brazil, Argentina and Mexico reaffirmed the call to 'modernise' the organisation's human rights bodies. The United States staunchly opposed major changes to the existing system. However, its position was hampered by its long-standing refusal to ratify the American Convention on Human Rights, which established the human rights bodies under question.

In January 2012, the OAS Permanent Council approved a major report on changes to the Inter-American Commission on Human Rights. Among other things, it called for greater universality in the application of its human rights reporting and more explicit consideration of economic, social and cultural rights (Organization of American States 2012). From Washington's perspective, the changes threatened to enfeeble the OAS human rights system rather than strengthen it. As written by one analyst, representatives from Venezuela and Ecuador 'insisted on recommendations opening the door to reducing the transparency and independence of the Commission, as well as burdening it with mandates to monitor new "social" and "economic" rights unrelated to basic freedoms' (Johnson 2012). The United States held to the status quo. On human rights, the OAS simply needed to train its sights on Washington's 'radical' leftist detractors.

American officials adopted a similar approach in the debates over the OAS Social Charter. First introduced in 2005, the Social Charter was a Venezuelan-backed project aimed at advancing the hemispheric agenda on social and economic rights. It was formally adopted by the General Assembly in June 2012, with an action plan approved by the Permanent Council in February 2015. The Charter enjoyed strong support from NLL governments, who sought to use it to shift the politics of inter-American system towards issues of development and social and economic justice. Its drafters viewed it as a 'humanistic model' of development in opposition to neoliberalism (Wikileaks 2005a). Although eventually approved by acclamation, the Social Charter drew the ire of US officials, who consistently sought to steer the project away from its 'Bolivarian' origins and anti-neoliberal posture.

Numerous embassy cables referenced the United States' 'displeasure' and/or 'misgivings' over the Social Charter, which was described variously as 'ideologically driven', 'unacceptable' and 'harmful' (Wikileaks 2005b, 2005c, 2005d). Although the United States eventually offered nominal support to the initiative, the Charter was seen as a distraction from the OAS's traditional work. Perhaps more to the point, US officials were critical of the Charter's socio-economic platform, which ran against the neoliberal view that poverty reduction should be pursued via the private sector rather than state-based programmes. The United States emphasised that member states should not let the process 'become a "feel-good" flow of words . . . whose final product is a series of lofty promises that everyone knows will go unfulfilled'. Rather, the Charter should be grounded in free markets and the existing programmes of the Washington-based IFIs (US Department of State 2005).

Officially, and rhetorically, the strengthening of the OAS human rights regime remained an important objective of US policymakers, one that fuelled broader discussions on reforming the organisation as a whole. This did not mean extending the inter-American human rights system to address those rights based in the economic, social and cultural spheres, however. As Washington contemplated the reconstitution of its institutional power in Latin America, initiatives like the Social Charter became proof the OAS need to be 'pruned'. It also suggested the OAS was, like the region, increasingly independent of the United States.

A left turn in the inter-American system: the OAS and the NLL

Like all inter-governmental organisations, the OAS is an arena of contestation as well as an instrument of co-operation. 'The US government views the OAS as a mechanism for building alliances with Latin American nations, gaining support on critical issues, and exerting leadership in hemispheric affairs.' Meanwhile, 'Latin Americans see the organization, in part, as a means to moderate and contain Washington's power and influence' (Inter-American Dialogue 2006: 6). As the region moved to the left in the 2000s, the left turn spilled over into the internal politics of the OAS. The 2005 election of José Miguel Insulza as the ninth Secretary General signalled the beginning of a new era.

Insulza, a socialist, had served in the Chilean government of Salvador Allende in the early 1970s. He was the preferred candidate of the region's left-leaning governments (including both the 'moderates' and 'radicals'). In the early rounds of voting Insulza came in ahead of Francisco Flores Pérez, former president of El Salvador and the United States' favourite for the position. Washington subsequently shifted its support to another candidate, Luis Ernesto Derbez, Mexico's foreign minister, who was likewise unable to garner enough votes to defeat Insulza. The United States engineered his withdrawal from the race to break an incipient diplomatic stalemate (several countries had remained undeclared in their support, and elections are traditionally by consensus). It was the first time in the

OAS's history that a candidate initially opposed by the United States was elected to lead the organisation (Rohter 2005).

Insulza's victory marked a loss for Washington. Publicly, the Bush administration downplayed its significance. Privately, however, the administration's concerns were palpable. The United States expended considerable diplomatic energy in an attempt to influence the vote. Leaked cables reveal that the State Department had counted on the backing of Caribbean and Central American nations to ensure a victory for Flores (Wikileaks 2005e). Speaking with Undersecretary of State Douglas Feith days after Insulza's election, Colombian President Uribe agreed that it was a setback for the US and Colombian governments, stating: 'We can put the best face on it, but no amount of make-up can disguise that it was a defeat.' Chávez's ability to marshal support for Insulza was particularly worrisome given Venezuela's status as a 'threat to regional stability and to US and Colombian interests', according to Feith (Wikileaks 2005f).

As an affiliate of South America's 'moderate' left, Insulza occupied the middle ground between the 'radical' governments of the Andean region and the United States and its allies. But some officials maintained that Insulza's hesitancy to denounce Chávez showed his true sympathies. Despite several acerbic diplomatic exchanges with the Venezuelan president,[1] Insulza remained cordial with leaders from the ALBA bloc, including Evo Morales and Rafael Correa. For the Bush administration especially, the OAS was 'soft' on Chávez and his 'populist' allies, showing the 'weakness' of the institution. Hector Morales, US Permanent Representative to the OAS, felt Insulza and the OAS were 'unbalanced'. He highlighted the importance of 'improving OAS efficiency and effectiveness' by 'pruning' its mandates. He also insisted that new regional organisations needed to complement the OAS rather than compete with it (Wikileaks 2008a).

Insulza was re-elected in 2010, remaining in the post until 2015. In light of the tensions with Insulza over the coup Honduras and other issues, the State Department flirted with blocking his re-election. However, Secretary Clinton later offered nominal support for Insulza, a shift that came as he was drawing heightened criticism from Republican lawmakers and elements of the US press. The *Washington Post* (2010), for example, called on Obama to replace Insulza, whom it criticised as 'unabashedly cater(ing) to the region's left-wing leaders', which, according to the editorial, 'frequently meant ignoring the democratic charter'. In addition to coddling 'authoritarian leaders' in Venezuela and Nicaragua, the *Post* denounced Insulza 'for the lifting of Cuba's ban from the OAS, even though there (had) been no liberalization of the Castro dictatorship'. With the new left making its presence felt in the halls of the OAS, it was the disputed status of Cuba, the old-left stalwart, which signalled a change of direction in the institution's agenda.

Cuba, the NLL and the OAS

As noted above, the decades-long exclusion of Cuba from the OAS served as an enduring symbol of the organisation's subservience to Washington. In the 2000s, the status of Cuba re-emerged as a 'hot-button' issue within the organisation, one that pitted the United States against the overwhelming majority of the body's membership. The NLL governments transformed the debate over Cuba into one of the signature topics of the OAS-sponsored Summits of the Americas. Disagreements over the status of Cuba came to dominate the General Assembly, crowding out other issues. With new IOs in the making, Cuba's exclusion from the OAS reminded Latin Americans that the institution had frozen in time the privileges and biases of Washington's Cold War security agenda; that it remained, above all, a manifestation of US power.

In the aftermath of the Castro-led Cuban Revolution the United States sought to isolate the country—to restrain its influence and undercut the appeal of the Cuban model. The core feature of this punishing, hard-line approach was an economic embargo, initiated in the early 1960s, that persisted well into the post-Cold War period, even as the original rationale for the policy grew untenable with the collapse of the Soviet Union. In fact, the embargo was tightened and codified into law in the 1996 Cuban Liberty and Democratic Solidarity Act (also called Helms-Burton), pushed through Congress by a well-financed Cuban American lobby desperate to squeeze the communist regime and force it from power. Working through the Cuban American National Foundation (CANF), right-wing activists in the exile community all but 'captured' US policy towards the island, forestalling any and all efforts at implementing a different approach, at least for a time (Haney and Vanderbush 2005). With the death of CANF leader Jorge Mas Canosa in 1997, the lobby slowly began to fracture, even as the Bush administration doubled-down on the embargo, heightening restrictions on travel and commerce. However, the changing demographics of the Cuban American population gradually produced a more moderate form of exile politics. Younger voters and more recent arrivals to the United States were more likely to favour a policy of engagement, including an end to the embargo. This altered the national political context (Florida, home to the majority of Cuban Americans, is the largest 'swing state' in presidential elections), providing an opening for the Obama administration to abandon 'regime change' as the overarching objective of US policy (LeoGrande 2015: 467–80; Lowenthal 2010: 119). Although US Cuba policy was never entirely a domestic issue, it was wrapped up in the ability of a highly organised ethnic constituency to 'punch above its weight' on the national stage.

Obama's decision to normalise diplomatic relations with Cuba, dramatically announced in December 2014, was preceded by efforts to bring Cuba back into the OAS fold. (The embargo would remain in place pending an act of Congress.) In June 2009, the General Assembly passed a resolution nullifying the 1962 act that excluded Cuba from participation in the organisation. However, at the urging of the United States, additional language was included: 'The participation of the Republic of Cuba in the OAS will be the result of a process of dialogue initiated at the request of the Government of Cuba, and in accordance with the practices, purposes, and principles of the OAS' (Organization of American States 2009: 12). Secretary of State Clinton was integral in helping to secure the consensus resolution, which allowed Cuba to reintegrate only *after* it complied with said 'practices, purposes, and principles'. The Obama administration viewed the language as a victory for its diplomacy, and for the OAS (Wikileaks 2009a). Conservatives in Congress viewed the move as a capitulation to the Castro regime.

The consensus resolution highlighted the shifting politics of the inter-American system, even though Cuba's readmission was incomplete. Washington was constantly playing defence on the issue, particularly in the context of the dialogue to transform the Rio Group into CELAC, which includes Cuba but excludes the United States and Canada. US officials were acutely aware that Latin American delegations opposed Cuba's continued exclusion, with representatives calling the policy 'anachronistic', 'callus', 'unjust' and 'violent' (Wikileaks 2009b). During the 2009 General Assembly meetings, for example, 'every speaker except for Canada and the United States voiced their enthusiasm for real hemispheric dialogue and cooperation, which many claimed had been jeopardized by the 1962 resolution' barring Cuba (Wikileaks 2009b). Washington's efforts illustrated the degree to which it continued to value the OAS's role. Moreover, that the Obama administration was able to pre-empt Cuba's unconditional return demonstrated the level of US influence within the institution, even at a time when its traditional leadership of the body was being challenged.

As the United States and Latin America jousted over Cuba's isolation from the OAS, it remained unclear whether the Cuban government wanted readmission, and at what cost. Debate centred on the Inter-American Democratic Charter, which provided the leverage to tie Cuba's eventual return to a form of liberalisation that Washington would recognise as democratic. Havana's participation in the Summit of the Americas was more manageable. The Obama administration's decision to normalise diplomatic ties with Havana was impacted by the pushback that had built up in the Summits process (LeoGrande 2015: 480–3). For instance, by the time of the Sixth Summit of the Americas in Colombia in 2012, several leaders boycotted the meeting over Cuba's exclusion, with others threatening to do so in the future. The impasse meant the Summit concluded, unusually, without a major agreement or formal communiqué. Cuba was invited to the Seventh Summit in Panama in 2015. It was there that Obama and Raúl Castro shook hands during the first meeting between Cuban and American presidents in over fifty years.

Ultimately, the United States could expect to make little headway on revitalising the inter-American system with the Cuba issue festering. However, similar controversies emerged in regards to Venezuela, Cuba's ally. Working through various channels, the State Department routinely used the institution to press its case that the Chávez government was not committed to the Democratic Charter, with limited success. Chávez's domestic politics and regional influence became major focal points of US activity in the OAS during the consolidation of the NLL in the mid- to late 2000s. Meanwhile, Venezuela championed alternatives to the OAS. It would not be alone in this project.

Latin America's new regionalism

Just as its influence within the OAS was challenged by the NLL, the United States' institutional power was also undermined by the emergence of new forums, initiatives and organisations that were constructed without US input, and which largely excluded US participation. While the OAS remained the pre-eminent institution of hemispheric co-operation, its centrality was offset by the creation and utilisation of alternate IOs, fashioned precisely because the OAS had been dominated by US interests (Council on Foreign Relations 2015; Lowenthal 2010: 112; Meyer 2014: 26–7; Riggirozzi *et al.* 2015). This dynamic was particularly acute in the realm(s) of security co-operation and conflict resolution.[2] Because the various forms of power in US hegemony are interlinked, Washington's efforts to reinforce its coercive power, as detailed in Chapter 4, impacted its institutional power in the region, largely in a countervailing way.

For starters, the United States' determination to 'harden' its military posture vis-à-vis Latin America hastened the formation of the South American Defense Council, part of UNASUR (Battaglino 2012). Although it is not a military alliance, the security forum, created in 2009, helped address lingering tensions in the Andean sub-region following the crisis of 2008 (discussed below). Along with Brazil, its chief architect, the Chilean government of Michelle Bachelet also provided key leadership. And although Brazil 'sold' the new forum to the United States as a means of countering the Chávez government, the project came to fruition through support from the Bolivarian bloc. 'A driving force behind the group's formation was a concern with developing a uniquely South American approach in the face of an unattractive US vision based on its impunity for regional affairs', remarked the Council on Hemispheric Affairs (2009).

To an extent, Washington welcomed the formation of the South American Defense Council to work alongside existing multilateral bodies (Wikileaks 2008b). Brazil's leadership of the venture appeared to offer the United States a roundabout way of developing closer military ties with Brasilia. Once the Council became operational, though, Washington did express concerns that it could facilitate 'anti-Americanism' (Wikileaks 2009c). And despite some hints at north–south dialogue, Brazilian officials were clear that, in the words of Nelson Jobim, then Defense Minister, 'there is no possibility of (full) participation by the United States because the council is South American' (Suggett 2008). While occasionally expressing support for the project, then, the US Department of State (2008) was careful to argue that it should not get in the way of 'true' hemispheric co-operation, as represented by the OAS. For their part, military analysts expressed slightly more unease with the prospect of a South American military forum closed to the United States (Cope and Mora 2009: 68; Deare 2009). Furthermore, privately, US officials felt Brazil's argument that the Council could help to 'bring Chávez into the mainstream' was 'impractical' given his support for the project (Wikileaks 2008c). The momentum behind the new forum gathered pace following Colombia's 2008 military attack on insurgents in neighbouring Ecuador, an event that had profound implications for Latin America's new regionalism.

The Andean crisis of 2008

On 1 March 2008, Colombian military forces crossed into a remote jungle area of neighbouring Ecuador to carry out an operation against a guerrilla encampment of the FARC, Colombia's oldest insurgent group. Colombian forces killed twenty-four people in the bombing raid, including a high-level FARC commander. The episode set off a diplomatic crisis, which led the governments of Ecuador, Venezuela and Nicaragua to cut diplomatic ties with Colombia. Ecuadoran President Correa staunchly protested the violation of his country's sovereignty. Chávez dispatched troops to the Venezuelan–Colombian border in support of Correa. President Uribe accused both Chávez and Correa of supporting the FARC, claiming that computer files uncovered in the raid proved that the leftist leaders had financial ties to the insurgent group (Forero 2008). According to one US military analyst, it was 'the worst crisis in Inter-American diplomacy' in a decade (Marcella 2008: v). War between Colombia and its neighbours seemed a distinct possibility.

Just days later, however, the crisis was resolved, and outside of OAS channels. On 7 March, the heads of state of the Rio Group met in the Dominican Republic for an annual summit.[3] The gathering provided an opportunity for the leaders to address Colombia's incursion into Ecuadoran territory and the various claims and counterclaims made by Correa, Chávez and Uribe. The proceedings concluded with dramatic images of the three presidents shaking hands and embracing. The Rio Group (2008) issued a declaration that collectively 'denounce(d) (the) violation of the territorial integrity of Ecuador' while noting, 'with satisfaction, the full apology' offered by President Uribe. The declaration reiterated states' 'respect for sovereignty, abstention from the threat or use of force, and non-interference in the internal affairs of other states', while also committing signees to 'counter threats to the security of all states . . . from the action of irregular groups'. By the end of the summit all parties to the conflict had re-established full diplomatic and commercial ties.

The Bush administration unambiguously supported Colombia's 'right to self-defense' over Ecuador's claims to sovereignty and non-intervention (Marcella 2008: 8). Correa and Chávez argued that the United States had attempted to use the controversy to undermine their respective governments (by linking them to the FARC, a terrorist group under US law). The Bush administration encouraged Colombia and Ecuador to take the incident to the OAS, which convened its permanent council on 4 March. The following day, the OAS issued a declaration reaffirming the principles of territorial integrity and non-intervention, but without textually condemning the raid (US Senate Committee on Foreign Relations 2008). These actions failed to defuse the tensions. As noted above, it took the Rio Group summit to ultimately bring about a resolution. Because Washington was a sponsor of Colombia's counter-insurgency policies, and because the United States has traditionally dominated the OAS, its actions alone were insufficient. That said, the Rio Group declaration did reference Articles 19 and 21 of the OAS Charter (which established non-interventionism as a principle of the inter-American system).

In the weeks following the raid, the United States pushed for an OAS resolution emphasising the need for states to 'take collective action against international terrorism'. The OAS passed another resolution largely mirroring its earlier statement. 'The US joined the consensus that passed the OAS resolution but caveated its vote by inserting a clear reference to the obligation of states not to support international terrorism' (Walser 2008: 6). Washington's language here was a condemnation of Chávez and Correa as much as it was a defence of its Colombian client. A Senate report on the crisis made reference to the potentiality of Venezuela as a 'state sponsor of terrorism', a designation that carries the automatic implementation of targeted economic sanctions. The report recommended the development of security and border-protection plans to prevent the recurrence of crisis (US Senate Committee on Foreign Relations 2008). These were to be developed through the OAS. As an added benefit, the plans would help constrain Venezuela, and in a manner that would avoid overt intervention by the United States. The report concluded:

> It is better for the United States' long term interests in the region to be seen as respectful of the ongoing process established in the OAS, which up to now has been beneficial in defusing tensions. On this occasion, rather than 'speaking softly and carrying a big stick' the better posture for the USG to assume is one of speaking with gentle persuasion, and wise counsel, and letting those 'sticks' that may need to be wielded be ones of a multi-lateral rather than a unilateral nature . . . This does not mean that support for terrorism is accepted, or that US interests should be made vulnerable to the timetable or whims of the collective will of Latin nations.
>
> (US Senate Committee on Foreign Relations 2008: 12)

It is instructive that, in the wake of the attack, Correa proposed the creation of an OAS without the United States (Marcella 2008: 21), presaging the transformation of the Rio Group into CELAC. Meanwhile, the State Department saw the crisis as detrimental to the institutional status quo. Secretary of State Condoleezza Rice commented that 'the easing of tensions stemming from the Rio Group Summit in Santo Domingo came as a surprise to OAS delegations and generated uncertainty as to the OAS role' (Wikileaks 2008d). It was the actions of the Rio Group that put pressure on the OAS to again take up the Colombia–Ecuador dispute after its initial declaration failed to end the hostilities. Officials understood that, for Latin American heads of state, the absence of the United States and Canada from Rio Group meetings made them 'more open and frank than OAS meetings' (Wikileaks 2008e).

The United States was keen for an OAS resolution partly to bolster Colombia's counter-insurgency policy. Washington used the discussion to lean on several countries to 'soften' their criticisms of Colombia's actions (Wikileaks 2008d). Working through the OAS, US representatives pressured their Colombian counterparts to take a tougher stance in defence of their security policies, noting that Washington 'did not agree that Colombia's actions constituted a violation of international law' (Wikileaks 2008d). Although the United States did not block the adoption (by consensus) of an OAS resolution criticising Colombia's incursion, it attached a proviso to the agreement that defended the right to self-defence as established in the OAS charter (Organization of American States 2008). By relying on the institution to protect Uribe's counter-insurgency policy, the Bush administration was able to, in Secretary Rice's words, score a 'clear win' for the United States and Colombia (Wikileaks 2008f).

Overall, the episode demonstrated that, while the OAS remained relevant, its importance in the institutional space had been undermined. This 'dilution' of US institutional power had direct bearing on its ability to use coercive leverage in a 'smarter' way. Increasingly, the hemispheric consensus on international co-operation was being formed via new institutional channels. Outside of the OAS framework, Washington had less capacity to impact regional mediation. The Rio Group cum CELAC excluded US participation, as did the Union of South American Nations (UNASUR, which also excluded Canada, Mexico and the Central American and Caribbean countries on geographic grounds). UNASUR was brand new when, in 2008, the governments of South America used the forum to address an emerging conflict in Bolivia, one that threatened to destabilise the government of Evo Morales.

Political violence in Bolivia: UNASUR takes charge

In September 2008, nineteen peasants were massacred in the department of Pando, Bolivia, with dozens more injured and hundreds forced to flee the area. The incident, which became known as the 'Pando massacre', was one of the most violent episodes in a low-intensity conflict between supporters and opponents of the MAS (Movement towards Socialism) government of Evo Morales, Bolivia's leftist president. The dynamics of the conflict overlaid geographic divisions between the poorer highlands—Morales' support base comprised of an indigenous peasant majority—and the wealthier, lowland departments, which had long controlled Bolivia's lucrative natural gas industry, nationalised by Morales on 1 May 2006. Amidst MAS efforts to rewrite the constitution, the eastern lowlands departments (called the *media luna*, or half-moon, because of their crescent-like shape) had pushed for increased autonomy from the central government, partly to maintain elite control over the region's natural resources (Human Rights Watch 2008). Clashes were not limited to Pando, but occurred elsewhere in the *media luna*. Instigators of the violence were often anti-MAS vigilante groups. It often transpired in the context of peasant activism supportive of the government's land redistribution and nationalisation programmes (Amnesty International 2009).

The Pando massacre came at a fragile time for Morales. He had strengthened his governing position through the 2008 recall referendum, in which he won 67 per cent of the national vote, a greater share than in his initial election in 2005 (53 per cent). Yet he was under duress from the country's well-financed opposition, and the small-scale clashes between his supporters and the separatist elements of the country's elite threatened to erupt into a wider conflagration. Additionally, the opposition had the backing of the United States, which regarded Morales as a radical populist hostile to US interests. La Paz accused the Bush administration of attempting to organise a 'civic coup' against Morales, leading to the ejection of the US ambassador from the country. Embassy documents show that staff met routinely with members of the opposition, leading some analysts to speculate that Washington was orchestrating an extra-legal attempt to remove the democratically elected Morales from power (Burbach 2008).

In the days after the massacre, Michelle Bachelet of Chile called an emergency meeting of UNASUR, a multilateral group comprising twelve South American nations created in May 2008 to function alongside existing regional groups such as Mercosur and the Andean Community of Nations. Bachelet was *pro tempore* president of UNASUR at the time. The resulting 'Declaration of La Moneda' proclaimed the group's full support for the constitutional government of Evo Morales. The heads of state 'energetically rejected' all civic coups and any attempts at the 'rupture of the institutional order that could compromise the territorial integrity of Bolivia' (Bachelet 2008). The organisation also created a commission to investigate the Pando killings. Bolivia's political opposition soon fractured, with some elements returning to the constitutional process. This dialogue was actively supported by UNASUR, leading to a period of relative calm in the country. UNASUR effectively 'put out the fire' in Bolivia (Zibechi 2008). Its management of the conflict, and its support for Morales' democratic mandate, may have prevented the civic coup that La Paz insisted was in the making.

The United States, for its part, condemned the Morales government while remaining all but silent on the issue of opposition violence. Following the expulsion of the US ambassador, and without referencing the UNASUR declaration, the Bush administration announced in September 2008 that it was suspending the Andean Trade Preference Act for Bolivia, ostensibly because, as stated by President Bush, the country had 'failed to cooperate with the United States on important efforts to fight drug trafficking'. The move was detrimental to Bolivia's textiles industry, and was criticised by Bolivian officials as 'discriminatory and political' (Partlow 2008). The Obama administration doubled-down on the decertification of Bolivia's drug control efforts in September 2009. Bilateral ties remained frosty for years, even after the violence in Bolivia dissipated.

There were similarities between the resolution of the conflict in Bolivia and that between Ecuador and Colombia. From Washington's vantage, the ability of South America to manage its own crises (including through the regional leadership of Brazil in forums like UNSAUR) could benefit US objectives. At the same time, these institutions encroached on the role of the OAS. Although the capacities of the newer organisations remained limited, they augmented the region's newfound autonomy (Meyer 2010: 8; Riggirozzi 2012; Riggirozzi *et al.* 2015). This was true despite the fact that they lacked some of the formal mechanisms possessed by the OAS. In the analysis of one Bolivian military officer, it was the 'overbearing relationship' of the United States in the OAS that provided the impetus for the creation of UNASUR (Cordero 2009: 4); its value as a forum for co-operation lay in the fact that it excluded the United States, disabling Washington's ability to play 'spoiler' on issues like the Bolivian conflict. The United States had diminished capacity to steer mediational processes towards outcomes that buttressed its multidimensional hegemony.

In the case of the Pando massacre, US officials were displeased with UNASUR's vindication of the Bolivian government's position. Embassy documents repeatedly placed scare quotes around the word 'massacre', indicating that, for the United States, 'both sides' were to blame for the violent confrontation (in contrast to the prevailing opinion of most observers). Officials saw Morales' use of the UNASUR intervention as a means of criticising the United States for its support of the opposition. Cables noted that Morales found it 'encouraging that "South American countries could solve their own problems", a nod to on-going Morales complaints about undue US influence in the OAS and UN'. The embassy also questioned the impartiality of the UNASUR report. Members of Bolivia's opposition lobbied the US embassy for 'other international institutions to do a separate report'. Ultimately, US officials concluded that 'UNASUR's first foray into member state investigation (was) a supreme disappointment, favoring an Evo lovefest fuelled by political interests instead of honestly trying to deconstruct a complicated violent conflict' (Wikileaks 2008g). They also expressed concerns that the OAS was side-lined, a trend that represented an 'ideological' challenge to the United States. As the embassy in Chile quoted one of its contacts: 'the successful UNASUR summit marked the decline of the OAS, an organization with a US apellido, or last name' (Wikileaks 2008h).

Strengthening the OAS

In US discourse on Latin America, it became commonplace to hear that the OAS was nearing irrelevance (Kerry and Menendez 2010; Riggirozzi *et al.* 2015). As the analysis in this chapter makes clear, however, the rise of the NLL made the OAS more relevant to US hegemony. Even as the OAS seemed to be escaping Washington's grasp, the United States worked through the organisation to pursue its objectives. It allowed the United States to, for example, successfully lobby against Venezuela's 2006 bid for a temporary seat on the UN Security Council and 'exploit Chavez's gaffes' to try and 'drive a wedge between Chavez and the region', in the words of one cable (Wikileaks 2006g). A more streamlined and stronger OAS would entail the reformation of US institutional power at a moment when 'nascent projects, imbued with a range of strategic objectives', were producing the 'partial unravelling of the age-old tug of the US's hegemony in the region' (Tussie 2010: 25).

The Latin American initiatives that emerged in the 2000s were certainly distinct. In general, ALBA was treated with the greatest suspicion. Launched by Chávez to foster economic integration amongst Latin America's anti-neoliberal governments, it was seen as the most precarious (and ideological) of the new bodies, dependent on Venezuelan oil revenue. Publicly, the Bush and Obama administrations downplayed ALBA, partly to deprive Chávez of the rhetorical exchanges that nurtured his anti-imperialist image. However, there was some alarm at ALBA's expansion into 'an increasingly vocal and coordinated grouping that demands attention' (Wikileaks 2010). With CELAC, Washington's concerns were mitigated by the perception that it was rife with divisions and lacking in details. Some, however, saw the creation of a forum so close in membership to the OAS as highly problematic (Kerry and Menendez 2010; Wikileaks 2008i). If CELAC was an uncertainty, UNASUR, another Brazilian-led initiative, was more substantive. To the degree that the United States viewed CELAC and UNASUR as fairly benign, it was due to the complex bilateral relationship with Brazil (Meyer 2010; Sweig 2010), which the United States viewed as both a competitor and a partner.

The Obama years witnessed a partisan divide on the OAS, one that mirrored divisions between the administration and Congress on Cuba. In 2010, Democratic Senators John Kerry and Robert Menendez called for the United States to again 'make the OAS relevant'. The need to improve the organisation was prompted by CELAC, the creation of which, they felt, set off 'alarms bells' (Kerry and Menendez 2010). They introduced a bill calling for the 'increased use' of the OAS as the 'primary multilateral diplomatic entity for regional dispute resolution' (US Senate 2010). Republicans were generally more critical. A report by Senator Richard Lugar highlighted the OAS's financial precariousness while arguing that it had failed to address the erosion of democratic practices. It criticised the leadership of Secretary General Insulza, accusing him of focusing more on politics than on the efficacy of the organisation (US Senate Committee on Foreign Relations 2010).

On the House side, Republican condemnation was more strident, the influential Cuban-American faction holding sway. Florida Representative Ileana Ros-Lethinen, who once openly advocated for the assassination of Fidel Castro (Associated Press 2006), emerged as an especially combative opponent. In July 2011, Connie Mack, Chairman of the Western Hemisphere Subcommittee, introduced a bill that threatened to withhold portions of US funding unless the OAS condemned the constitutional reforms in Venezuela as undemocratic. He argued, 'if the OAS finds that it is unable to make itself effective, there remains no reason for its continued existence' (US House of Representatives 2011). The House Committee on Foreign Affairs subsequently voted along party lines to cut off all US funding for the OAS. The $48.5 million annual contribution represented more than half of the OAS budget. Though the measure had little chance of becoming law, its message was clear. Ahead of the vote, Congressman David Rivera stated bluntly: 'the OAS is an enemy of the US' (Rogin 2011). As congressional debate meshed with the broader policy discourse, criticisms were routinely levelled at Insulza, Cuba and Venezuela, as well as the consensus approach to decision-making within the OAS and its treatment of liberal democracy in general.

For the Obama administration, the OAS was no enemy. Although it had slipped from Washington's grip, Latin America's new regionalism meant a reformed OAS was essential to US objectives in the hemisphere. During her tenure as Secretary of State, Hillary Clinton (2010) called for the urgent financial and political restructuring of the OAS, saying there was 'serious work to be done to bolster the institution'. She criticised the organisation's 'proliferation of mandates'. In stark contrast to initiatives like the Social Charter, the United States would seek to strengthen the targeted application of the Inter-American Democratic Charter. As she pressed for Honduras to be readmitted after the 2009 coup, Clinton called on the OAS to 'consider more precise guidelines for what constitutes an unconstitutional alteration'. For representatives of the NLL, OAS weakness was evident in its muted response to the 2002 coup against Chávez, as well as its inability to achieve ousted Honduran president Zelaya's reinstatement. For the Bush and

Obama administrations, however, the coups were ancillary to the populist, illiberal processes of constitutional reform that preceded them.

The clashing partisan views on the OAS converged on the belief that it needed to be refocused on the solidity of (neo)liberal democracy; on protecting and extending polyarchic governance, as Robinson (1996) would have it. In October 2013, Obama signed into law the 'Organization of American States Revitalization and Reform Act', passed by wide margins in Congress. The bill asserted that the OAS should remain the primary multilateral entity in the region. It outlined a strategy for the State Department to streamline the organisation's agenda (Council on Foreign Relations 2015; Meyer 2014: 25). The legislation directed the OAS to review its core functions (namely dispute resolution and the promotion of democratic governance and institutions) and reduce unrelated mandates. The act suggested a modified fee structure to shore up the organisation's finances. Finally, it stipulated that the OAS work more closely with the Inter-American Development Bank, a proposition that seemed to run against the notion that it needed to do less to be more effective.

To an extent, Washington's reforms dovetailed with ongoing changes in the OAS, which had already begun to reprioritise certain aspects of its work (Meyer 2014: 21–7). Congressional threats and the Obama administration's cajoling likely played a part in this even before the passage of the 2013 legislation. But these changes were not simply imposed by Washington. There is an ideological dimension here which is much more diffuse. Moreover, considering the rules of the OAS, and given the nature of institutional power, the United States cannot force the multilateral body to adhere to its commands. An overly direct and coercive posture would be counterproductive. Instead, it must find or produce a consensus that allows the organisation to continue to play the mediator's role, even as the mechanisms and pathways of this process lead to outcomes in line with the wider renewal of US hegemony.

Conclusion

As the United States works through international institutions to pursue its foreign policy goals, the maintenance of an amenable institutional landscape becomes an objective in and of itself. In the Western hemisphere, the OAS remained critical to US institutional power, which was diminished in two respects: first, within the OAS, as a reflection of the left turn in Latin American politics; and second through the creation of new regional forums that exclude the United States altogether, and which erode the United States' ability to operate via the inter-American system to pursue mediated outcomes in its self-described national interest. The changing institutional terrain clearly impacted on the structural power of the United States as well, as seen in Chapter 3. And as detailed in Chapter 4, Washington's efforts to reconstitute its coercive power in Latin America negatively affected its institutional power in the region, as Latin American states, led by NLL governments, worked to build alternate forums of security co-operation and conflict management. Meanwhile, the OAS was used by the United States to expose, and challenge, 'populist' governance on the part of 'radical' leftist governments. The ideological manifestation of US power is further analysed in Chapter 6. As the preceding analysis illustrates, US institutional power was, and is, bound up with other forms of power in the international relations of the Western hemisphere. The inter-locking character of the various forms of hegemonic power comes into greater focus.

Constructed at the behest of the United States, the OAS has dutifully served US hegemony since the early Cold War. By of the end of the 2000s, however, the OAS shared the institutional space with several rival projects. Spurred by NLL governments in Brazil and Venezuela, initiatives such as CELAC and UNASUR bridged ideological divisions in the region, while ALBA helped to co-ordinate the foreign and economic policies of those countries most directly at odds with US hegemony. Although these organisations were but new competitors to the OAS, their emergence stimulated discussions in Washington on the utility of the more established inter-American system. The need to strengthen the OAS was realised once it had escaped US 'control' and was beset with competition from newer multilateral institutions constructed without US input. The United States sought to protect the centrality of the OAS to inter-state co-operation while reinforcing the OAS's commitment to polyarchic democracy, all while attempting to reassert greater influence over the organisation itself. As an established institution, the OAS helped the United States co-ordinate its diplomatic response to the region's new left. However, the reformation of the United States' institutional power in the Americas remains, like US hegemony, an open-ended prospect, realisable but contested.

Notes

1 Insulza's first major row with Chávez occurred in 2007, when the Venezuelan government revoked the broadcast licence of a television station partial to the anti-Chávez opposition. The OAS strongly condemned the move. Spats between Chávez and Insulza occurred again in 2010 and 2011 over human rights issues, leading Chávez to denounce OAS interference in Venezuela.
2 Following 9/11, the United States used the OAS to advance its security agenda in the region. However, the US global security agenda diverged from dominant concerns in Latin America, which tended to focus more on criminal violence than international terrorism. Additionally, many Latin American countries were critical of the Bush administration's foreign policy in the War on Terror, and this impacted regional perceptions of the OAS (Inter-American Dialogue 2006: 17–19).
3 The Rio Group, not to be confused with the Rio treaty, was created in 1986. Its membership was eventually extended to include twenty-four Latin American and Caribbean countries. It did not develop a secretariat, and, considering its wide membership, remained a relatively minor player within Western hemispheric affairs. In contrast to CELAC, which grew out of the Rio Group forum, the latter advocated the strengthening of the OAS (Atkins 1999: 195–6).

References

Amnesty International (2009). 'Bolivia: Victims of the Pando Massacre Still Await Justice', 9 September. Available online at www.amnesty.org/en/press-releases/2009/09/bolivia-victims-pando-massacre-still-await-justice-20090909/ (accessed 20 January 2016).

Associated Press (2006). 'Lawmaker Admits Call for Castro's Assassination', 24 December. Available online at www.washingtonpost.com/wp-dyn/content/article/2006/12/23/AR2006122300850.html (accessed 31 January 2016).

Atkins, G. P. (1999). *Latin American and the Caribbean in the International System*, fourth edition, Boulder: Westview Press.

Bachelet, M. (2008). 'Presidencia Pro-Tempore de UNASUR, S.E. Presidenta de La República de Chile, Informe de la Comisión de UNASUR sobre los Sucesos de Pando: hacia un alba de justicia para Bolivia', November.

Barnett, M. and R. Duvall (2005). 'Power in Global Governance', in *Power in Global Governance*, edited by M. Barnett and R. Duvall, Cambridge: Cambridge University Press: 1–32.

Battaglino, J. (2012). 'Defence in a Post-Hegemonic Regional Agenda: The Case of the South American Defence Council', in *The Rise of Post-Hegemonic Regionalism: The Case of Latin America*, edited by P. Riggirozzi and D. Tussie, New York: Springer: 81–100.

Burbach, R. (2008). 'The United States: Orchestrating a Civic Coup in Bolivia', Transnational Institute, 18 November. Available online at www.tni.org/en/archives/act/18943 (accessed 20 January 2016).

Clinton, H. R. (2010). 'Address to the Organization of American States General Assembly', 7 June. Available online at www.state.gov/secretary/rm/2010/06/142804.htm (accessed 13 July 2013).

Cope, J. A. and F. O. Mora (2009). 'Hemispheric Security: A New Approach', *Current History*, 108(715): 65–71.

Cordero, O. (2009). 'UNASUR and its Future Impact on the Americas', US Army War College.

Council on Foreign Relations (2015). 'The Organization of American States', 19 April. Available online at www.cfr.org/latin-america-and-the-caribbean/organization-american-states/p27945 (accessed 12 January 2016).

Council on Hemispheric Affairs (2009). 'The Paradox of South American Integration: The Founding of a Defense Council', 12 March. Available online at www.coha.org/the-paradox-of-south-american-integration-the-founding-of-a-defense-council/ (accessed 12 January 2016).

Deare, C. A. (2009). 'Time to Improve US Defense Structure for the Western Hemisphere', *Joint Forces Quarterly*, 53(2): 35–6.

Forero, J. (2008). 'Latin American Crisis Resolved: Colombia Apologizes at Regional Summit', *Washington Post*, 8 March: A09.

Guevara, E. (1964). 'Colonialism is Doomed', Che Guevara Internet Archive. Available online at www.marxists.org/archive/guevara/1964/12/11-alt.htm (accessed 12 January 2016).

Haney, P. and W. Vanderbush (2005). *The Cuban Embargo: Domestic Politics of American Foreign Policy*, Pittsburgh: University of Pittsburgh Press.

Human Rights Watch (2008). 'Bolivia: Investigate Killings in Pando', 16 September. Available online at www.hrw.org/news/2008/09/16/bolivia-investigate-killings-pando (accessed 20 January 2016).

Hurrell, A. (2005). 'Power, Institutions, and the Production of Inequality', in *Power in Global Governance*, edited by M. Barnett and R. Duvall, Cambridge: Cambridge University Press: 33–58.

Inter-American Dialogue (2006). 'Responding to the Hemisphere's Challenges', Task Force on the Organization of American States, June.

Johnson, S. (2012). 'Time to Rethink the OAS?' Center for Strategic and International Studies, 8 June. Available online at https://csis.org/blog/time-rethink-oas (accessed 23 January 2016).

Kerry, J. and R. Menendez (2010). 'Make the OAS Relevant', *Miami Herald*, 17 March. Available online at www.americasquarterly.org/node/1380 (accessed 24 January 2016).

LeoGrande, W. M. (2015). 'Normalizing US–Cuba Relations: Escaping the Shackles of the Past', *International Affairs*, 91(3): 473–88.

Lowenthal, A. F. (2010). 'Obama and the Americas', *Foreign Affairs*, 89(4): 110–24.

Mann, M. (1986). *The Sources of Social Power Volume 1: A History of Power from the Beginning to A.D. 1760*, Cambridge: Cambridge University Press.

Mann, M. (2012). *The Sources of Social Power Volume 3: Global Empires and Revolution*, Cambridge: Cambridge University Press.

Marcella, G. (2008). 'War without Borders: The Colombia-Ecuador Crisis of 2008', US Strategic Studies Institute, December.

Meyer, P. J. (2010). 'Brazil-US Relations', Congressional Research Service, 5 March.

Meyer, P. J. (2014). 'Organization of American States: Background and Issues for Congress', Congressional Research Service, 29 August.

Organization of American States (2008). 'Resolution of the Twenty-Fifth Meeting of Consultation of Ministers of Foreign Affairs', 17 March.

Organization of American States (2009). General Assembly, Thirty-Ninth Regular Session, Proceedings, Volume 1, 'Resolution on Cuba', June.

Organization of American States (2012). 'OAS Permanent Council Approved the Report of the Working Group to Strengthening the Inter-American Human Rights System', 25 January. Available online at www.oas.org/en/media_center/press_release.asp?s Codigo=E-018/12 (accessed 23 January 2016).

Organization of American States (2016). Homepage. Available online at www.oas.org/ (accessed 12 January 2016).

Partlow, J. (2008). 'US Trade Move Shakes Bolivia', *Washington Post*, 19 October. Available online at www.washingtonpost.com/wp-dyn/content/article/2008/10/18/ AR2008101801883.html (accessed 20 January 2016).

Reuters (2009). 'Castro says Cuba Doesn't Want to Rejoin "Vile" OAS', 15 April. Available online at http://uk.reuters.com/article/2009/04/15/us-cuba-castro-oas-sb-idUKTRE53E07K20090415/ (accessed 12 January 2016).

Riggirozzi, P. (2012). 'Region, Regionness and Regionalism in Latin America: Towards a New Synthesis', *New Political Economy*, 17(4): 421–43.

Riggirozzi, P., A. F. Cooper, R. P. Montalbán, J. Byron and O. Stuenkel (2015). 'Re-Thinking the OAS: A Forum', *Americas Quarterly*, Winter. Available online at www.americasquarterly.org/content/re-thinking-oas-forum (accessed 28 January 2016).

Rio Group (2008). 'Declaration of the Heads of State and Government of the Rio Group on the Recent Events between Ecuador and Colombia', 7 March.

Robinson, W. I. (1996). *Promoting Polyarchy: Globalization, US Intervention, and Hegemony*, Cambridge: Cambridge University Press.

Rogin, J. (2011). 'House Panel Votes to Defund the OAS', *Foreign Policy*, 20 July. Available online at http://thecable.foreignpolicy.com/posts/2011/07/20/house_panel_ votes_to_defund_the_oas (accessed 25 January 2016).

Rohter, L. (2005). 'OAS to Pick Chile Socialist US Opposed as its Leader', *The New York Times*, 30 April. Available online at http://query.nytimes.com/gst/fullpage.html?res=9 D0CE6DF1E31F933A05757C0A9639C8B63 (accessed 12 January 2016).

Shaw, C. M. (2004). *Cooperation, Conflict, and Consensus in the Organization of American States*, New York: Palgrave Macmillan.

Suggett, J. (2008). 'Venezuela and Brazil Advance on South American Defense Council', Venezuela Analysis, 15 April. Available online at http://venezuelanalysis.com/news/3361 (accessed 12 January 2016).

Sweig, J. E. (2010). 'A New Global Player: Brazil's Far-Flung Agenda', *Foreign Affairs*, 89(6): 173–84.

Tussie, D. (2010). 'Hemispheric Relations: Budding Contests in the Dawn of a New Era', in *Inter-American Cooperation at a Crossroads*, edited by G. Mace, A. F. Cooper and T. M. Shaw, New York: Palgrave Macmillan: 23–42.

US Department of State (2005). 'Remarks on Hurricane Katrina and the Social Charter of the Americas: Ambassador John F. Maisto, US Permanent Representative to the Organization of American States', 1 September. Available online at http://2001-2009.state.gov/p/wha/rls/rm/2005/53049.htm (accessed 24 January 2016).

US Department of State (2008). 'Secretary of State Rice: Remarks with Brazilian Foreign Minister Celso Amorim', 13 March. Available online at http://2001-2009.state.gov/secretary/rm/2008/03/102228.htm (accessed 13 July 2013).

US House of Representatives (2011). Opening Statement, Chairman Connie Mack, Western Hemisphere Subcommittee, Markup on H.R. 3401 and H.R. 2542, 15 December.

US Senate (2010). 111th Congress, 2nd Session, S. 3087, 8 March.

US Senate Committee on Foreign Relations (2008). 'Playing with Fire: Colombia, Ecuador, and Venezuela', 28 April.

US Senate Committee on Foreign Relations (2010). 'Multilateralism in the Americas: Let's Start by Fixing the OAS', 26 January.

Walser, R. (2008). 'The Crisis in the Andes: Ecuador, Colombia, and Venezuela', Heritage Foundation, 2 May.

Washington Post (2010). 'Mr. Obama Should Press for Change at the OAS', 10 February: A16.

Wikileaks (2005a). 'Venezuelan Embassy's Seminar on the Social Charter of the Americas', 21 June. Reference ID: 05LIMA2751.

Wikileaks (2005b). 'Canada: Response to Demarche on OAS Social Charter', 18 February. Reference ID: 05OTTAWA537.

Wikileaks (2005c). 'Honduras Demarche on Chavez Social Charter Event; GOH to be Represented by OAS Permrep', 26 August. Reference ID: 05TEGUCILGALPA1776.

Wikileaks (2005d). 'Canadian Views on Chavez and the Social Charter', 2 September. Reference ID: 05OTTAWA2650.

Wikileaks (2005e). 'OAS SYG: GOH Believes Derbez and Insulza have Solid CARICOM Support, but USG Can Still Sway Outcome', 31 March. Reference ID: 05TEGUCIGALPA697.

Wikileaks (2005f). 'Under Secretary Feith Meets with President Uribe', 10 May. Reference ID: 05BOGOTA4360.

Wikileaks (2006a). 'Venezuelan Elections Wrap Up: Observers Endorse Results', 8 December. Reference ID: 06CARACAS3571.

Wikileaks (2006b). 'Venezuelan Elections: Issues for Future International Observers to Watch', 11 December. Reference ID: 06CARACAS3598.

Wikileaks (2006c). 'OAS EOM Final Report on Venezuela Elections—Weaker Still', 8 May. Reference ID: 06CARACAS1231.

Wikileaks (2006d). 'Embassy's Assessment of OAS Monitoring of Peruvian Elections', 24 April. Reference ID: 06LIMA1549.

Wikileaks (2006e). 'Elections: Dead Heat after Correa Surge', 15 November. Reference ID: 06QUITO2808.

Wikileaks (2006f). 'OAS Mission Leader: Political Stakes Much Higher in November National Election', 13 March. Reference ID: 06MANAGUA565.

Wikileaks (2006g). 'Is Chavez Losing It?' 3 May. Reference ID: 06CARACAS1169.

Wikileaks (2008a). 'Exchanging Views on the OAS and the Summit of the Americas with Canada', 1 August. Reference ID: 08OTTAWA1028.

Wikileaks (2008b). 'Thoughts on the Visit of the Defense Minister Jobim to Washington', 31 March. Reference ID: 08BRASILIA429.

Wikileaks (2008c). 'Ambassador's Meeting with Minister of Defense Jobim', 20 February. Reference ID: 08BRASILIA236.

Wikileaks (2008d). 'Colombia-Ecuador Dispute: OAS Resolution 930', 12 March. Reference ID: 08STATE25971.

Wikileaks (2008e). 'FM Morales and OAS Rep on Rio Group, OAS Ministerial, HR Report', 13 March. Reference ID: 08SANTODOMINGO373.

Wikileaks (2008f). '38th OAS General Assembly: Colombia Scores a Win', 16 June. Reference ID: 08STATE64684.

Wikileaks (2008g). 'UNASUR Endorses Evo's Version of Pando "Massacre"', 5 December. Reference ID: 08LAPAZ2543.

Wikileaks (2008h). 'Chileans Generally Upbeat on UNASUR Outcome', 18 September. Reference ID: 08SANTIAGO853.

Wikileaks (2008i). 'Brazil's Latin America/Caribbean Summit: Concentric Circles or Circling the Wagons?' 1 October. Reference ID: 08BRASILIA1301.

Wikileaks (2009a). 'OAS General Assembly: US Diplomacy Prevails on Cuba', 15 June. Reference ID: 09STATE61676

Wikileaks (2009b). '2009 OAS General Assembly Wrap-up Report', 23 June. Reference ID: 09STATE64971.

Wikileaks (2009c). 'Ecuador's UNASUR Agenda: An Anti-American Tone?' 7 August. Reference ID: 09QUITO703.

Wikileaks (2010). 'Ortega and the US: New-found True Love or Another Still-born Charm Offensive', 25 February. Reference ID: 10MANAGUA115.

Wyss, J. (2012). 'OAS Rights Body Slammed at Annual Meeting', *Miami Herald*, 5 June. Available online at www.miamiherald.com/2012/06/05/v-print/2834901/oas-rights-body-slammed-at-annual.html (accessed 13 July 2013).

Zibechi, R. (2008). 'UNASUR Puts Out its First Fire in Bolivia: Brazil Makes the Difference', Center for International Policy, 5 December. Available online at www.cipamericas.org/archives/1584 (accessed 20 January 2016).

6 Reinscribing 'populism'

US ideological power and the 'radical' left

References to populism are sprinkled throughout this book. As seen in Chapter 3, opposition to US-backed 'free trade' is portrayed as populist. Chapter 4 addresses how Washington perceives populism as a threat to its coercive power. And, as alluded to in the previous chapter, populism is understood as undermining the liberal democratic values codified in the OAS. Indeed, for some observers, it was populism itself that best explained the rise of Latin America's new left (Edwards 2010; Reid 2007). However, 'populism' is not an objective condition. It is a discursive construct, one that takes on different meanings in different contexts. Through a discourse analysis of speeches and official documents and texts, this chapter examines the populist construct in relation to US ideological power. As the analysis demonstrates, the depiction of (some) NLL agents as 'populists' facilitates the renewal of US hegemony by affixing certain meanings to the region's anti-neoliberal, counter-hegemonic governments. The construction of 'populism' represents a move to recoup the power lost amidst the ascendency of 'nationalist', 'leftist', 'socialist', 'Bolivarian', 'pan-Latin American' and 'anti-imperialist' ideas and values.

The focus on discourse is closely related to what Barnett and Duvall term 'productive power', which works through diffuse and constitutive social processes 'that are effected only through the meaningful practices of actors'. This involves 'the discursive production of the subjects, the fixing of meanings, and the terms of action, of world politics' (2005: 20–1). Productive power runs through those phenomena that produce identities, ideas and knowledge. Barnett and Duvall define discourses as 'the social processes and the systems of knowledge through which meaning is produced, fixed, lived, experienced, and transformed' (2005: 20). Like structural power, this involves the constitution of subjects (and, in the case of productive power, [inter-]subjectivity). Transformation is possible, and important, because agents play an active role in inter-subjective processes of identity formation and the production of meaning in social relations. Along these lines, the United States has been discursively imbued with an identity that naturalises its hegemony, an identity it has helped to construct via its foreign policy (Campbell 1992; Hunt 2009 [1987]; Schoultz 1998; Weldes 1999).

This type of power is ideological because it legitimates the actions of more powerful actors—those with the greater capacity to shape the meanings embedded in discursive and representational practices in a plurality of settings/contexts. But, as noted by Michael Mann (1986: 23), though ideologies always play a role in legitimating material interests, they do more than that. Ideology cannot be reduced to the raw manipulation of weaker actors by their dominant superiors. Ideological power, for Mann, is more diffuse. It is involves the search for, and creation of, meaning; the influence of shared norms and values; and the ritualised and aestheticised practices of social interaction (2012: 6–7). This broadly cultural conceptualisation resonates with Gramscian theory and its emphasis on (contested) 'common sense' and the construction of hegemonic consensus. It also dovetails with Barnett and Duvall's notion of productive power. Just as Mann's wider project places ideological power alongside other, more 'material' forms of power, this chapter utilises an understanding of discursive power that differs from post-structuralist accounts.

My discourse analytic approach is pluralistic. It blends interpretivist techniques with the theoretical commitments of Norman Fairclough's critical discourse analysis, which holds that texts should be studied in relation to extra-discursive structures (1992: 60; 2003: 2–15). In interpretivist fashion, Milliken's notion of predicate analysis highlights the use of binaries and the definitional language practices of privileged actors. 'Predications of a noun construct the thing(s) named as a particular sort of thing, with particular features and capacities' (Milliken 1999: 232). This focus on construction is central to the studies of David Campbell (1992) and Jutta Weldes (1999). I also draw on the methodological intervention of Lene Hansen,[1] who points to the compatibility of different forms of textual and discourse analysis (2006: xviii), and who, like Milliken, Campbell and Weldes, explores the constitutive power of representations. I argue that the word 'populist' conveys certain meanings for those actors inscribed with the label; it *represents* them in a certain way. That said, 'not all representations are equally lasting', not all discourses are equally fluid and 'meaning and materiality must be studied together' (Neumann 2008: 73–4). The construction of 'populism' does not take place in a 'discursive echo chamber', in which 'discourses constitute other discourses that in turn constitute other discourses and so on without any relationship to other social structures or indeed to any notion of political economy or national interests' (Stokes 2009: 89). Given the realist ontology of this project, it is important to emphasise that ideological power is interlinked with other forms of power in US hegemony.

I therefore adopt a 'thin' conceptualisation of discourse to focus primarily on the instrumentalist use of language within US foreign policy. Discourse here is largely rhetorical. The depiction of certain Latin American governments as 'populist' is (partly) an attempt to undermine the counter-hegemonic project they represent. The populist construct facilitated Washington's distinction between the 'good left' and the 'bad left' in Latin America; it animated the division between the 'responsible', forward-looking centre-left governments in Brazil and Chile from 'dangerous' states implementing 'anachronistic' economic policies, such as Venezuela, Bolivia and Ecuador (Castañeda 2006). And if 'populism' was a means by which policymakers in Washington made sense of the NLL, it also worked to delegitimise certain governments. Ideologically, in condemning those who self-identify as 'Bolivarians' or socialists, the populist construct legitimated the renewal of US power in structural, coercive and institutional settings. It also shaped the interests of US policy, which was moved to thwart to the proliferation of populist governance.

The first section of this chapter outlines the meanings embedded in the wider discourse on populism by sketching the two dominant approaches to the concept in the academic literature. I start with the view that populism—a notoriously vague concept—is best seen as a discourse that constitutes 'the people' as a unitary actor. I then look at how the meanings of populism have been impacted by the history of the 'populist model' in Latin America. The subsequent section uses discourse analytic techniques to gauge the meanings of populism in US discourse on the NLL. I examine the metaphor of the 'pied pipers of populism' in the Bush administration's trade policy. I then turn to two competing collocations (frequent conjunctions of words) in US discourse: 'radical populism' and 'false populism', teasing out the inconsistencies in their application to NLL leaders. Finally, I examine the parameters of the populist construct by looking at the silences in the discourse; that is, cases in which it was not applied (with regards to Colombia's Uribe, for example). The analysis aims to relate ideological power to the other forms of power in the renewal of US hegemony, which has been challenged by the nationalist and anti-imperialist discourses of the region's 'radical' left.

Populism in the Latin American context

The creative capacity of US ideological power does not generate meaning 'out of thin air'. Established knowledge of 'populism' provides the ideational resources from which the contemporary discourse on the NLL is constructed. To an extent, these meanings are conditioned by the extra-discursive phenomena surrounding the populist 'model'. In Latin America, the expression of 'populism' is wrapped up in nationalist, anti-imperialist and Bolivarian ideas, which, as noted in previous chapters, challenge the coercive and institutional power of the United States in the region. Moreover, the 'populist' tag is applied almost exclusively to the anti-neoliberal faction of the NLL. This has implications for structural power in the political economy of the Western hemisphere, as left-leaning governments are dissuaded from pursuing 'statist' alternatives to US-backed 'free trade'.

In its various guises, populism is rooted in the cultures and societies that produce it. There is a large body of literature on populism in Latin America, much of which tackles populist movements, governments and leaders in specific national settings. This section reviews the two dominant strands of the literature on populism: one which conceptualises it as a particular discursive style; and another which sees it as a model of political-economic organisation. Though there are some tensions between the discourse-driven and historicist strands of the literature, they are not irreconcilable. In fact, they reinforce one another, and most analyses of populism account for elements of both; some studies even make explicit reference to the relationship between the discursive and extra-discursive 'faces' of populism (Cammack 2000). Importantly for this chapter, broad under-standings of the concept influence US discourse on the NLL, which utilises 'populism' as a convenient epithet. The representation of certain states or leaders as 'populist' is deeply normative, but it stems from the concept's significance as an analytical attribution. For instance, populism becomes 'undemocratic' because it runs counter to Washington's equation of democracy with polyarchy—'thin', elite-led democracy conducive to processes of socio-economic neoliberalisation (Robinson 1996).

The discursive approach to populism

The discursive construction of populism in US foreign policy is enabled by the looseness of the concept. Populism is a notoriously vague term, yet it has been widely used in the Latin American context since the 1930s. Although concerns over populism have grown more prominent in US policy, populism itself is hardly new. However poorly understood, populism provides policymakers with a way of internalising the complex phenomena associated with the collapse of the Washington Consensus. To quote Álvaro García Linera, vice-president of Bolivia under Evo Morales, 'populism is a bag into which they put everything they do not understand' (Hawkins 2010: 50). It is a useful heuristic, and more. In Washington's approach to the region, populism is viewed as inimical to liberal democracy, a deviation from responsible economic policymaking and a threat to US interests and security. Of course, these qualities are far from self-evident when we consider the literature on the concept, which highlights its deeply contested status (Canovan 1999; Taggart 2000).

Ernesto Laclau writes that 'a persistent feature of the literature on populism is its reluctance—or difficulty—in giving the concept any precise meaning' (2005: 3). For Laclau, populism is virtually synonymous with politics itself. In his theoris-ing, populism denotes a mode of articulation that constitutes 'the people' as such. It is the discourse of populism that allows this subject to make demands on an enemy—the 'other' that is also discursively constructed through Laclau's logic of equivalence/difference (2005: 77–93). Similarly, Panizza highlights the modes of identification and the processes of naming that allow for the emergence of populism as a dimension of politics. He contends that 'while there is no scholarly agreement on the meaning of populism, it is possible to identify an analytical core around which there is a significant degree of academic consensus' (Panizza 2005: 1). This core is comprised of the identification of 'the people' as a sovereign, unitary actor in an antagonistic relationship with a powerful 'other'—the oligarchy, the elite or a foreign power (Canovan 1999; Laclau 2005; Panizza 2005: 4). In this view, populism is fundamentally *discursive*. Carlos de la Torre, for example, defines populism as 'a style of political mobilization based on strong rhetorical appeals to the people and crowd action on behalf of a leader' (2000: 4).

Populism is unique in that, 'unlike other equally contested concepts, such as democracy, it has become an analytical attribution rather than a term with which most political actors would willingly identify' (Panizza 2005: 1). With few exceptions, leaders and political parties avoid association with the term, making it largely objectionable from a normative standpoint. Much of this has to do with the insinuation that the populist model is top-down, anachronistic and autocratic. 'In Latin America', writes de la Torre (2000: ix), 'populism is generally viewed in negative terms. For most it implies an abnormality, an anomaly, and a passing phenomenon that will eventually, and hopefully, go away . . . Populism is also associated with leaders who manipulate, followers who are betrayed, and overall backwardness'. Cammack notes that the conventional view on Latin American populism 'feeds off a literature critical of the dangers of forms of mass politics in which unscrupulous demagogues stimulate mob rule' (2000: 149). Charismatic leaders are thus closely associated with the concept, particularly in Latin America, where it overlaps the image of the *caudillo*, or strongman.

In general, populism is ambiguous in terms of the left–right scale. It denotes a kind of demagogic agitation in right-wing criticism, while, for the left, it implies the subornation of socialist struggle to base-level prejudices and habits, as displayed in some fascist movements (Williams 1983 [1976]: 238). In Latin America, populism has generally been associated with the left, as sketched out below. Insofar as it represents a discursive style, however, there is no reason why this should automatically be the case. Moreover, there is disagreement about the degree to which populism is compatible with liberal democracy. Despite its uneasy relationship with liberalism, populism need not be undemocratic (Arditi 2007; Canovan 1999). Even if the dynamics of populist mobilisation culminate in the leadership of a charismatic figurehead who skirts the protocols of established institutions, populism is more appropriately viewed as a mode of democratic politics than an alternative to it. Also important is the sense of conflict that derives from the antagonism between the different poles of the socio-political hierarchy (the people versus the oligarchy), which, in Latin America at least, has given the impression of populism as something born out of crisis. In this vein, populism can offer the promise of compromise—between unruly masses and the established order; or between revolutionary movements and the reactionary forces of the status quo. The ambiguity of 'the people' is key here, as it can take on different meanings at different points in time.

Indeed, the precise purpose of the appeal to 'the people' that constitutes the 'populist moment' unfolds in the context of structural changes in capitalist society (Cammack 2000: 152). Even a discursive approach to populism (such as that employed in this chapter) must contend with its relationship to the material/extra-discursive realm. As outlined below, the 'model' of Latin American populism shifted with wider political and economic trends, as the purpose of the populist appeal seesawed from developmentalist to neoliberal and then anti-neoliberal. This impacts US ideological power because Washington's discourse *on* populism (i.e. debates over which leaders or governments are populists) is contingent on discourses *of* populism in the region (antagonistic rhetoric deployed by Latin American leaders against the oligarchy, elites or foreign powers). These discourses are themselves conditioned by structural shifts and the actions of other agents. Along these lines, NLL leaders in Latin America have frequently targeted the United States as an enemy of 'the people'. As discussed in Chapter 1, Chávez, Morales, Correa and Ortega made anti-*Yanqui* and/or anti-imperialist appeals a major part of their campaigns. In this manner, 'populist', anti-neoliberal politicians problematised the common sense acceptance of US 'leadership', with implications for the power of the hegemon across various dimensions of inter-American relations.

The historical dynamics of the populist model in Latin America

The focus on the discursive aspects of populism by the likes of Laclau and Panizza contrasts with a historicist literature that views populism as a distinct configuration of politico-economic forces that emerge at a particular stage in the modernisation process. From this vantage, populism is a model of political economy that involves a multiclass alliance in support of state-directed economic development (Dornbusch and Edwards 1990; Hennessy 1969). This arrangement is held together by a strong executive, often headed by a charismatic leader who cultivates direct ties with his/her constituents; even in this strand of the literature 'populist' leaders were often defined by their rhetorical appeals to 'the people'. Latin American populism was traditionally viewed in relation to the region's mid-twentieth century industrialisation process. However, this depiction of populism was undermined by the neoliberalisation of the region beginning in the 1970s, which, as it gained momentum in the 1980s and 1990s, accommodated populist political strategies (Demmers *et al.* 2001). The 'metamorphoses' of Latin American populism during and after the Cold War called into question its conceptualisation as a singular model of 'statist' economic development.

From the Great Depression through the early Cold War, Latin American populism was associated with the reformist, non-communist left. It was epitomised by a select group of influential, independent and nationalistic leaders, with Argentina's Juan Perón the paradigmatic example. Due to the conceptual leeway provided by its vagueness, however, it has been used to designate a diverse set of regimes, movements and individuals, from Mexico's PRI (*Partido Revolucionario Institucional*) and Peru's APRA (*Alianza Popular Revolucionaria Americana*) to the governments of Panama's Omar Torrijos and Cuba's Fidel Castro, among others. The origins of the populist model are often traced to the 1930s–1960s era, which saw widespread migration from the countryside to the cities. Featuring distinct urban and rural configurations, the model was, on the whole, mass-based and multiclass, mobilising not only industrial workers and marginalised city-dwellers but large swaths of the peasantry as well. Classical populism would come to be associated with import substitution industrialisation. In describing the governments of Perón and Brazil's Getúlio Vargas, Hennessy wrote that, 'in general, they (were) neo-socialist but emphasizing redistribution of wealth rather than increasing productive capacity. Salvation can only come from the state, which must protect national industries against foreign competition by protective tariffs, by nationalizing strategic foreign-owned companies and by stringent profit-remittance legislation' (Hennessy 1969: 29). By targeting foreign economic influence, expressions of classical populism in Latin America challenged US power in the region. This was manifest in the 'anti-Americanism' of leaders like Perón.

Originally, the economic component of Latin American populism was as important as its political face. 'The "old populism" of the post-war era emerged as a reaction to the failure of liberal political institutions and economic policies evident in the depression of the 1930s and the events that followed', fostering a 'state-centred matrix of economic development' that was interventionist and redistributive (Panizza 2000: 145–7). Populism, in this view, was a means of constructing a kind of 'embedded liberalism'. The model was corporatist and featured the clientelistic dynamics of patronage politics. There was also a cultural element. Hennessy (1969) pointed to the personalist relationships intrinsic to the region's industrialising economy. Moreover, the success of the populist leadership style, he felt, was facilitated by the prevailing Catholicism of Latin American countries, which reinforced a *caudillo* ethos in secular society. A more common cultural understanding of the 'golden age' of populism focused on the nationalistic and anti-oligarchic language of populist movements and their ability to articulate an anti-establishment message to unite emergent blocs against the traditional land-owning elite.

The classical populism of Latin America gave way in the 1980s and 1990s to a neoliberal variant. Populist discourse was articulated in the service of a more market-oriented and globalised capitalism (Cammack 2000: 156–9; Demmers *et al.* 2001). This trend was driven by the socio-political necessities of the neoliberal turn in economic policy as much as the personal predilections of those leaders that defined this shift—a group that included Carlos Menem in Argentina, Fernando Collor de Mello in Brazil and Alberto Fujimori in Peru. In other words, the practicalities of implementing a policy agenda that was opposed by the bulk of the so-called 'popular classes' (peasants and workers) required a strong executive able to use personalised appeals for change to counteract the vested interests of the developmentalist state. This represented a major departure from the embedded liberalism of the classical model.

For example, in examining the case of Peru's Fujimori, who employed traditional populist rhetoric before implementing a neoliberal structural adjustment scheme, Roberts concluded that populism could be reconciled with its 'putative antithesis, neoliberalism' (1995: 83). Contrary to widely held assumptions at the time, Fujimori's government showed that a personalistic and top-down regime with an eclectic ideology and multiclass backing could pursue clientelistic economic policies in the service of a broader neoliberalisation project. Weyland's analysis corroborated this account (2003), highlighting the ways in which appeals to the informal sector and a targeting of the political class as the new enemy factored into the emergence of what he dubbed 'neoliberal neopopulism'. There was an anti-organisational strain of populism that made it conducive to what Tickell and Peck dubbed the 'roll-back' phase of neoliberalism (2003: 169). Paradoxically, populism was used to dislodge the model of embedded liberalism it had helped to propagate. The ascendant 'neopopulism', as Weyland put it, would actively 'protect the market from interference by special interests and rent-seeking groups' (2003: 1098). In contrast to the 'populism' of the NLL, this 'neopopulism' was generally welcomed as evidence of a deepening Washington Consensus.

Latin American populism changed again amidst the crises of the (Post-) Washington Consensus, returning to a more state-centric or Keynesian posture. Much of the commentary on Latin America's 'left turn' focused on the ostensible upsurge of populism in the 2000s (Castañeda 2006; Edwards 2010; Reid 2007). Roberts wrote that 'the explosive rise of Hugo Chávez in Venezuela demonstrated that even more traditional, statist variants of populism remained potentially potent in Latin America's neoliberal era' (2007: 4). He noted that Chávez 'symbolised the revival of populism's historic nationalist and anti-market thrust'. Following Chávez's election in 1998, 'mass protest movements toppled a series of pro-market presidents in Ecuador, Argentina, and Bolivia, and new left-of-center governments were elected into office throughout much of South America'. Suddenly, 'the Washington Consensus was in tatters, and a social backlash had repoliticized development policy, offering group solidarity, collective action, and an interventionist state as alternatives to the material insecurities of market individualism' (Roberts 2007: 11). Chávez's anti-elitist rhetoric and mass-based organisational structure seemed to conform to the traditional model. It was simultaneously labelled 'radical', however, an appellation rarely attached to the far-reaching policy changes implemented by the likes of Menem, Collor de Mello and Fujimori.

Populism did not return with Chávez, for it had never really gone away. Yet, for many, Chávez represented the quintessential populist politician (Castañeda 2006; Hawkins 2010). In the international relations of the Western hemisphere, the relevance of the NLL was owed to the fact that it extended well beyond Venezuela. Chávez merely embodied the greater trend. Given Venezuela's immense oil wealth, Chávez's bombastic style and his ambitions to counter US hegemony in the region, Washington's fixation on the Venezuelan leader was unsurprising. For US officials, the populist label was the simplest way of capturing the Chávez phenomenon; of distilling the complexity of his regime into an easy-to-grasp categorisation. Chávez was a 'radical populist', 'false populist' or 'pied piper of populism' before he was a 'revolutionary', 'nationalist', 'leftist' or 'socialist', although these predicates were also present in the discourse (Hawkins 2010; Sullivan 2010). But Chávez was not alone. In 2007, a congressional report on Latin America sounded the alarm on a 'new form of populism in several countries', with the Andes its epicentre (Sullivan *et al.* 2007: 2).

The regimes Washington deemed 'populist' were those that challenged neoliberalism in a manner that, from the perspective of the historicist literature, would seem to earn them the label (through, for example, the nationalisation of key industries and an increase in social spending for the poor). In addition to Chávez and his Venezuelan supporters (*Chavistas*), Morales, Correa and Ortega were pigeonholed as populists. The anti-neoliberal projects associated with these leaders coalesced in ALBA, which was depicted as a populist institution. Other leaders, such as Zelaya in Honduras and the Kirchners in Argentina, would occasionally be linked to Chávez. Candidates running for office who were saddled with the populist tag included Andrés Manuel López Obrador in Mexico and Ollanta Humala in Peru, both of whom lost close elections in 2006. For his part, 'Chávez himself resisted the label and referred to populism either as a pejorative or in terms of what (could be called) "economic populism"' (Hawkins 2010: 51). It was not a term that left-ist politicians, or their supporters, embraced. If 'populism' was never particularly popular, US discourse stripped the term of its ambiguity, inscribing the concept with purely negative attributes.

'Populism' in US discourse on the New Latin Left

Together, the discursive and extra-discursive dynamics of populism—at least in its 'classical' sense—fostered understandings of the concept as coupling an antagonistic political style with a statist model of economic development. This knowledge provided the ideational resources underpinning Washington's ide-ological approach to Latin America at the time of the NLL's rise. Structural shifts in the political economy altered the characteristics of populism in Latin America, even as the idea of populism remained contested and ambiguous (Cammack 2000; Roberts 1995; Weyland 2003). Politicians' discursive appeals to 'the people' took on different meanings during the rise of the NLL than they did during the Washington Consensus era, when charismatic leaders worked to 'globalise' their economies. These neoliberal policies were often controversial, and occasionally clientelistic (Demmers *et al.* 2001). Yet, importantly, these governments were rarely classified as 'populists' by US officials. In contrast, Chávez, Morales, Correa and Ortega were routinely marked as such. More to the point, these leaders were constructed as certain *kinds* of populists—'radical', 'false', 'authoritarian', and so on.

Washington's response to the NLL was initiated by the 'hard-liners' of the Bush administration.[2] The discourse analysis carried out in this chapter focuses primarily on the diplomatic speech and official texts, documents and reports of that era. After President Obama assumed office he rhetorically 'reset' US–Latin American relations to bolster the flagging image of the United States. Obama was less likely to evoke populism in his speeches. However, the Obama administration continued to perceive, discuss and address Latin American populism as a poten-tial threat to US interests. This was evident in the shifting views on Honduran President Zelaya, for example, as detailed in Chapter 4. Testifying before the Senate in 2010, Dennis Blair, Obama's Director of National Intelligence, stated: 'elected populist leaders are moving toward a more authoritarian and statist political and economic model, and they have banded together to oppose US influence and policies in the region' (Blair 2010: 30). James Clapper, Blair's replacement, told Congress the following year that 'populist efforts to limit dem-ocratic freedoms' were damaging otherwise positive trends in the region (2011: 21). In outlining the Obama administration's second-term strategy for the region, Roberta Jacobson (2013), Assistant Secretary of State for Western Hemisphere Affairs, emphasised the problems posed by 'populist leaders'.

Leaving aside the problematic assertion that elected leaders were pursuing an 'authoritarian' model, the 'populists' did present an ideological challenge to US hegemony. The Washington Consensus was no longer the dominant, common-sense ideology that it was in the 1990s. In conjunction with the rise of the NLL, Bolivarian 'populism' fed off of nationalist, anti-imperialist and pan-Latin American values at odds with US power in its coercive and institutional guises. By articulating a rationale for anti-neoliberal policies (called '21st Century Socialism' by proponents), Latin American 'populists' also destabilised the structural power of the United States (via opposition to US-backed free trade regimes). Through all of this, the legitimacy of US hegemony was increasingly called into question. Its renewal would entail a push to shore up the ideological purchase of (neo)liberal values through a condemnation of populism. Discursively, 'populist' leaders were assigned certain meanings that delegitimised their political, economic and foreign policies. This was done partly through the deployment of binaries that represented these governments as undemocratic, backward and irresponsible.

Latin America's 'pied pipers of populism'

The classical model of Latin American populism centred on a state-directed economy that protected domestic industries from foreign competition. This is antithetical to 'free trade'. Chapter 3 analysed the ways in which the United States utilised formal trade agreements to lock in processes of neoliberal restructuring. As I further clarify here, Latin American states that departed from this agenda were dubbed populists. Because of the conflation of free trade with liberal ideas, 'populism' functioned in opposition to (neo)liberal (polyarchic) principles in US discourse. In one enlightening example, Deputy Secretary of State Robert Zoellick argued in a 2005 speech on CAFTA:

> The region is setting its course for the future: down one path travel modern, democratic leaders who believe in economic reform, adaptations to the challenges and openings of the global economy, democracy, and better social conditions for all their peoples. Down the other travel the pied pipers of populism, who hold out the false promise of autarky achieved by the dangerous means of political authoritarianism and personalized power.
>
> (Zoellick 2005)

Zoellick's 'pied pipers' metaphor set up a modern/populist binary that flowed from, and reinforced, the United States' identity as an open and democratic (and thus non-populist) hegemon. The discursive antagonism between populist 'autarky' and the modern promise of free trade was illustrated by the persistent deployment of the populist label amidst the debate over bilateral FTAs with Peru, Panama and Colombia. In buttressing the United States' self-image as a benevolent exemplar for the hemisphere, Zoellick's metaphor legitimated Washington's ongoing efforts to neoliberalise the region's political economy through free trade.

As a manifestation of US ideological power, then, the populist construct was closely related to US structural power as well. Whereas the heuristic of populism allowed US policymakers the ability to comprehend the region's changing politics, the pied piper metaphor fastened certain meanings to these changes in the discursive sphere.

The 'pied pipers of populism' were, quite plainly, Chávez and the other opponents of Washington's economic policies (a group that would include Morales, Correa, Ortega and, at times, other NLL figures). It was a turn of phrase that Zoellick used on multiple occasions, and not just with US audiences. In addressing the OAS General Assembly, for example, he told delegates that 'the pied pipers of populism will only lead people backwards, while globalization and the rest of the world looks ahead' (Zoellick 2006). After leaving the Bush administration to join Goldman Sachs, Zoellick penned an editorial for *The Wall Street Journal* in which he called for the formation of an Association of American Free Trade Agreements. In defending the decades-old effort by Washington to liberalise trade in the Western hemisphere, he argued for the passage of the FTAs with Colombia, Peru and Panama, writing:

> The US cannot afford to lose interest in its own neighborhood. The pied pipers of populism in Latin America are taking advantage of the genuine frustrations, especially in indigenous communities, of people who have not been able to climb the ladder of opportunity. We should not let these populists dictate the debate.
>
> (Zoellick 2007)

However alliterative or comical, Zoellick's 'pied pipers' metaphor keyed off of some of the uglier stereotypes in the history of US–Latin American relations. In European folklore, the legend of the pied piper took a number of forms. In most versions, the story centred on a piper who rids a rat-infested town of their vermin by using seductive music to drown the pests in a river. After the townspeople refuse to pay the piper for his services, he enacts his revenge by luring away the children of the village. In contemporary usage, a pied piper is a metaphor for a fanciful, flamboyant figure ('pied' refers to his multi-coloured, jester-like garb) who leads his followers astray by making irresponsible promises. The element of danger—indeed of impending doom—remains central to the picture of the pied piper as a spiteful predator. Zoellick's pied pipers of populism are wily politicians (mis)leading their people down the path of economic ruin for reasons stemming from their own fiendish personalities. In addition to the trope of Latin misrule, the evocation of the piper's followers as children conjures earlier images of the Latino-as-child, which were pervasive in the US press during the Spanish-American War and throughout the early part of the twentieth century (Hunt 2009 [1987]: 46–91; Schoultz 1998). The childish followers of populist presidents invariably fall under the spell of the promise of a better lot in life; a promise that unites 'the people', implicates the powerful and, in contemporary Latin America, generally takes the guise of nationalistic, anti-imperialist or anti-neoliberal politics. In other words, they were easily duped by deceitful, *caudillo*-like demagogues.

As was the case with Zoellick's framing of CAFTA, the call to combat the burgeoning influence of populist leaders formed an important plank in the Bush administration's rhetorical efforts to secure the passage of the bilateral accords. Beyond the issue of trade, however, trepidation over the wider ramifications of Latin American populism also appeared in the administration's diplomacy and security policy. Zoellick's binary separating 'modern, democratic leaders' from dangerous, deceitful authoritarians would become well-worn in Washington's diplomatic approach to Chávez, Morales, Correa, Ortega and others. Populism was (and is) represented as inimical to liberal democracy, despite the elected status of those leaders harnessed with the populist label. The Bush administration also referred to the anti-free trade members of the NLL as 'false populists', apparently calling into question their mass-based appeal. This kind of conjunction, or collocation, where words co-occur together in a habitual pattern, can be significant in grasping the wider meanings transmitted in a specific discourse (Fairclough 2003: 131, 213). The oft-repeated expression 'false populism' co-existed with another collocation in the administration's speech: 'radical populism', which surfaced frequently in the language of Pentagon officials, who portrayed the phenomenon as threatening US security.

'Radical populism' as a security threat

For military strategists, populism constituted a potential security threat to the United States, particularly if it adopted 'radicalised' or 'anti-American' forms. As noted in Chapter 1, the anti-neoliberal faction of the NLL was represented as 'radical', a word which takes on highly pejorative terms in diplomatic discourse. As the left turn in Latin America deepened in the mid-2000s, 'radical populism' took its place alongside drugs, terrorism and gang violence as the most prominent 'non-traditional threats' to the United States in the Western hemisphere (Barry 2005; LeoGrande 2006; Wikileaks 2007a). The combination of these issues gave Southcom renewed purpose in a region that had witnessed the diminished likelihood of traditional armed conflict. Among other things, radical populism provided a rationale for the changes to US military and security strategy analysed in Chapter 4, from the reformation of the Navy's Fourth Fleet to changes in the Defense Department's basing posture. US ideological power contributed to the construction of Chávez, Morales and others as 'extremist', and dangerous, including through the deployment of the 'radical populist' collocation. This facilitated the (attempted/ongoing) reconstitution of US coercive power.

In testimony before Congress in 2004, General James Hill, Commander of Southcom, outlined the changing security environment confronting the US military in Latin America. In Southcom's annual posture statement, Hill juxtaposed an established set of threats (namely narco-terrorists, urban gangs and Islamist groups) alongside a nascent threat: 'radical populism'. Hill related this to socioeconomic developments:

Traditional threats are now complemented by an emerging threat best described as radical populism, in which the democratic process is undermined to decrease rather than protect individual rights. Some leaders in the region are tapping into deep-seated frustrations of the failure of democratic reforms to deliver expected goods and services. By tapping into these frustrations caused by social and economic inequality, the leaders are at the same time able to reinforce their radical positions by inflaming anti-US sentiment.

(Hill 2004)

Danger exists because populism lends itself to radicalism and anti-democratic manoeuvring. Radicalism here is manifest in the degree of opposition to the United States, which becomes no more than a method of political manipulation— even when anti-Americanism permeates the broader population.

Populism in and of itself is not a threat. Rather, the threat emerges when it becomes radicalized by a leader who increasingly uses his position and support from a segment of the population to infringe upon the rights of all citizens. This trend degrades democracy and promises to concentrate power in the hands of a few rather than guaranteeing the individual rights of the many. Anti-American sentiment has also been used to reinforce the positions of radical leaders who seek to distract the populace from their own shortcomings. Anti-American sentiment also troubles our partner nations as well, as elected leaders must take into account the sometime very vocal views of their constituents.

(Hill 2004)

General Bantz Craddock sounded similar themes in Southcom's 2005 posture statement. Referring to social movements in Bolivia, Ecuador and Peru, Craddock pointed to 'anti-US, anti-globalization, and anti-free-trade demagogues, who, unwilling to shoulder the burden of participating in the democratic process and too impatient to undertake legitimate political action, incite violence against their own governments and their own people' (Craddock 2005). Like Hill, Craddock related the emerging security threat to deteriorating socio-economic conditions. Stating that 'the roots of the region's poor security environment are poverty, inequality, and corruption', he added that 'the free market reforms and privatization of the 1990s have not delivered on the promise of prosperity for Latin America. Unequal distribution of wealth exacerbates the poverty problem' (Craddock 2005). Populism was an indicator that Washington should bolster those countries amenable to responsible policymaking: 'We cannot afford to let Latin America and the Caribbean become a backwater of violent, inward-looking states that are cut off from the world around them by populist, authoritarian governments' (Craddock 2005). Responsible partners needed increased economic and military assistance.

In the 2008 threat assessment prepared by the intelligence community for the Senate Armed Services Committee, J. Michael McConnell, Director of National Intelligence, underscored the role of Venezuela in supporting and inspiring the leaders of Bolivia, Nicaragua and Ecuador to strengthen their presidentialist systems, weaken civil liberties and pursue 'economic nationalism at the expense of market-based approaches' (McConnell 2008: 33). Foregrounding its socio-economic appeal, he stated: 'the persistence of high levels of poverty and striking income inequalities will continue to create a potentially receptive audience for radical populism's message'. Again, the 'anti-US rhetoric' of the leaders of these states was taken as evidence of their radicalism (McConnell 2008). The colloca-tion of 'radical populism' was present in the internal communications of the State Department, as well, as evidenced in leaked embassy cables (Wikileaks 2005, 2006, 2007a, 2007b). In this context, it was widely attached to leaders/govern-ments in the Andean region. In the public discourse, however, US officials were relatively cautious in applying the label to specific figures, particularly when dis-cussing radical populism as a security threat.

Radical populism generated serious attention from thinkers and planners in the US military. In a monograph for the Army War College's Strategic Studies Institute (SSI), Steve Ropp detailed the implications of South American populism from the vantage of the US military's academicians. Ropp's concerns emanated from the uncertainty associated with populist politicians operating in the context of representative democracies. He focused on the stresses that generate 'bursts of populist turbulence', citing the 'harsh economic realities' experienced in South America as a result of 'the transition to open market economies in the 1990s', which 'increased income inequality in most countries, led to a rise in urban unem-ployment, and to a widening gap between the wages of skilled and unskilled workers' (Ropp 2005: 7). He highlighted the possibility of Chávez's influence spreading, pointing to a potential disruption to the US energy supply through a 'petro-alliance' of populists (Ropp 2005: 12–13).

Whereas Ropp explored populism as an outcome of liberal democratic practices set against a range of social stresses, SSI scholar Gabriel Marcella took populism to be a product of the 'authoritarian impulse' embedded in the Latin American psyche; an impulse produced by the combination of the preference for civic rebelliousness among Latin Americans (as opposed to voting) and the overall inef-fectiveness of Latin American governance (Marcella 2007: 9–15). Contemporary Latin American populism strives for radical change, brought on by a 'culture of resentment' fed by 'social exclusion and persistent poverty' (Marcella 2007: 5).

> The transnational culture of resentment is reshaping international security, creating alliances of opportunity between state and nonstate actors that cross borders. Much like revolutionaries and terrorists of the past, its members are motivated out of a profound sense of victimization by what they believe to be injustices perpetrated by some combination of capitalism, bad government associated with democracy, Western materialism, and modernity, and by the pervasiveness of American power, wealth, and influence. The sense of vic-timization needs an agent to make it politically powerful. In Latin America, that agent is authoritarian populism, which is always latent in the political culture of the region.
>
> (Marcella 2007: 6)

Marcella's essentialist account drew an even more explicit link between populism and the backlash against the Washington Consensus than Ropp's, although, for Marcella, this had more to do with the cultural resentment of America than the actual (material) impact of American foreign economic policy. Like Ropp, Marcella paid close attention to the influence of Chávez, who came in for a rather hyperbolic appraisal. He wrote that 'an anti-democratic, deeply anti-American Venezuelan state that de facto supports drug trafficking' was 'a growing problem for regional security'. The Chávez government was a 'personalistic and militarized authoritarian system' and a 'populist dictatorship' that was pursuing a 'primitive' form of socialism (Marcella 2007: 39–43). There was little room for nuance in Marcella's condemnation. The basic argument of the SSI strategists was found throughout the official discursive terrain: the radicalism of populist governments was axiomatic; it was a security threat and a recipe for economic backwardness. In another SSI monograph, Hal Brands contrasted radical populism with a 'post-radical' centre-left that adhered to market reforms and safeguarded democracy (2009: 32–7). There was, quite simply, a good, pragmatic left and a bad, radical left, with populism the dividing line.

The writings of the SSI analysts reinforced the dichotomy between populism's backward and authoritarian tendencies and the modern democracy exemplified by the United States. Yet there were inconsistencies in the broader populist construct—tensions which US discourse could only partially smooth over. In placing anti-US leaders (as 'dictators') at the service of the few rather than the many, 'radical populism' cohered with the insincerity of the 'false populists' in the Bush administration's trade rhetoric, as detailed below. However, the former implies that the governments of Chávez, Morales and Correa were genuinely populist, even vigorously so, and that their populism was therefore particularly pronounced in some significant way. In this sense, the two collocations were barely compatible. There was further tension between the Pentagon's acknowledgement that contemporary Latin American populism has roots in the social and economic conditions of the Washington Consensus and the insistence that a failure to extend the neoliberal model (through the FTAs) would result in an emboldened group of populist demagogues. Whereas strategic discourse highlighted the increased levels of inequality and poverty that played into populism, on economic policy Washington advocated neoliberalisation to combat its appeal. As the United States sought to recoup its ideological power by denigrating the NLL's Bolivarian leaders, this re-constitutive process would remain open and ongoing. The counter-hegemonic ideology of the 'populists' thrived amidst Washington's condemnation, which further empowered the NLL's anti-imperialism.

The turn towards 'false populism' in US discourse

The Bush administration was widely seen as softening its rhetoric toward the NLL during Bush's second term. A series of electoral victories for left-wing and 'anti-American' candidates in Bolivia (Morales in 2005), Ecuador (Correa in 2006) and Nicaragua (Ortega in 2006) demonstrated the growing appeal of the anti-neoliberal left. With the popularity of the United States at an historic low (Hakim 2006), and with Chávez's influence on the rise, US strategy grew more conciliatory in tone. 'The tenor of US political rhetoric changed in the second half of 2006', wrote one congressional researcher. Despite a series of verbal attacks by Chávez and others, 'President Bush ignored the taunts and US officials emphasised that they wanted to focus on a positive agenda of US engagement with Latin America' (Sullivan 2010: 14). Fallout from the Iraq War, among other considerations, ensured there was little momentum for retaining a more aggressive stance in the Americas. With the legitimacy of US hegemony under duress, renewing US ideological power would require a less bellicose posture. 'Radical populists' became 'false populists' in Washington's approach to the region.

Consider, for example, Washington's change of tack on Evo Morales. During Bolivia's 2002 presidential campaign, the US ambassador to the country stated publicly that 'if Bolivians elected those who want Bolivia to become a major cocaine exporter again, the future of US assistance to the country (would) be put in jeopardy' (Muñoz-Pogossian 2008: 148). Referencing Morales, a former coca grower who vehemently opposed US eradication efforts, the comments boosted the leftist's poll numbers. Although Morales lost in 2002, he would capture the presidency three years later. By then, the United States was no longer threatening to cut off financial assistance or alter Bolivia's access to US markets. As noted by James Dunkerley, Bush himself even made the obligatory telephone call congratulating Morales on his victory, no doubt aware that Bolivia's first indigenous president had referred to himself as '"Washington's worst nightmare". Even after the new government had (re)nationalised the hydrocarbons industry, halted the mandatory eradication of coca, and hosted three visits by Hugo Chávez in six months, the United States expressed little more than tight-lipped irritation' (Dunkerley 2007: 134). Morales would soon be joined by Correa, Ortega and others in articulating the 'Bolivarian' message of 'Twenty-first Century Socialism'.

As the NLL took on a more ideological purpose, and having determined that directly attacking Chávez, Morales, Correa and Ortega could be counterproductive, the charge of 'false populism' became a proxy for those leaders hostile to Washington's interests. Secretary of State Condoleezza Rice was among the first to use the phrase. Rice's vision for US policy in Latin America, set out in a 2005 interview, signalled a heightened awareness that the administration's confrontational approach had failed to curtail Washington's geopolitical backsliding. Maintaining that the United States would pursue good relations with 'governments from across the political spectrum', Rice praised Brazil and Chile, calling attention to their 'stable and sound economic policies'. In contrast, however, and without naming names, Rice stated:

> Now, there are places where people are giving easy answers, a kind of false populism, I'll call it, where there are easy answers: 'We can be out of poverty tomorrow if we'll just do these things'. That's not helpful. But when you have sound economic policies and people care about social justice and better lives for their people, the United States is going to be friends with those governments.
>
> (Rice 2005)

The 'false populism' line quickly became a hallmark of the Bush administration's rhetoric. During an address to the Council of the Americas, Nicholas Burns, Under Secretary of State for Political Affairs, claimed Washington's promotion of democracy, free markets and social justice was ecumenical. 'We impose no ideological litmus test on potential partners in the region', he said, 'and do not fear political differences. We have forged productive relationships with governments from across the political spectrum, from the Lula administration in Brazil and the Bachelet administration in Chile to the Calderón and Uribe administrations in Mexico and Colombia' (Burns 2007). In defending Plan Colombia, Washington's aid package for the country, Burns stated: 'While some of its neighbors have embraced false populism and authoritarian leaders, Colombia has embraced democratic governance and open markets'. He added that a defeat of the FTA 'would be a huge victory for those—like Hugo Chávez—who promote an authoritarian, populist highly personalized model of government, drawing upon the failed economic policies of decades past.'

President Bush grew to appreciate the 'false populism' line, using it in numerous speeches over his final years in office. It typically surfaced in the context of the debate over the Panama, Peru and Colombia FTAs. According to Bush, the passage of these agreements would 'help counter the false populism promoted by hostile nations' (Bush 2007a). Citing Colombia's Uribe, he stated in November 2007 that:

> These friends of America are waiting to see what Congress will do with the trade agreements we have concluded with our neighbors in the region. People are watching the actions of the US Congress very carefully. Champions of false populism in the region are watching Congress. They will use any failure to approve these trade agreements as evidence that America will never treat democracies in the region as full partners.
>
> (Bush 2007b)

Counterintuitive though it was, the notion that Latin American populists would use the failure of the bilateral FTAs as evidence of US fickleness became a persistent theme in Bush's messaging. In his remarks with Peruvian President García on the signing of the US–Peru accord, for example, Bush repeated that 'those who espouse the language of false populism will use (the) failure of these trade agreements as a way of showing America doesn't—isn't committed to our friends in the hemisphere' (2007c). As he advocated the ratification of agreements with Colombia and Panama, Bush continued to position populism in opposition to the self-evident benefits of free trade and democracy. In his final State of the Union, Bush (2008) said of the Colombia FTA: 'If we fail to pass this agreement, we will embolden the purveyors of false populism in our hemisphere. So we must come together, pass this agreement, and show our neighbors in the region that democracy leads to a better life.'

But why *false* populism? Was this to say that the populism of Chávez and his allies was less than fully fledged? And why the insinuation that the failure to ratify the FTAs would provide fodder to the United States' populist adversaries, precisely those leaders who most vehemently opposed the 'free trade' of US foreign economic policy? These questions appeared all the more conspicuous when considering the collocation of 'radical populism', which both preceded the 'false populist' label and co-existed with it in US foreign policy discourse. Here, the 'radical' predicate strengthened the dominant meaning of populism; radical signifies extremism, and, like the word 'populist' itself, conveyed meanings of danger and demagogy. In other words, both halves of the 'radical populist' collocation point in the same direction, whereas the deceptiveness implied by the 'false' prefix seems to undermine the dominant construction of these leaders as true populists. How did these apparent inconsistences in meaning function ideologically?

As discussed above, populism is seen as a mass-based movement or phenomenon that challenges the entrenched interests of the elite. To label it false is to deny that the leader, government or movement in question represents 'the people'. It suggests that those posing as populists do not, in fact, serve the interests of the many against the few. With the populism of charismatic leaders placed in opposition to liberal democracy, a paradox emerged in US discourse on the NLL. Those leaders striking an anti-US pose were constructed as *populists* as their commitment to democracy was made suspect, but they were *false* in that their commitment to the people was somehow ephemeral or misleading. This contradiction, which held that the United States' adversaries are populists and non-populists at the same time, was elided in Washington's denunciation of the region's anti-neoliberal governments. Ultimately, the 'false populism' collocation removed the ambiguity that tends to envelop the term, giving 'populism' a decidedly negative flair. The 'radical' adjective does something similar. In diplomatic speech, a leader who is 'false', 'radical' or both is untrustworthy if not downright illegitimate. Here the populist construct is not an analytical device as much as an attempt to *represent* NLL governments in a certain normative light.

The parameters of the 'populist' construct

Discursive power functions through the construction of meaning. This process implies a certain amount of stability, if not closure. Discourses are also fluid, and open, creating elements of ambiguity and uncertainly in the very 'blank spots which a discourse has to leave in silence to present itself as stable' (Hansen 2006: 128). Discourse analysts often look to what Weldes refers to as 'telltale silences' to gauge the taken-for-granted assumptions underpinning social action, and to locate the boundaries of a given construct (1999: 59–60, 93–4). The absences in official US discourse on Latin American populism are as telling as the contemptuous evaluations of the false/radical populists themselves. These silences help to hone in on the meaning of populism in US ideology.

The treatment of Colombia's Álvaro Uribe poses an enlightening contrast to the ascribed 'populists' of the NLL. On issues of political style and governance, the presidency of the rightist Uribe had a number of parallels with that of the leftist Chávez. Like Chávez, Uribe's popularity enabled his supporters to spearhead a change in the Colombian constitution that allowed him to successfully run for re-election. The popularity of both leaders helped to reconfigure party politics in their respective countries. Uribe was embroiled in a major corruption scandal that called into question his commitment to the norms and institutions of liberal governance—a scandal that involved his family and the country's paramilitary forces. Weyland likened Uribe's political strategy to the neoliberal populists of the 1990s (2003: 1109). One scholar wrote that Uribe's failed bid for a third term constituted a 'populist push' that threatened the separation of powers in Colombia (Posada-Carbó 2011: 150). Uribe displayed a confrontational style in dealing with political opponents and cultivated a highly personalised method of governing, which included weekly neighbourhood council meetings that allowed him to establish direct links with the electorate (Posada-Carbó 2011: 138–9). And yet, for Washington, Uribe strode directly opposite the 'champions of false populism', in Bush's 2008 State of the Union.

Due to the complexities of Colombia's decades-long civil conflict, Uribe's heavy-handed law-and-order project (which he labelled 'democratic security') was distinct in the region, garnering enthusiastic support from the United States. As one would expect, his discourse never cohered with that of the NLL governments, meaning that his relationship to 'the people' did not involve mobilising the 'popular classes' against the oligarchy or US hegemony. What is more, Uribe's 'economic policies (were) orthodox and neoliberal in nature, aimed at reducing state spending (except on the state security forces) and with little in the way of redistribution to the poorer sectors of society' (Dugas 2003: 1117). In 2006, after two years of negotiations, he signed an FTA with the United States. By aligning his government with Washington's objectives, Uribe demonstrated that populism—defined as a style of political mobilisation—could still be of service to US hegemony. This was demonstrated previously by Fujimori, Menem and other leaders in the 1980s and 1990s. Any acknowledgement of this, however, would undermine the construction of 'populism' as synonymous with an irresponsible statism and a radical hostility to the United States. Uribe's classification as a non-populist—as the antithesis of Chávez—demonstrates the degree to which Washington equates populism with anti-Americanism and anti-neoliberal policies. Leaked embassy cables contain hundreds of references to populism but not one reference to Uribe as such. Ostensibly, Uribe was a bulwark *against* populism.

Given the meanings inscribed in the concept, it is entirely 'natural' that the United States would be free from any association with such a pejorative term. This is despite the fact that several initiatives could have been construed as pandering directly to 'the people', and outside of established institutional channels. For example, Washington deployed a naval ship, the *Comfort*, to administer free health services to residents in a number of countries. The Bush administration also announced a scholarship programme for Latin American students. According to the US military, these kinds of initiatives helped the United States cultivate a 'softer', 'smarter' image in Latin America (Stavridis 2010). Although one commentator derided 'the pale imitations of the Venezuelan and Cuban educational and health programs announced on President Bush's 2007 trip to Latin America' (Lowenthal 2009: 18), the administration chose to describe its efforts as part of a commitment to 'social justice' (White House 2007). 'Populism' was exclusive to the 'radicals' of the 'bad left'. Of course, the United States was firmly outside of the classification. So too were its more neoliberal allies/partners, whether rightists like Uribe or the reformist governments in Brazil, Chile and Uruguay.

In 2007 and 2008, the Hudson Institute, a Washington think tank, held several forums on radical populism in Latin America, including one that featured a keynote address by Francis Fukuyama. In his comments, Fukuyama argued that any strategy for combating radical populism—which he described as a 'symptom' of a wider 'disease'—must engage with the social issues downplayed during the Washington Consensus era, such as poverty and inequality (Hudson Institute 2007: 5–6). From this vantage, he praised the *Bolsa Família* and *Oportunidades* programmes of Brazil and Mexico, respectively. For Fukuyama, these conditional cash transfer programmes avoided the kind of patronage politics that typify radical populism.[3] However, given the vagueness of 'populism', which Fukuyama left undefined, it was unclear exactly why the *Bolsa Família* and *Oportunidades* programmes escaped the populist stain. Both provided money to poor families in exchange for their co-operation in governmental efforts to boost participation in education and health services, and both helped parties in power win allegiance from poor voters. This is made more puzzling by the fact that Fukuyama acknowledged that the popularity of *Oportunidades*, which was developed by the PRI but expanded under the government of Vicente Fox, may have been decisive in helping Felipe Calderón (from Fox's party) narrowly defeat leftist Andrés Manuel López Obrador in Mexico's 2006 contest (Hudson Institute 2007: 9). The PRI, which retained power for decades using heavy doses of clientelism, had embraced neoliberalism in the 1980s and 1990s.

Fukuyama didn't need to remind his audience that the architects of these programmes were the pro-US, centre-right government of Mexico and the 'moderate', centre-left government of Brazil. Fox, like Uribe, had been a close and important ally of the Bush White House, particularly on economic matters. A former union leader, Lula had been widely viewed as a 'populist' in Washington policy circles, including after his initial election to the presidency. (CIA director George Tenet [2003] linked Lula directly to the 'transnational threat' of 'Latin America's rising populism'.) In accordance with his fidelity to macroeconomic orthodoxy, however, Lula was eventually established as a pragmatic if lukewarm partner of the United States. The populist label was no longer appropriate, despite the continued adulation Lula received from large portions of the Brazilian electorate, concentrated amongst the country's poorer sectors. As an exemplar of the 'good left' in Latin America, his social programmes could not be 'populist', it seems, although they certainly contributed to the popularity of his government and party.

Conclusion

The discursive construction of Latin American populism is by no means the only manifestation of US ideological power in inter-American relations. The ideology of US hegemony is expansive and multifaceted, and discourses, by their nature, are fluid and interlacing. As discussed in Chapter 2, neo-Gramscian theory has highlighted the ways in which the Washington Consensus functioned ideologically and discursively to normalise and legitimate the neoliberalisation of the region's political economy. In the Post-Washington Consensus era, as detailed in this chapter, the populist construct expedites the renewal of this hegemony. The various ideas, values and discourses associated with the NLL's counter-hegemony (most notably those related to nationalism, Bolivarianism and Twenty-first Century Socialism) could be reduced to this handy term. The populist construct represented a means of distinguishing the anti-neoliberal, anti-American agents of the NLL from its more reformist elements—of dividing the 'good' left from the 'bad'. With this binary in place, the condemnation populism constituted an attempt to undercut 'bad' leaders/governments as backward and undemocratic.

In arguing that populism is a discursive construct, I am not making the case that it doesn't 'exist' in the 'real world'. As the ideational aspects of the constitutive appeal to 'the people' intersect with changes in the politico-economic sphere, the discourse(s) of political leaders in Latin America is/are shaped by structural changes in the extra-discursive realm. Populism is an amorphous concept, connecting intellectual conjecture to the material realities of inter-American relations, in which the charge of populism functions largely as an epithet. But Washington's fixation on populism cannot be attributed to an identifiable increase in populist practices on the part of Latin American governments; by any 'objective' measure, populist politics persisted during the Washington Consensus years. Despite this conceptual haziness, 'populism' gained considerable purchase within US policy in the 2000s. It was stripped of the ambiguously positive overtones associated with its root (*populus*, Latin for 'people') and equated with an alarming extremism. This move (re)inscribed targeted governments as radical, irresponsible and authoritarian.

Notwithstanding its frequent use in official US discourse, the construct rested on tenuous foundations (e.g. the inconsistences in its application; the apparent contradictions between 'radical' and 'false' adjectives). The reconstitution of US ideological power remained an ongoing and contested process, not least because of the agency of those dubbed populists in US discourse. However, in reinforcing the self-understandings of US foreign policy (as non-populist, democratic, forward-looking and so on), the populist construct legitimated the utilisation of power in its structural, coercive and institutional guises. The construct also *shaped* US interests; populist governments are not only imprudent when it comes to economic policy, they are autocratic and a potential threat to US security. Given the meanings of 'populism', which were extended and refined through the metaphors, collocations and silences of US discourse, Washington was positioned (and, more to the point, *positioned itself*) in opposition to the 'radical', 'Bolivarian' faction of the NLL, including, most prominently, the governments of Venezuela, Bolivia and Ecuador. Notably, the agency of these states played a role in this dynamic, including through the deployment of counter-hegemonic discourses. As we see, then, ideological power is mutually imbricated with the other forms of power in international politics, which, in the context of hegemony, exist in relation to the (counter-)powers of oppositional forces. These dialectical themes recur throughout this book. They are given additional consideration in the concluding chapter.

Notes

1 My reading of US foreign policy discourse corresponds to models 1 and 2 of Hansen's (2006) four-model framework, which limits the research to official speech/texts and to those of the wider foreign policy debate. In contrast, models 3 and 4 of her typology focus on cultural representations and marginal political discourses, respectively.
2 Many of these figures were associated neoconservatism. The group included Defense Secretary Donald Rumsfeld, who articulated his concerns on populism during a trip to Latin America in 2005. Also influential in the Bush administration at this time were Otto Reich, Assistant Secretary of State for Western Hemisphere Affairs and a staunch anti-Castro Cuban American, and Roger Noriega, who succeeded Reich in this post. The administration 'softened' its discourse in Bush's second term under the guidance of Assistant Secretary of State Thomas Shannon. Whereas Rumsfeld, Reich and Noriega were often viewed as hard-line ideologues, Shannon was seen as a more traditional and pragmatic diplomat. He later became US Ambassador to Brazil and Under Secretary of State for Political Affairs in the Obama administration.
3 As an example of patronage politics, Fukuyama mentioned Venezuela's 'Cuban eye clinics', which he described as a tool of Chávez's 'demagogy' (Hudson Institute 2007: 8). This was a reference to *Misón Milagro*, a government health initiative staffed by Cuban doctors that provided free eye care clinics and eye surgery to Venezuelans.

References

Arditi, B. (2007). *Politics on the Edges of Liberalism: Difference, Populism, Revolution, Agitation*, Edinburgh: Edinburgh University Press.

Barnett, M. and R. Duvall (2005). 'Power in Global Governance', in *Power in Global Governance*, edited by M. Barnett and R. Duvall, Cambridge: Cambridge University Press: 1–32.

Barry, T. (2005). '"Mission Creep" in Latin America—US Southern Command's New Security Strategy', International Relations Center, July.

Blair, D. C. (2010). 'Annual Threat Assessment of the US Intelligence Community for the Senate Select Committee on Intelligence', 2 February.

Brands, H. (2009). 'Dealing with Political Ferment in Latin America: The Populist Revival, the Emergence of the Center, and Implications for US Policy', Strategic Studies Institute, September.

Burns, N. (2007). 'Under Secretary Burns: Promoting Peace and Prosperity in Colombia', 22 October. Available online at www.as-coa.org/article.php?id=648 (accessed 28 July 2013).

Bush, G. W. (2007a). 'President's Radio Address', 13 October. Available online at http://georgewbush-whitehouse.archives.gov/news/releases/2007/10/20071013.html (accessed 21 February 2016).

Bush, G. W. (2007b). 'Remarks at the White House Forum on International Trade and Investment', 6 November. Available online at http://georgewbush-whitehouse.archives.gov/news/releases/2007/11/20071106.html (accessed 21 February 2016).

Bush, G. W. (2007c). 'President Bush and President Garcia of Peru Sign H.R. 3688', 14 December. Available online at http://georgewbush-whitehouse.archives.gov/news/releases/2007/12/20071214-8.html (accessed 21 February 2016).

Bush, G. W. (2008). 'President Bush Delivers State of the Union Address', 28 January. Available online at http://georgewbush-whitehouse.archives.gov/news/releases/2008/01/20080128-13.html (accessed 21 February 2016).

Cammack, P. (2000). 'The Resurgence of Populism in Latin America', *Bulletin of Latin American Research*, 19(2): 149–61.

Campbell, D. (1992). *Writing Security: United States Foreign Policy and the Politics of Identity*, Minneapolis: University of Minnesota Press.

Canovan, M. (1999). 'Trust the People! Populism and the Two Faces of Democracy', *Political Studies*, 47(1): 2–16.

Castañeda, J. (2006). 'Latin America's Left Turn', *Foreign Affairs*, 85(3): 28–43.

Clapper, J. R. (2011). 'Statement for the Record on the Worldwide Threat Assessment of the US Intelligence Community for the Senate Select Committee on Intelligence', 16 February.

Craddock, B. (2005). 'Posture Statement of General B Craddock, United States Southern Command', Senate Armed Services Committee, 15 March. Available online at www.america.gov/st/washfile-english/2005/March/20050316170548ASrelliM0.2706873.html (accessed 27 July 2013).

De la Torre, C. (2000). *Populist Seduction in Latin America: The Ecuadorian Experience*, Athens: Ohio University Press.

Demmers, J., A. E. Fernández Jilberto and B. Hogenbloom, eds (2001). *Miraculous Metamorphoses: The Neoliberalization of Latin American Populism*, London: Zed Books.

Dornbusch, R. and S. Edwards (1990). 'Macroeconomic Populism', *Journal of Development Economics*, 32(2): 247–77.

Dugas, J. C. (2003). 'The Emergence of Neopopulism in Colombia? The Case of Álvaro Uribe', *Third World Quarterly*, 24(6): 1117–36.

Dunkerley, J. (2007). 'Evo Morales, the "Two Bolivias" and the Third Bolivian Revolution', *Journal of Latin American Studies*, 39(1): 133–66.

Edwards, S. (2010). *Left Behind: Latin America and the False Promise of Populism*, Chicago: Chicago University Press.

Fairclough, N. (1992). *Discourse and Social Change*, Cambridge: Polity Press.

Fairclough, N. (2003). *Analysing Discourse: Textual Analysis for Social Research*, London: Routledge.

Hakim, P. (2006). 'Is Washington Losing Latin America?' *Foreign Affairs*, 85(1): 39–53.

Hansen, L. (2006). *Security as Practice: Discourse Analysis and the Bosnian War*, Oxford: Routledge.

Hawkins, K. A. (2010). *Venezuela's Chavismo and Populism in Comparative Perspective*, Cambridge: Cambridge University Press.

Hennessy, A. (1969). 'Latin America', in *Populism: Its Meanings and National Characteristics*, edited by G. Ionescu and E. Gellner, London: Weidenfeld and Nicolson: 28–61.

Hill, J. T. (2004). 'Testimony in Front of the US House Armed Services Committee', 24 March. Available online at www.america.gov/st/washfile-english/2004/March/20040325145251ASrelliM0.9962274.html (accessed 27 July 2013).

Hudson Institute (2007). 'Radical Populism in Latin America', transcript by Federal News Service, Washington, DC, 6 November.

Hunt, M. H. (2009 [1987]). *Ideology and US Foreign Policy*, New Haven: Yale University Press.

Jacobson, R. (2013). 'Statement Before the Subcommittee on the Western Hemisphere of the Committee on Foreign Affairs', 28 February. Available online at www.state.gov/p/wha/rls/rm/2013/205468.htm (accessed 27 February 2016).

Laclau, E. (2005). *On Populist Reason*, London: Verso.

LeoGrande, W. M. (2006). 'From Red Menace to Radical Populism: US Insecurity in Latin America', *World Policy Journal*, 22(4): 25–35.

Lowenthal, A. F. (2009). 'Renewing Cooperation in the Americas', in *The Obama Administration and the Americas: Agenda for Change*, edited by A. F. Lowenthal, T. J. Piccone and L. Whitehead, Washington, DC: Brookings Institution Press: 1–21.

Mann, M. (1986). *The Sources of Social Power Volume 1: A History of Power from the Beginning to A.D. 1760*, Cambridge: Cambridge University Press.

Mann, M. (2012). *The Sources of Social Power Volume 3: Global Empires and Revolution*, Cambridge: Cambridge University Press.

Marcella, G. (2007). 'American Grand Strategy for Latin America in the Age of Resentment', Strategic Studies Institute, September.

McConnell, J. M. (2008). 'Annual Threat Assessment of the Intelligence Community for the Senate Armed Services Committee', 27 February.

Milliken, J. (1999). 'The Study of Discourse in International Relations: A Critique of Research and Methods', *European Journal of International Relations*, 5(2): 225–54.

Muñoz-Pogossian, B. (2008). *Electoral Rules and the Transformation of Bolivian Politics: The Rise of Evo Morales*, New York: Palgrave Macmillan.

Neumann, I. B. (2008). 'Discourse Analysis', in *Qualitative Methods in International Relations: A Pluralist Guide*, edited by A. Koltz and D. Prakash, New York: Palgrave Macmillan: 61–92.

Panizza, F. (2000). 'Editorial: New Wine in Old Bottles? Old and New Populism in Latin America', *Bulletin of Latin American Research*, 19(2): 145–7.

Panizza, F. (2005). 'Introduction: Populism and the Mirror of Democracy', in *Populism and the Mirror of Democracy*, edited by F. Panizza, London: Verso: 1–31.

Posada-Carbó, E. (2011). 'Colombia After Uribe', *Journal of Democracy*, 22(1): 137–51.

Reid, M. (2007). *Forgotten Continent: The Battle for Latin America's Soul*, New Haven: Yale University Press.

Rice, C. (2005). 'Rice Outlines US Vision for Western Hemisphere', 29 April. Available online at http://archives.uruguay.usembassy.gov/usaweb/paginas/370a-00EN.shtml (accessed 21 February 2016).

Robinson, W. I. (1996). *Promoting Polyarchy: Globalization, US Intervention, and Hegemony*, Cambridge: Cambridge University Press.

Roberts, K. (1995). 'Neoliberalism and the Transformation of Populism in Latin America: The Peruvian Case', *World Politics*, 48(1): 82–116.

Roberts, K. (2007). 'Latin America's Populist Revival', *SAIS Review*, 27(1): 3–15.

Ropp, S. (2005). 'The Strategic Implications of the Rise of Populism in Europe and South America', Strategic Studies Institute, June.

Schoultz, L. (1998). *Beneath the United States: A History of US Policy toward Latin America*, Cambridge, MA: Harvard University Press.

Stavridis, J. (2010). *Partnership for the Americas: Western Hemisphere Strategy and US Southern Command*, Washington, DC: National Defense University.

Stokes, D. (2009). 'Ideas and Avocados: Ontologising Critical Terrorism Studies', *International Relations*, 23(1): 85–92.

Sullivan, M. P. (2010). 'Venezuela: Issues in the 111th Congress', Congressional Research Service, 8 February.

Sullivan, M. P., C. W. Cook, J. F. Hornbeck, N. Olhero, C. M. Ribando, C. Veillette and M. A. Villarreal (2007). 'Latin America and the Caribbean: Issues for the 110th Congress', Congressional Research Service, 31 August.

Taggart, P. (2000). *Populism*, Buckingham: Open University Press.

Tenet, G. (2003). 'DCI's Worldwide Threat Briefing', 11 February. Available online at www.cia.gov/news-information/speeches-testimony/2003/dci_speech_02112003.html (accessed 21 February 2016).

Tickell, A. and J. Peck (2003). 'Making Global Rules: Globalization or Neoliberalism?' in *Remaking the Global Economy*, edited by J. Peck and H. W. Yeung, London: Sage: 163–81.

Weldes, J. (1999). *Constructing National Interests: The United States and the Cuban Missile Crisis*, Minneapolis: University of Minnesota Press.

Weyland, K. (2003). 'Neopopulism and Neoliberalism in Latin America: How Much Affinity?' *Third World Quarterly*, 24(6): 1095–115.

White House (2007). 'Fact Sheet: Advancing the Cause of Social Justice in the Western Hemisphere', Office of the Press Secretary, 5 March.

Wikileaks (2005). 'Democracy Promotion Strategy-Dominican Republic', 12 October. Reference ID: 05SANTODOMINGO4606.

Wikileaks (2006). 'Ecuador Update: Correa Moves into Second Place', 15 September. Reference ID: 06QUITO2309.

Wikileaks (2007a). 'Iran-Russia-Venezuela Triangle Threatens Regional Stability', 13 November. Reference ID: 07BRASILIA2132.

Wikileaks (2007b). 'Scene Setter for Deputy Secretary Negroponte', 1 May. Reference ID: 07LIMA1591.

Williams, R. (1983 [1976]). *Keywords: A Vocabulary of Culture and Society*, London: Fontana Press.

Zoellick, R. (2005). 'From Crisis to Commonwealth: CAFTA and Democracy in our Neighborhood', 16 May. Available online at http://2001-2009.state.gov/s/d/former/zoellick/rem/46320.htm (accessed 20 February 2016).

Zoellick, R. (2006). 'Remarks to General Assembly of the Organization of American States', 5 June. Available online at http://2001-2009.state.gov/s/d/former/zoellick/rem/2006/67552.htm (accessed 20 February 2016).

Zoellick, R. (2007). 'Happily Ever AAFTA', *Wall Street Journal*, 8 January: A17.

7 Conclusion

For generations, Latin America was known as the United States' 'backyard', and with good reason. As detailed in Chapter 1, the literature on the international politics of the Western hemisphere points to a uniquely asymmetrical relationship between the superpower and its southern neighbours. This is captured elegantly in the revisionist titles on the topic. Galeano (1973), taking cues from the *dependistas*, wrote of the *Open Veins of Latin America* feeding waves of imperial plunder. Peter Smith (2000) likened US policy to the *Talons of the Eagle* bearing down on those countries geographically and metaphorically *Beneath the United States*, in Schoultz's phrasing (1998). Loveman's history of the Western hemisphere demonstrated that there was *No Higher Law* above the imperatives of American foreign policy (2010), while Grandin documented the ways in which the region was transformed into the *Empire's Workshop* (2006a). Even orthodox accounts generally begin by acknowledging the preponderant power of the United States (Brands 2012; Pastor 2001). The diminishment of the political left after the Cold War deepened Washington's influence (Castañeda 1994). During the 2000s, however, the narrative of US dominance was turned on its head. This was due largely to trends in the region itself—to the rise of the New Latin Left. The ebb of this 'Pink Tide' left behind a changed hemispheric landscape.

More than his ascendency to office, Hugo Chávez's ability to survive a US-backed coup attempt in 2002 seemed to portend a fresh defiance of Washington's agenda. That same year, Brazil elected Lula of the left-wing Workers' Party to the presidency. In addition to Venezuela and Brazil, from 2000 to 2012 twelve other Latin American countries elected left-leaning presidents to replace leaders of a more conservative or 'pro-market' persuasion. In 2005, José Miguel Insulza, who had served in the Chilean government of Salvador Allende, was elected Secretary General of the OAS, despite opposition from the United States. Latin American countries created a series of new organisations that limited US participation in regional co-operation. The FTAA collapsed. Venezuela, Bolivia and Ecuador began nationalising their energy and mineral resources. The neoliberal Washington Consensus—initially formulated with Latin America in mind—was declared dead (Panizza 2009). So too was the Monroe Doctrine, though not for the first time (Erikson 2008). The Council on Foreign Relations, the United States' most prominent foreign policy think tank, released a report proclaiming a 'new reality' for the United States and its dwindling influence in the region (2008). Washington had 'lost' Latin America—or so it seemed.

In the conventional reading of US–Latin American relations, the United States was content to turn the page on its long history of interventionism. Hoping to re-set relations, Obama (2009) acknowledged that the United States had 'sought to dictate (its) terms' in the past, that it had been 'disengaged', and that it had failed to fulfil the promise of true partnership. For many, the United States was too distracted to fret over the prospect that it was losing control of its backyard. The site of intense superpower rivalry as recently as the 1980s, Latin America simply didn't matter all that much anymore. The War on Terror, Iraq, Afghanistan and the rise of China dominated Washington's security agenda. Some alleged that the United States had 'ignored' or 'neglected' its neighbourhood (Emerson 2010; Valenzuela 2005), allowing the region to become fully autonomous (Crandall 2011; Sabatini 2012). This book paints a different picture. The logic of hegemony as a social relationship means the hegemon does not simply yield to political challenges 'from below'; it internalises counter-hegemony in an ongoing dialectic of contestation and hegemonic reconstitution.

By the end of the Obama presidency commentators were less interested in the imminent 'loss' of Latin America. The tone had shifted again. The political cycle that saw the left come to power throughout much of the region was drawing to a close. On the heels of the 2015 victory of centre-right presidential candidate Mauricio Macri in Argentina, Brazilian president Dilma Rousseff was impeached amidst a corruption scandal the following year. The leftist Maduro government in Venezuela was shaken by economic crisis and political unrest. With the decline of global commodity prices, the tensions in the extractivist model of 'Twenty-first Century Socialism' came to the fore. Social movements, which initiated the Pink Tide through their early challenges to the Washington Consensus, found themselves in opposition to some of the policies of the governments they helped elect, especially in the resource-rich Andes. Organisations created largely at the behest of progressive leaders, such as ALBA and UNASUR, confronted new diplomatic and budgetary uncertainties. As stated by Raúl Zibechi, 'the overwhelming feeling (was) that the region may have missed its best chance in a long time to put an end to US dominance and its own "backyard" status' (2016: 27).

For its part, the Obama administration's commitment to establishing diplomatic relations with Cuba showed that Latin America was more than an afterthought for US policymakers. The decision to engage the Castro government was not taken lightly; despite the changing demographics of the Cuban American population, it came with an element of political risk, and was made with an eye towards the broader hemispheric context (LeoGrande 2015). Speaking in Havana, Obama (2016) said he wanted to 'bury the last remnant of the Cold War in the Americas', remove the 'shadow of history' and 'open debate and dialogue' between the age-old adversaries. The White House's drive to normalise relations with Cuba was part and parcel of Washington's efforts to normalise relations with the region as a whole. Cuba presented an opportunity—the possibility of revitalising the OAS and its affiliated Summit of the Americas to build towards a new and more accommodating consensus. This is not anathema to hegemony, of course, but a crucial component.

Over the preceding chapters, I have endeavoured to elucidate processes of change and continuity in the international politics of the Western hemisphere. To do so, I carved US hegemony into its 'moving parts', the multiple and overlapping forms of power that (re)produce the asymmetries of inter-American relations. In this concluding chapter, I review the main arguments of the book. I highlight its contributions to the burgeoning literature on power in IR, with the aim of under-scoring the potential contributions of critical perspectives to this robust debate. I also review the limitations of the present project so as to identify avenues for future research. Finally, and in this spirit, I briefly consider the implications of my analysis for the future of US–Latin American relations.

Despite the fact that Washington did not articulate a sweeping foreign policy project in response to the rapid political shifts in Latin America in the 2000s (there was no Alliance for Progress-type programme to combat the rise of Bolivarian 'populism', no co-ordinated 'rollback' akin to the Reagan administration's violent counter-insurgency), the United States *did* react to these changes. It recalibrated its military strategy to attend to the region's shifting geopolitics, as examined in Chapter 4. As analysed in Chapter 5, Washington sought to reinforce the central-ity of the OAS to the institutional environment, thus giving it greater capacity to influence events 'at a distance'. Ideologically, as highlighted in Chapter 6, the discursive construction of Latin American 'populism' facilitated the renewal of US hegemony by affixing certain meanings to the region's anti-neoliberal govern-ments. The Bush and Obama administrations utilised free trade agreements to push forward the Washington Consensus agenda, as chronicled in Chapter 3, reinforc-ing its structural power. And although this structural power is not deterministic, its constitutive element is *immediate*, as agents are enabled and constrained through the internal relations of pre-existing patterns of political economy. The book's empirical account thus began with Washington's unyielding efforts to neolib-eralise Latin America as a kind of baseline for the more expansive foray into hegemonic power in its various dimensions and manifestations.

Power, hegemony, resistance

My reading of the history of US–Latin American relations, outlined in Chapter 1, generates the critical disposition underpinning this project. The interventions and repression of the Cold War gave way to a more consensus-based relationship in the new century. But, without question, the United States remained hegemonic. Definitions of hegemony abound. In realist and liberal paradigms, it is gener-ally theorised as military preponderance or multilateral leadership. I maintain that it is better conceptualised as an asymmetrical social relationship patterned by multiple and overlapping forms of power and counter-power. It encompasses a tenuous and ever-changing balance between force and consent, as realised in the economic, geopolitical, institutional and ideological spheres of international relations. In contrast to imperialist rule, hegemony invites forms of resistance that track the powers that shape and reshape the interactions between the hegemon and its subordinates. Indeed, it implies a counter-hegemony that is both constitutive of the hegemonic relationship and a potential threat to its durability. Thus, it is a dialectical social process, not a static order. Its periodic reconstitution is contingent on the agency of hegemonic actors as well as those forces that engender resistance through oppositional or revolutionary action.

I have sought to capture the fullness of the concept of hegemony alongside the tensions inherent in its actualisation. My inquiry was based on the philosophical foundations of historical materialism, including its realist ontology. The structural, institutional and ideological purchase of the neoliberal Washington Consensus is of major significance here because, although the emergence of the NLL elicited talk of a 'post-neoliberalism', US foreign policy remained committed to the liberalisation of the region's political economy. The Post-Washington Consensus embodied the renewal of hegemony in its multiple dimensions. The United States rededicated itself to the protection and augmentation of ongoing processes of neoliberalisation. In accordance with a 'dual logic' (Stokes and Raphael 2010: 15, 35–8), this served the interests of US national capital while simultaneously creating a regional political economy in the interests of international capital. Building on neo-Gramscian approaches to hegemony (Cox 1996; Gill 2008; Morton 2007; Persaud 2001; Robinson 1996; Rupert 1995, 2000), I applied the insights of this literature to the hemispheric policies of the United States. My analytical focus on *US* hegemony was just that; it pertained to the power and position of the United States qua national actor in its relations with the nation-states of Latin America. There is distinction here with a strand of Marxian scholarship on globalisation, best represented by William Robinson's writings on the transnational capitalist class (2014) and by Hardt and Negri's notions of 'empire' (2000). The 'statism' of the present study responds to diverse disciplinary calls to get 'back to basics' on the matter of state power (Finnemore and Goldstein 2013). I aimed to confront head-on the complexity of power in inter*national* relations.

Conceptually, power is just as slippery as hegemony, if not more so. Both concepts are deeply, if not essentially, contestable. It is preferable to see power broadly rather than narrowly, as something that is inherently multidimensional (Lukes 2005: 1). Clearly, there is value in analysing the various expressions of power in global politics. Different forms of power have a degree of autonomy from each other, even as they overlap and interweave in the messiness of 'real world' social relations (Mann 2012: 15–16). More than simply delineating ideal types of power at an abstract level, then, these forms need to be positioned in relation to one another, and analysed together (Barnett and Duvall 2005a, 2005b; Mann 1986, 2012). By operationalising power in different ways, we gain a deeper, more complete picture of hegemonic renewal. Indeed, it is the conjunction between different forms of power that allows us to speak of a comprehensive, dynamic and multifaceted hegemony, in contradistinction to crude and outdated understandings of imperial domination. That the United States does not directly intervene in Latin America like it did during the Cold War does not prove that the hemisphere has become a 'post-American' space (Crandall 2011; Zakaria 2008), to use vogueish terminology.

Competing theoretical commitments lead scholars to view power in various ways, often emphasising one form of power over others. This is not to say that different views/forms of power are incommensurable; that there is a necessary sequence to their arrangement or application; or that one or more forms of power can or should be subsumed to a 'master' theory of the concept. 'The inevitable question, then, is how exactly should we think about the relationship between these forms of power?' In answering their own query, Barnett and Duvall settle on an additive, pluralistic approach. Rejecting the 'gladiatorial' competition that characterised IR's 'paradigm wars', they note that, in most contexts, all forms of power are operating simultaneously, and that to reject one outright would risk overlooking a fundamental element of the social relationship under investigation (Barnett and Duvall 2005b: 67). There is no single form of power that has 'ultimate primacy' or 'determinacy' over other forms (Mann 1986: 3; 2012: 16). Rigorous empirical analysis requires examining the ways in which the various forms of power in the international sphere mould one another in particular historical settings.

Having four forms of power in my US hegemony framework is not an attempt to wipe away or circumvent the differences that split IR as a discipline. Problems of ontology and epistemology are vital and unavoidable. The meta-theoretical approach underpinning this project merits discussion, particularly given its impact on the ways in which the four forms of power were operationalised. Taking Gramscian-inflected historical materialism as my starting point, I positioned US hegemony in relation to global capitalism, which has imbued this primacy with a structural depth that transcends the foreign policy projects of specific administrations. As noted above, the fortification of a neoliberal political economy was a long-standing objective of US foreign policy in Latin America, and the ideational and material importance of neoliberalism was seen from the outset of this book, as with the typologisation of the New Latin Left into two strands, anti-neoliberals and neoliberal reformers. At the same time, US hegemony was not—and is not—*reducible* to the (Post-)Washington Consensus. Coercive force matters, even when latent.

Finally, any empirical analysis of hegemony must account for what Gramsci deemed the 'revolutionary tide(s)' traversing the 'flow of the historical current' (cited in Morton 2007: 212). Power and resistance are 'mutually implicated', Barnett and Duvall write (2005a: 22–3), 'because the social relations that shape the ability of actors to control their own fates are frequently challenged and resisted by those on the "receiving end"'. The drive for hegemonic reconstitution is brought about by the (counter-)powers of those on the receiving end of the asymmetrical relationship. The various agents interact in a messy tangle—not only states (the primary focus of my inquiry), but classes and social movements, amongst other actors. There is a give-and-take element that spans the various forms of power that comprise US hegemony: structural, coercive, institutional and ideological. Insofar as there is an 'outcome' on the horizon, however, it remains hazy. The dialectical process stays in motion; the moment of hegemonic renewal is elusive. The only certainty is continued contestation.

Contested futures

Gramscian theory is far from uniform, but it has been crucial in enabling a more open, flexible form of Marxism (Gill 1993; Morton 2007), allowing for a serious and sustained critique of the role of the United States in world politics and the international political economy (Cox 1996; Gill 2008; Robinson 1996; Rupert 1995). This book updates this tradition, extending neo-Gramscian and historical materialist insights to IR's re-energised emphasis on state power. As with any study, it has limitations. The book's scope excluded substantive examination of actors from outside the Western hemisphere. I avoided drawing direct links between US foreign policy in the Americas and elsewhere, sidestepping consideration of American 'grand strategy'. The following paragraphs place the preceding chapters in a wider context. In doing so, they suggest potential pathways for future research, while recognising that, in the contested terrain of inter-American relations, contingencies are sure to arise.

A hegemon in decline?

While the NLL was emerging as a political force in the early 2000s, IR was fixated on the question of American empire. By the end of the decade, however, the discourse had shifted to the durability (or fragility) of American unipolarity. Thus was rekindled the debate over American decline, a speculative discussion that has recurred in waves. Prior to the end of the Cold War, Paul Kennedy's bestseller *The Rise and Fall of the Great Powers* stimulated interest in the relative decline of the United States, as brought about by 'imperial overstretch'. Kennedy wrote, 'decision-makers in Washington must face the awkward and enduring fact that the sum total of the United States' global interests and obligations is nowadays far larger than the country's power to defend them all simultaneously' (1987: 515). The collapse of the Soviet Union buried this notion, which returned with a vengeance in the post-Iraq War, post-financial crisis climate. For some, the Obama presidency revealed a country coming to grips with its decline in a prudent and measured way (Quinn 2011), even if Obama himself was wont to put an energetic face on the perseverance of 'American exceptionalism'. The unexpected rise of Donald Trump indicated that declinist anxieties had incubated in the body politic, and that further decline overseas could be tethered to growing divisions at home. His election raised serious questions concerning the direction of US foreign policy and the future of American power, and was a definite turning point, even when compared to past presidential transitions. Nevertheless, this book has pointed to the importance of structures, institutions and ideologies to the actions of the United States in the international arena, while also highlighting the historical continuities in its foreign policy objectives—goals that tend to precede and outlive individual administrations.

'Decline' can be seen in a number of ways (as in the decline of American leadership, or the loss of legitimacy). It is closely connected to the debate on polarity, at least within IR's dominant rationalist paradigms. To quote Layne (2012), the end of unipolarity means the end of *Pax Americana*, and, though declinists may have jumped the gun previously, 'this time it's real'. However, leading realist and liberal scholars remain split on the implications of global economic trends. For Layne and others, the idea that the United States can sustain its global hegemony is, at best, an illusion. In stark contrast, Brooks and Wohlforth (2008) see the unipolar arrangement, and thus American primacy, as uniquely stable. Ikenberry writes:

> Ironically, the prospect of a decline in American relative power generates incentives for a renewed commitment by the United States to open and rule-based order. In the end, it is these liberal features of the international order that will slow down and mute the consequences of a return to multipolarity.
>
> (2011: 156)

Needless to say, there is considerable disagreement over the consequences of the changing distribution of material capabilities, both for state behaviour and for the international system itself. This has led to widely divergent interpretations of the United States' role in the shifting global order. If Trump's election scrambled these interpretations, his individual influence was tied to a host of actors, institutions and structures, including the very foreign policy and military establishments his campaign lambasted.

Assuming the United States is in decline (since the issue is largely one of time-scale), what kind of decline will it be? Contemporary debates over US 'grand strategy' flow from this question. Those who view decline as imminent have tended to advocate strategic retrenchment. Layne, for example, has long advocated 'offshore balancing'. By curtailing global commitments, he argues, such a strategy would insulate the United States from future great power conflict. It would mitigate against relative decline by conserving resources, lowering the United States' politico-military profile and ending 'ideological crusading' on behalf of democracy (Layne 2009). In the wake of neoconservatism's unceremonious demise, offshore balancing gained a certain élan. However, those who saw American 'leadership' as desirable and durable—and US decline as overstated—continued to push for a more activist grand strategy. Brooks, Ikenberry and Wohlforth called for 'deep engagement'. Such a strategy would help the United States continue to 'underwrite the global economy in a general sense', while allowing the United States 'to structure it in ways that serve the United States' narrow economic interests' (Brooks *et al.* 2012: 42). Similarly, Joseph Nye (2011) argued that 'smart power'—in which Washington uses its foreign policy resources more wisely—would reverse the decline of American leadership, and thus help the country manage the 'power shifts' on the horizon. Although Obama's foreign policy was restrained compared to Bush's heavy-handed unilateralism, his administration remained committed to a 'traditional' (i.e. liberal, postwar) vision of hegemony. The vaunted pivot to Asia, for example, was not so much strategic retrenchment as strategic reorganisation. 'Rather than pull back from the world', wrote Hillary Clinton (2011), the United States needed to 'press forward and renew (its) leadership'. In contrast, Trump's ad hoc, hyper-nationalist vision blended 'isolationist' appeals with militaristic bombast. Multilateral leadership would be downplayed in favour of a more aggressive and unilateral posture, one with little apparent concern for the institutions of the liberal order.

Debates over American decline are sure to persist, guided mainly by conventional scholarship. To date, they have been inattentive to the complexities and multifaceted nature of power in the international system. Critical voices could do much to invigorate and broaden the discussion. There are questions that go unasked, for example, on the functionality of the discourse of decline to US hegemony. Is an activist foreign policy an easier sell if the fading superpower is rumoured to be in decline? And what of global capitalism in the supposed twilight of American hegemony? Moreover, decline may have a disproportionate impact on US–Latin American relations. It seems reasonable to ask whether multipolarity makes Latin America *more* relevant to US interests. Will the dwindling 'reach' of US foreign policy compel the United States to refocus on its backyard? Does Latin America matter more in the context of a possible rivalry with China? And does hegemonic renewal in the Western hemisphere offer clues to the direction of US strategy elsewhere? There is much for future research to contend with in this area.

The 'rise of the rest' and China's role in the Western hemisphere

Contemporary debates over American foreign policy parallel wider disciplinary debates over the future of the global order. In concert with declinist anxieties, much of this speculation was driven by the 'rise of the rest' (Acharya 2014; Mabee 2013: 209–35; Nye 2011; Zakaria 2008). In 2001, Goldman Sachs proclaimed that the future of the world economy lay with the so-called BRIC nations (Brazil, Russia, India and China), and events afterward—especially the 2008 financial crisis—reinforced this perception. More established actors, including the European Union and Japan, also factored into the equation. As measured by the distribution of the world's economic resources, many detected a world moving rapidly towards multipolarity (Nye 2011; Zakaria 2008). Although the debate over polarity is driven largely by realists and liberals, the inclusion of critical voices would help to elucidate the implications of these shifts for the future of global politics, and the direction of US foreign policy therein. What would a multipolar world mean for the Americas?

In this context, Brazil's rise has become an important subject in and of itself. In 2012 Brazil overtook the UK to become the world's sixth largest economy. The country hosted the World Cup and summer Olympics in succession in 2014 and 2016. It has a diverse economy featuring strong agricultural, mining, manufacturing and service sectors, with considerable potential in offshore oil. Its GDP far surpasses that of any other Latin American country. It was only marginally affected by the global financial crisis of the late 2000s, although it slipped into recession in the context of declining commodity prices in the mid-2010s. The Lula and Rousseff governments served as a kind of model for 'moderate' left-wing leaders. Brazil has been extremely active in regional affairs, from the expansion of Mercosur to the creation of UNASUR. Some observers have suggested that Brazil is becoming hegemonic within South America (Burges 2008; Crandall 2011: 89). This is certainly debatable, especially in light of Rousseff's expulsion, a controversy that upended the country's politics. Yet, it is important to consider the implications of Brazil's growing influence, which, given the country's size, is likely to persevere in one fashion or another. 'The new conventional wisdom suggests that Brazil is now poised to make its name on the global stage and balance the other power in its neck of the woods, the United States' (Sweig 2010: 173). Inter-American relations may revolve increasingly around Washington's multi-faceted 'partnership' with Brasilia. Will Brazil resume its rise? Will this spell the waning of US hegemony in Latin America? Additional study is warranted.

In truth, the 'rise of the rest' is mainly about China. More than the European Union, Japan, India or Russia, China has made its presence felt in the Western hemisphere in recent years, with uncertain consequences for inter-American relations. In 2004, Chinese President Hu Jintao made a historic, high-profile trip to Latin America, visiting Argentina, Brazil, Chile and Cuba. He signed a number of economic deals along the way, touring the region again in 2010. In 2006, China and Venezuela finalised a series of major co-operation agreements in trade, energy and infrastructure development. Chávez visited China six times to deepen bilateral ties. Hu's successor, Xi Jinping, made his own high-profile tour of Latin America in 2013, promising billions of dollars in loans. As the United States 'pivoted' to Asia, Beijing reached out to the 'new world'. Through forums like the BRICs and its affiliated development bank (launched in 2014 and head-quartered in Shanghai), Latin America has become integral to China's policy of South–South co-operation. The Chinese have shown considerable interest in utilising CELAC as a way of co-ordinating their actions in the hemisphere, as initiated in a five-year strategic plan announced at the China–CELAC summit in Beijing in 2015.

As noted in Chapter 2, Sino-Latin American relations have centred mainly on trade. Chinese exports to Central and South America have boomed across a number of sectors. Latin American exports to China—concentrated in a few commodities, such as copper, oil, soybeans and iron ore—grew steeply. Between 2000 and 2009, for instance, total trade between China and Latin America increased by over 1,000 per cent, fuelling the region's commodities boom (Jenkins 2012). Chinese investment has also steadily increased, though at a slower pace. China remains the single largest trading partner for a number of Latin American countries, including Brazil. (China also represents a potential economic competitor to Latin America in the global export of manufactured goods.) Chinese loans to Latin American countries have outpaced those made by US-based IFIs, and they generally include fewer policy conditionalities (Ellis 2014; Gallagher *et al.* 2012). By 2015, annual Chinese lending to the LAC region surpassed $29 billion, more than the World Bank and Inter-American Development Bank combined, and a major source of counter-cyclical finance in the post-commodity boom era (Ray *et al.* 2016). Additionally, China's model of state-directed growth generated considerable interest in Latin America as the countries of the region moved away from the Washington Consensus.

'In addition to expanding economic ties', wrote Ellis, 'China is establishing an array of new political, social, and cultural links with Latin America' (2009: 3). The 'One China' policy and the status of Taiwan provided much of the impetus. The People's Republic of China has engaged in an intense contest with the Republic of China (Taiwan) over diplomatic recognition; a majority of the countries worldwide that extend recognition to Taiwan are in the Western hemisphere, concentrated mainly in Central America and the Caribbean. Beijing was active in trying to win over small countries using foreign aid, with intermittent success. China has also engaged with Latin American countries in the security realm, through arms sales, military exchanges and joint exercises (Ellis 2009; Marcella 2012). The nominally-communist state's emphasis on South–South co-operation helped facilitate ties with some of Latin America's left-wing governments, including Venezuela and Cuba, even as China insisted that its foreign policy was non-ideological. For the first time since the Cold War, an extra-hemispheric power is impacting the region in a major way.

In the early stages of Beijing's outreach, one congressional report dryly noted: 'Some observers believe increased Chinese interest and economic linkages with Latin America constitute a significant future threat to US influence and interests in Latin America' (Dumbaugh and Sullivan 2005: 5). Conservative elements of the US foreign policy establishment have proved alarmist at times. But, on the whole, Beijing has been deferential to Washington's historical position. As stated by Jiang Shixue, 'China understands the sensitive character of its deepening ties with Latin America . . . and in no way should China's growing presence be interpreted as a challenge to US hegemony in the hemisphere' (2008: 28). There is a consensus that China's actions are driven by commerce (Ellis 2009, 2014; Jenkins 2012), and despite the presence of key flashpoint issues, such as energy, there is unlikely to be an out-and-out 'rivalry' between Beijing and Washington in the foreseeable future. Although it may complicate the international relations of the Western hemisphere down the line, I would contend that China's role in the Americas has not overridden the hegemony/counter-hegemony dialectic at the core of this book. Nevertheless, future research should remain attentive to the evolution of this 'triangular relationship'. Assuming China emerges as a truly *global* power, the scope of its interests in the Western hemisphere may expand, potentially leading to heightened tensions, particularly if it views itself (or is viewed in Washington) as a peer competitor to the United States.

The future of US–Latin American relations

The continuity thesis of US foreign policy, introduced in Chapter 1, posits that the objectives of US statecraft have remained relatively consistent over time. The notion of hegemonic renewal certainly reinforces this position. That said, hegemony is a fluid social process, and the dynamism of international relations offers the prospect of meaningful change. In this vein, critical IR theory implies a normative commitment not generally found in mainstream scholarship. Critics of US foreign policy—IR scholars, revisionist historians, political commentators, public intellectuals, journalists, activists—have an extensive history of tackling issues of import to Latin America, partly because the region served as a laboratory for US imperialism for so long. In the first decade of the twenty-first century these critics found cause for optimism. In praising changes in Latin America across both 'moderate' and 'radical' governments, Greg Grandin wrote that, 'more than just giving one another room to maneuver, Latin America's new leftists have produced . . . their own consensus, a common project to use the centrifugal forces of globalization to loosen Washington's unipolar grip' (2006b: 23). Maintaining this consensus was always going to be challenging given the diversity among NLL governments and eventual electoral setbacks.

In an interview with the *Financial Times* in 2013, renowned linguist and social critic Noam Chomsky lauded the successes of Latin Americans in addressing poverty and inequality. 'For the last couple of hundred years Latin America has been pretty much under the control of the imperial powers', he said. In the new millennium, though, 'the countries have chosen their own paths independently of the demands of the great powers, particularly the US'. Although the United States remains 'far and away the most powerful state', Latin America provides 'the most striking case' of the 'diversification of power in the world'. He noted that Washington had fewer options to dispatch unwanted governments than it did previously. True to form, however, Chomsky emphasised that these gains had not diminished Washington's desire to exercise control (Kenard 2013). This sentiment—call it guarded optimism—was surprisingly widespread among critics of US foreign policy, and was not limited to North America. It was, of course, Latin Americans themselves that posed the question of US hegemony at this juncture.

The turn away from the left in the mid-2010s tempered enthusiasm for the belief that Latin America had won a post-hegemonic future. In breaking with the orthodoxy of the Washington Consensus, NLL governments made great strides in combating poverty and, to a lesser extent, addressing the region's seemingly intractable levels of economic inequality. But they largely failed to create lasting, transformative and adaptable models that could withstand the vicissitudes of the global capitalist economy. This was always going to be a tall order, especially for a collection of governments that were generally reformist in orientation. Moreover, the NLL was dependent on a kind of social mobilisation that proved difficult to sustain. For Castañeda, the chronicler of the collapse of the Latin American left after the Cold War, the Pink Tide 'may have been undone by high expectations as much as anything else' (2016). Progressive administrations, he argued, after benefitting greatly from the commodities boom, were unable to overcome the scourge of corruption, as individual leaders and parties clung to power using 'authoritarian' tactics. Among critics, he was not alone in sensing an abrupt conclusion to the political cycle that had characterised the first fifteen years of the new century (Sabatini 2015; Vargas Llosa 2015). More sympathetic voices also saw the end of an era (Zibechi 2016). 'There's much at stake', wrote Grandin (2015), 'for, in addition to having presided over a return of social-democratic redistribution, the

South American left over the last decade and a half created an effective counter-balance to the United States'. This extended from matters of trade and political economy to issues of international security.

In the United States, the consolidation of the nationalist right, channelled through the rise of Donald Trump, raises numerous questions. Trump first gained traction as a presidential candidate by denigrating Mexican immigrants and calling for the construction of a massive wall along the southern border, to be paid for by Mexico itself. The Trump phenomenon portends the reorientation of American politics in a number of ways, including on issues of trade, globalisation and military strategy, as his campaign used a blend of racism, chauvinism and anti-globalist appeals to target white working-class voters. Although there isn't anything especially new about this form of politics in the United States (Rupert 2000), its wholesale capture of the White House in the package of a cavalier 'outsider' was a watershed. From a certain vantage, as noted above, Trump can be read as a response to American decline. His pledge to restore 'greatness' rested on the premise that the country was 'weak' and needed to be more assertive in its dealings abroad. Trump is a reminder of the potency of the 'Jacksonian' strand of American nationalism (Lieven 2016), which has the capacity to produce a more crudely militaristic foreign policy, if one (potentially) defined by a narrower understanding of national interests. Trump's obsession with Mexico and Mexican migrants is likewise a reminder of the importance of the racialised Latin 'Other' to the nationalism espoused by the American right.

Over the longer term, Trump-style nativism may be counterbalanced by the growing clout of Latinos in the United States (a trend which plays directly into the kind of reactionary politics catalysed by Trump himself). The demographics are clear. Latinos accounted for more than half of US population growth from 2000 to 2014. They are the fastest growing ethnic group among eligible voters, and, by 2060, are projected to make up over a quarter of the total population (Bell 2016: 3). Of course, Latinos are not a homogenous group. But they have tended to support the Democratic Party and are viewed as (marginally) more supportive of 'liberal' or left-leaning foreign and domestic policies when compared to the wider population (Bell 2016; Smeltz and Kafura 2015). Notwithstanding the idiosyncrasies of the Cuban American experience, in which the émigré community helped prop up an outdated, hard-line approach towards the Castro government, it is possible that Latino voters could constitute a moderating force on US foreign policy over time. In the Western hemisphere, this may take the form of a greater acceptance of the new-found and relatively fragile autonomy of Latin American countries.

Certainly, Latin Americans have so far exhibited increased confidence in regional and world affairs in the twenty-first century. Brazilian intellectual Emir Sader traced 'Latin America's growing importance in the world' from its ability to defy Washington's 'imperial hegemony' and forge ahead with alternatives to the North American agenda (2011: 156). In the title of his 2010 book, the Colombian writer Oscar Guardiola-Rivera provocatively asked: *What if Latin America Ruled the World?* He suggested that, as the United States itself grew more

'Latinised', the South would 'take the North into the 22nd Century'. Referencing the Community of Latin American and Caribbean States, Guardiola-Rivera even foresaw the potential for a 'United States of Latin America' (2010: 372). The peoples of the region are now authoring their own histories in an unprecedented manner, he asserted. Even in the twilight of the Pink Tide, one does not have to share his sanguinity to appreciate that Latin America has grown more autonomous. Many observers have reached this conclusion. And yet, there are questions gnawing at this new consensus. Will the countries of Latin America continue to develop in an autonomous direction? What would this mean for the power of the United States? In other words, how, and at what point, is hegemony overcome?

Beyond the din of current events and the vacillations of electoral politics, this book has pointed to deep-seated processes of hegemonic renewal. The leaders, movements and policies of the NLL have coloured Latin America's politics for a generation, with myriad implications for the citizens of the region—and for US foreign policy. Although the NLL problematised American pre-eminence, it seems premature to conclude that US hegemony has been eclipsed, particularly with the resurgence of right-wing forces in Argentina, Brazil and Venezuela, not to mention the electoral triumph of Trumpian conservatism in the United States. Writing in *Foreign Affairs* several decades ago, Abraham Lowenthal stated that 'the days of unchallenged US control of the Western hemisphere are numbered, if not already past' (1976: 199). The conflagrations of the 1970s and 1980s gave way to the Washington Consensus, an 'end of history' moment made possible by the organised destruction of the left in many Latin American countries. Lowenthal had encouraged the United States to do away with its 'hegemonic presumption'. Behind the platitudes of 'partnership', such a presumption persists. Just as importantly, however, hegemony is more than a project or a strategy; it is a complex and multi-layered social relationship. It encompasses the deployment of power both directly and at a distance—through coercive force, multilateral institutions, economic policy and diplomacy. Further, it is inextricably interlinked with processes of structural and discursive (re)production; with power in its more constitutive forms. Yet hegemony isn't eternal. If, at present, US hegemony in Latin America is being remade, the future of US–Latin American relations remains very much unwritten.

References

Acharya, A. (2014). *The End of American World Order*, Cambridge: Polity.

Barnett, M. and R. Duvall (2005a). 'Power in Global Governance', in *Power in Global Governance*, edited by M. Barnett and R. Duvall, Cambridge: Cambridge University Press: 1–32.

Barnett, M. and R. Duvall (2005b). 'Power in International Politics', *International Organization*, 59(1): 39–75.

Bell, A. T. (2016). 'The Role of the Latino Vote in the 2016 Elections', Center for Latin American and Latino Studies, American University, May.

Brands, H. (2012). *Latin America's Cold War*, Cambridge, MA: Harvard University Press.

Brooks, S. G. and W. C. Wohlforth (2008). *World Out of Balance: International Relations and the Challenge of American Primacy*, Princeton: Princeton University Press.

Brooks, S. G., G. J. Ikenberry and W. C. Wohlforth (2012). 'Don't Come Home, America: The Case against Retrenchment', *International Security*, 37(3): 7–51.

Burges, S. (2008). 'Consensual Hegemony: Theorizing Brazilian Foreign Policy after the Cold War', *International Relations*, 22(1): 65–84.

Castañeda, J. (1994). *Utopia Unarmed: The Latin American Left After the Cold War*, New York: Vintage Books.

Castañeda, J. (2016). 'The Death of the Latin American Left', *The New York Times*, 22 March. Available online at www.nytimes.com/2016/03/23/opinion/the-death-of-the-latin-american-left.html?_r=0 (accessed 20 September 2016).

Clinton, H. (2011). 'America's Pacific Century', *Foreign Policy*, November. Available online at www.foreignpolicy.com/articles/2011/10/11/americas_pacific_century (accessed 13 July 2013).

Council on Foreign Relations (2008). *US-Latin America Relations: A New Direction for a New Reality*, New York: Council on Foreign Relations.

Cox, R. W. (1996). *Approaches to World Order*, Cambridge: Cambridge University Press.

Crandall, R. (2011). 'The Post-American Hemisphere: Power and Politics in an Autonomous Latin America', *Foreign Affairs*, 90(3): 83–95.

Dumbaugh, K. and M. P. Sullivan (2005). 'China's Growing Interest in Latin America', Congressional Research Service, 20 April.

Ellis, R. E. (2009). *China in Latin America: The Whats and Wherefores*, Boulder: Lynne Rienner.

Ellis, R. E. (2014). *China on the Ground in Latin America: Challenges for the Chinese and Impacts on the Region*, New York: Palgrave.

Emerson, R. G. (2010). 'Radical Neglect? The "War on Terror" and Latin America', *Latin American Politics and Society*, 52(1): 33–62.

Erikson, E. (2008). 'Requiem for the Monroe Doctrine', *Current History*, 107(706): 58–64.

Finnemore, M. and J. Goldstein, eds. (2013). *Back to Basics: State Power in a Contemporary World*, Oxford: Oxford University Press.

Galeano, E. (1973). *Open Veins of Latin America: Five Centuries of the Pillage of a Continent*, New York: Monthly Review.

Gallagher, K., A. Irwin and K. Koleski (2012). 'The New Banks in Town: Chinese Finance in Latin America', Inter-American Dialogue, February.

Gill, S. (1993). 'Gramsci and Global Politics: Towards a Post-Hegemonic Research Agenda', in *Gramsci, Historical Materialism and International Relations*, edited by S. Gill, Cambridge: Cambridge University Press: 1–18.

Gill, S. (2008). *Power and Resistance in the New World Order*, second edition, New York: Palgrave.

Grandin, G. (2006a). *Empire's Workshop: Latin America, the United States, and the Rise of the New Imperialism*, New York: Owl Books.

Grandin, G. (2006b). 'Latin America's New Consensus', *The Nation*, 1 May: 23–7.

Grandin, G. (2015). 'Is This the End of the Latin American Left?' *The Nation*, 7 December. Available online at www.thenation.com/article/is-this-the-end-of-the-latin-american-left/ (accessed 20 September 2016).

Guardiola-Rivera, O. (2010). *What if Latin America Ruled the World? How the South Will Take the North into the 22nd Century*, London: Bloomsbury.

Hardt, M. and A. Negri (2000). *Empire*, Cambridge, MA: Harvard University Press.

Ikenberry, G. J. (2011). *Liberal Leviathan: The Origins, Crisis, and Transformation of the American World Order*, Princeton: Princeton University Press.

Jenkins, R. (2012). 'Latin America and China—A New Dependency?' *Third World Quarterly*, 33(7): 1337–58.

Kenard, M. (2013). 'BB Interviews . . . Noam Chomsky', *Financial Times*, 15 February. Available online at http://blogs.ft.com/beyond-brics/2013/02/15/bb-interviews-noam-chomsky/#axzz2X7ua3tqt (accessed 17 March 2016).

Kennedy, P. (1987). *The Rise and Fall of the Great Powers*, New York: Random House.

Layne, C. (2009). 'America's Middle East Grand Strategy after Iraq: The Moment for Offshore Balancing has Arrived', *Review of International Studies*, 35(1): 5–25.

Layne, C. (2012). 'This Time It's Real: The End of Unipolarity and the *Pax Americana*', *International Studies Quarterly*, 56(1): 203–13.

LeoGrande, W. M. (2015). 'Normalizing US-Cuba Relations: Escaping the Shackles of the Past', *International Affairs*, 91(3): 473–88.

Lieven, A. (2016). 'Clinton and Trump: Two Faces of American Nationalism', *Survival*, 58(5): 7–22.

Loveman, B. (2010). *No Higher Law: American Foreign Policy and the Western Hemisphere since 1776*, Chapel Hill: University of North Carolina Press.

Lowenthal, A. F. (1976). 'The United States and Latin America: Ending the Hegemonic Presumption', *Foreign Affairs*, 55(1): 199–213.

Lukes, S. (2005). *Power: A Radical View*, second edition, New York: Palgrave.

Mabee, B. (2013). *Understanding American Power: The Changing World of US Foreign Policy*, New York: Palgrave.

Mann, M. (1986). *The Sources of Social Power Volume 1: A History of Power from the Beginning to A.D. 1760*, Cambridge: Cambridge University Press.

Mann, M. (2012). *The Sources of Social Power Volume 3: Global Empires and Revolution*, Cambridge: Cambridge University Press.

Marcella, G. (2012). 'China's Military Activity in Latin America', *Americas Quarterly*, 6(1): 67–9.

Morton, A. D. (2007). *Unravelling Gramsci: Hegemony and the Passive Revolution in the Global Political Economy*, London: Pluto Press.

Nye, J. (2011). *The Future of Power*, New York: Public Affairs.

Obama, B. (2009). 'Remarks by the President at the Summit of the Americas Opening Ceremony', 17 April. Available online at www.whitehouse.gov/the-press-office/remarks-president-summit-americas-opening-ceremony (accessed 5 March 2016).

Obama, B. (2016). 'Remarks by President Obama to the People of Cuba', 22 March. Available online at www.whitehouse.gov/the-press-office/2016/03/22/remarks-president-obama-people-cuba (accessed 9 September 2016).

Panizza, F. (2009). *Contemporary Latin America: Development and Democracy Beyond the Washington Consensus*, London: Zed Books.

Pastor, R. (2001). *Exiting the Whirlpool: US Foreign Policy toward Latin America and the Caribbean*, second edition, Boulder: Westview Press.

Persaud, R. B. (2001). *Counter-Hegemony and Foreign Policy: The Dialectics of Marginalized and Global Forces in Jamaica*, Albany: State University of New York Press.

Quinn, A. (2011). 'The Art of Declining Politely: Obama's Prudent Presidency and the Waning of American Power', *International Affairs*, 87(4): 803–24.

Ray, R., K. Gallagher and R. Sarmiento (2016). 'China-Latin America Economic Bulletin 2016 Edition', Global Economic Governance Initiative, Boston University, March.

Robinson, W. I. (1996). *Promoting Polyarchy: Globalization, US Intervention, and Hegemony*, Cambridge: Cambridge University Press.

Robinson, W. I. (2014). *Global Capitalism and the Crisis of Humanity*, Cambridge: Cambridge University Press.

Rupert, M. (1995). *Producing Hegemony: The Politics of Mass Production and American Global Power*, Cambridge: Cambridge University Press.

Rupert, M. (2000). *Ideologies of Globalization: Contending Visions of a New World Order*, London: Routledge.

Sabatini, C. (2012). 'Rethinking Latin America', *Foreign Affairs*, 91(2): 8–13.

Sabatini, C. (2015). 'The Sad Death of the Latin American Left', *Foreign Policy*, 10 December. Available online at: http://foreignpolicy.com/2015/12/10/venezuela-brazil-chavez-maduro-rousseff-lula/ (accessed 20 September 2016).

Sader, E. (2011). *The New Mole: Paths of the Latin American Left*, London: Verso.

Schoultz, L. (1998). *Beneath the United States: A History of US Policy toward Latin America*, Cambridge, MA: Harvard University Press.

Shixue, J. (2008). 'The Chinese Foreign Policy Perspective', in *China's Expansion into the Western Hemisphere*, edited by R. Roett and G. Paz, Washington, DC: Brookings: 27–43.

Smeltz, D. S. and C. Kafura (2015). 'Latinos Resemble Other Americans in Preferences for US Foreign Policy', Chicago Council on Global Affairs.

Smith, P. (2000). *Talons of the Eagle: Dynamics of US-Latin American Relations*, second edition, Oxford: Oxford University Press.

Stokes, D. and S. Raphael (2010). *Global Energy Security and American Hegemony*, Baltimore: Johns Hopkins University Press.

Sweig, J. (2010). 'A New Global Player: Brazil's Far-Flung Agenda', *Foreign Affairs*, 89(6): 173–84.

Valenzuela, A. (2005). 'Beyond Benign Neglect: Washington and Latin America', *Current History*, 104(679): 58–63.

Vargas Llosa, A. (2015). 'Latin America Says "Adiós" to the Populist Left', *National Interest*, 4 December. Available online at http://nationalinterest.org/feature/latin-america-says-adi%C3%B3s-the-populist-left-14506 (accessed 20 September 2016).

Zakaria, F. (2008). *The Post-American World*, New York: W. W. Norton and Company.

Zibechi, R. (2016). 'Progressive Fatigue?' *NACLA Report on the Americas*, 48(1): 22–7.

Index